ISP Marketing Survival Guide: Proven Strategies and Secrets for Outmaneuvering the Competition

ISP Marketing Survival Guide: Proven Strategies and Secrets for Outmaneuvering the Competition

Christopher M. Knight

Wiley Computer Publishing

John Wiley & Sons, Inc.

NEW YORK · CHICHESTER · WEINHEIM · BRISBANE · SINGAPORE · TORONTO

Publisher: Robert Ipsen

Editor: Carol Long

Managing Editor: Angela Smith

Text Design & Composition: North Market Street Graphics, Lancaster, Pennsylvania

Designations used by companies to distinguish their products are often claimed as trademarks. In all instances where John Wiley & Sons, Inc., is aware of a claim, the product names appear in initial capital or ALL CAPITAL LETTERS. Readers, however, should contact the appropriate companies for more complete information regarding trademarks and registration.

This book is printed on acid-free paper. ∞

This publication is designed to provide accurate and authoritative information in regard to the subject matter covered. It is sold with the understanding that the publisher is not engaged in professional services. If professional advice or other expert assistance is required, the services of a competent professional person should be sought.

Library of Congress Cataloging-in-Publication Data:

ISBN 0-471-37679-5

Printed in the United States of America.

10 9 8 7 6 5 4 3 2 1

Contents

Introduction

"The only certain means of success is to render more and better service than is expected of you, no matter what your task may be."

OG MANDINO

Ever since the beginning of what has become a multibillion dollar industry, doomsayers have been saying that the Internet Service Providers (ISPs) will continue to consolidate until eventually all Internet access will be controlled by less than a few dozen providers, similar to the way in which the telecommunications industry has matured. They have been wrong, and continue to be wrong, but for how long is anyone's guess. As long as people need to get on the Internet, they will need someone to provide them with access, and as long as people continue to be dissatisfied with their provider of that access, there will be new opportunities for new players to jump into the industry with their solutions.

It is true that the cost to enter this market has gone down considerably, and the cookie cutter solutions for getting new ISPs launched continue to pop up left and right, but don't mistake this as an easy industry in which to become involved. The ISP industry, in my humble opinion, has crossed the start-up phase of the industry and is just heading for the high-growth stage, which will last for many, many years. If you're an ISP or about to start one, it means you are building a business that has or will have a moving foundation that may radically change before you cash out or exit. Your success and profitability or even survival totally depends on your ability to adapt, execute, change, and leverage the new external influences in the marketplace. You must also do this faster than your competitors, or risk being eaten for lunch. Unfortunately, many new ISPs spend their entire budget to get started, and then wonder why their ISP is not growing as fast as they'd like. For all of the current ISPs and ones yet to come that wish to grow, and grow fast on a shoestring budget in the shortest amount of time with the biggest impact, this book is for you.

This book is not designed to be a treatise on theory, but rather real-life, practical, quick, and brief tips, tricks, strategies, and ideas that you can use immediately, many within 24 hours of setting this book down. As you successfully build your ISP, you will begin to realize that knowing all of the answers is not what you are paid to do, but instead you need to know which questions to ask. This book is packed full of questions and checklists to help your thinking. It is my intent to help you to come up with new answers that are right for your specific business.

On the topic of ISP technology, I only reference technology as it relates to marketing. If you bought this book in order to understand ISP technology topics, you might want to check out the other Wiley ISP Survival Guide books such as Geoff Huston's *ISP Survival Guide* (ISBN 0-471-31499-4) or join some of the ISP-Tech e-mail discussion lists for assistance. If you need legal help, look for Wiley's upcoming *ISP Liability Survival Guide* in the spring of 2000 (ISBN 0-471-37748-1) written by Tim Casey, chief technical counsel for MCIWorldCom. Don't get me wrong, as there is plenty of tech talk in this book, but only if it relates to the business side of sales and marketing.

While I'm extremely gratified when I receive letters and e-mails from fans who have read my ISP-Planet.com articles online or my monthly ISP-Marketing column in *Boardwatch* magazine, if you really want the complete scoop, read this book. Think about how what you read here relates to your specific ISP business and then execute—take action toward your goals. Most of all, don't worry about whether your actions are right or wrong, just take your best shot and implement like crazy. Because you are smart, you will not repeat your mistakes, but the future of the ISP industry belongs to those who take action and forge forward without regard to whether their actions will succeed or fail. You must have faith in yourself, but never underestimate that faith alone will build a successful business—executable plans and the actions they demand build business.

It is getting harder to define what an ISP is. As the industry gets larger, an ISP is not only a business that provides modem dial-up Internet access, but any form of Internet access, including ISDN, T1, PRI circuits, DS3, ATM, cable access, satellite feeds, wireless access, and more. Many ISPs are large corporations who originally provided access for their employees and then decided to expand access for the friends and family of their employees, and all of a sudden, a new business unit was launched. As you will learn in the first chapter, you don't even have to own the network in order to play the ISP game. Non-facilities-based ISPs can also make thousands of virtual ISPs possible for specialized niche markets.

How This Book Is Organized

This book starts out explaining the basics of typical ISPs in terms of organization and structure. This sets the stage to help you begin planning your ISP marketing budget, strategy, and goal setting. I then describe your ISP exit strategy because it's one of the major baselines that will determine which marketing, advertising, and sales strategies you will deploy. You'll also be given resources on clearly identifying what makes your ISP unique and then a whopping set of ideas and strategies you can use in your ISP marketing arsenal. After we've focused on your marketing plans, we look at ways to save the customers you do have by reducing churn and improving customer service techniques. If you wish to grow your ISP via acquisition, I've outlined many of the strategies for successful purchasing of the subscriber bases of other ISPs. The book wraps up with ISP case studies, my personal recommended reading list, a must-read ISP resources collection if you're hungry for more, an ISP business plan sample that you can adapt for your own, and last, an ISP business glossary of common terms used in the ISP industry.

Chapter 1: Why Be an Internet Service Provider and Benefits of Being One

In this chapter, I provide an overview of the different types of ISPs (facilities-based versus non-facilities-based), along with an in-depth discussion on the advantages and disadvantages of each type. You will also get an extremely comprehensive list of 101 questions you need to ask yourself before you either start your ISP or continue running your existing ISP. If you need a healthy ISP reality checkup, start here.

Chapter 2: Planning Your ISP Exit Strategy as Part of Your Start-up

Most ISPs do not know what they are looking for in terms of outcome. You can't build a successful enterprise unless you know where you are going. This chapter helps you identify your ISP exit strategy, what your subscriber base is or could be worth soon, the various ways that ISPs are valued, and how all of this matters in your ISP marketing decision-making process. I have also included the top 10 things *not* to do when selling your ISP, along with many resources you can use to help find people that will help sell your ISP for you. While some books have exit strategies at the end of the book, I put the exit strategy near the front door. I believe that it is vitally important to know what and where the end will be for your ISP business before you attempt to go where you've never been before.

Chapter 3: Identifying Your Unique Selling Proposition

If you don't have a one-sentence positioning statement for your ISP, you will get one here, along with tools that you can use to identify which ISP niches are not right for the type of business you are or want to be running. I also describe techniques that you can use to deploy your new unique selling proposition for maximum return, along with four killer, but very simple, methods for ensuring that you own your market niche. Last, I wrap up this chapter with ISP goal-setting strategies to help keep you on track on your road to the top.

Chapter 4: The Only Three Ways to Grow Your ISP

In this chapter, I narrow it all down to the three lowest common denominators that will be the basis for all of your ISP sales-building plans and strategies. If you get lost, the three basic principles in this chapter will guide you to simplifying your marketing and business plans. Specifically, you get 21 strategies designed to increase the number of new subscribers you have, 14 ways to increase your average ticket price, and seven quick ideas for increasing the frequency between repeat business, which are all designed to help you build stronger profit pillars.

Chapter 5: Your ISP Marketing Arsenal

If you need more ISP marketing strategies than you can shake a stick at, start here. I cover everything from the basics that ISP marketing novices need to know, to the secrets I've learned the hard way. This is one of my favorite sections of the book. I also cover why most ISP marketing programs fail and what you can do about it immediately. You will also learn ISP branding basics that will help you create an incredible sales momentum for your business. In addition to ISP press releases and use of media opportunities to get the word out for your ISP, not to mention copywriting and headline-writing tips that can make or break the return you get on your next campaign, I debunk some of the greatest ISP marketing myths.

If you like beating the pants off your competitors and want to learn how to beat them at their own game before they even know what hit them with grassroots, boot-strapping campaigns that can make a real difference, you'll find this chapter useful.

You've got hidden assets at your ISP and this chapter will help you to identify and begin benefiting from those powerful weapons sitting literally right under your nose. I also describe the best of database and stealth/drip marketing ideas and ways that you can increase your sales conversion rates, especially when it comes from converting free trial memberships into life-long paying memberships.

This chapter may be the hardest to read section to section because I ask you to stop reading at certain points to suggest you go out and do some simple things. Many of these actions cost very little but can have incredible impact on the value of your ISP, not to mention your bottom line.

Chapter 6: What to Include in Your ISP Marketing Business Plan

This complete chapter is by our ISP Marketing guest expert, Jason Zigmont, CEO of HowToSell.net, who also shares with us his complete ISP Business Plan sample in Appendix A of this book.

In this chapter, you will learn the essential sections of what to include in your ISP business plan, including the executive summary, financial proposal, industry and market analyses, marketing plan, operating plan, organizational plan, and your financial plan. Jason not only includes what to put in your plan and why, but he packs in resources and tips to help speed your way to a profitable business plan that you can call your own.

Chapter 7: Strategies to Reduce Churn

While a lot of attention is aimed at helping you grow your subscriber base, we cannot forget to focus on the biggest deterrent to subscriber growth—churn and how to measure it. You'll get 12 inexpensive ways to reduce your churn immediately in this chapter. Though admittedly, it's a buzzword, I close this chapter with ways that you can increase your ISP's "stickiness" and keep your customers and the associated revenue stream longer.

Chapter 8: The Customer Service Role in Your ISP Marketing Strategy

This chapter covers how to attract, retain, and train a great customer service staff which you'll need in order to impress your existing customers, your soon-to-be customers, and to achieve or maintain the best reputation in your ISP niche, spurring positive word-of-mouth advertising. If you've ever wanted your staff to care as much as you do about delivering great service, this section covers employee incentive programs that, when tied with an excellent ISP marketing strategy, really work. Last, this chapter gives six tips that will help your technicians to better understand their role in your ISP's marketing plan and to get from them more participation in the service standards you've set.

Chapter 9: How to Acquire New Subscribers via Acquisitions of Other ISPs

For the ISPs reading this book with a hungry appetite for growth and the budget or capital to make it happen, this chapter can be very valuable. I describe how to identify the best ISP acquisition strategies for your ISP and niche. I've also included techniques for getting more bang for your acquisition buck, and what to do when your deals fall apart.

Chapter 10: ISP Case Studies

While this industry was less than eight years old at the time this book was written, there are many ISPs achieving great success and boldly going where no ISP has gone before. I've interviewed many ISPs that share their insights with us, along with their secrets, tips, and strategies from many different marketing perspectives. Hopefully, you'll be able to learn from others who have succeeded and failed using different models. You'll be able to identify what went right for them and apply those lessons learned to your own ISP business.

Who Should Read This Book?

This survival guide is for current Internet Service Providers and anyone associated with the ISP business or industry as well as those wanting to go into the ISP business. This audience also includes virtual ISPs, facilities-based ISPs, telecommunication providers, and CLECs who are introducing new products or want to improve their existing ISP division, cable companies who are or will be delivering ISP services soon, ISP wireless and satellite Internet access providers, vendors who provide services to ISPs, corporations that have a dial-up or Internet access network that they are attempting to turn into a profit center, Application Service Providers (ASPs), and, last, investors in ISPs who want to identify success criteria for the industry.

If you are in sales, marketing, advertising, or if the ISP bottom line is important to you, then this book has been designed for you. If you are an ISP technician and want to better understand how to start, build, grow, brand, and sell your ISP, there are literally hundreds if not thousands of tips in this book that you can read in a few short moments and begin implementing immediately.

If you either can't sleep or recently have awoke in a cold sweat wondering how you are going to maneuver your ISP through its next growth phase, or increase your positive cash flow, or you just need a book that not only gives you practical suggestions and tips but also stimulates your thinking by helping you discover the right answers for your ISP marketing strategies based on your unique situation, then this book will help.

Assumptions

I assume you know a bit about how the Internet works and the basics of the ISP industry. ISP technology is only discussed as it relates to marketing or sales functions. If you are an advanced marketer, you might want to skim to the middle of the book or start with Chapter 4, The Only Three Ways to Grow Your ISP, to get the many hundreds of ISP marketing solutions. If you are new to the ISP industry, or you are not new but your marketing is not working as effectively as you expect, I suggest starting at the very beginning of the book.

There are many risks in building a successful ISP business, and while many fail every day, many are growing faster than they ever dreamed possible. Your ISP can follow this path. This book's primary purpose is to help you increase your sales, increase your margin, increase the number of new customers you acquire, increase your average ticket price, and help you build an ISP that is worthy of being acquired some day at a premium and handsome profit for yourself and your investors.

That being said, let's jump right into the benefits of being an ISP.

Acknowledgments

First, I thank you, the reader, for helping make this book possible. Your interest, involvement, and contribution to the exploding ISP industry do make a difference. This book is dedicated to every ISP entrepreneur, business owner, investor, executive team, and everyone who is involved in the sales, marketing, and advertising departments that are critical in any ISP's growth, profitability, market capitalization, and success.

I'd like to express my appreciation to the team at internet.com who gave me the latitude and creative outlets to continue doing what I love best and in a bigger way than I ever imagined. Alan Meckler, Chris Cardell, Chris Baudouin, Chris Elwell, Gus Venditto, Susan Leiterstein, Ted Stevenson, Pat Fusco, David Arganbright, and the staff of internet.com Corporation have helped me grow personally and professionally. Without my involvement with internet.com and ISP-Planet.com, I'm not sure this book would have been completed. They are among the finest bunch of professionals I have ever met.

The ISP-Lists.com e-mail discussion list community has also been extremely instrumental in facilitating the research, interviews, case studies, and my own understanding of the extremely fast paced ISP industry. When I was building an ISP for the first time back in 1995 and 1996, it was the ISP-Lists.com community that helped me navigate every issue of starting, growing, funding, hiring, and building the network. Now, in 2000, it is the 25,000+ members of the ISP-Lists.com community that have made my job of writing this book much easier. The ISP-Lists.com community continues to be the best source on Earth for learning more about the ISP industry *from* the players who continue to shape our industry and I'm most grateful for the many teachers who showed up to show me the way.

Having come from an ISP background myself, I understand the many tireless all-nighters, the caffeine-buzzing, Generation-X propeller heads who know more than some of the college-educated IT professionals, and many other frustrations that go along with a typical ISP experience. I am not a techie. Fortunately I have been blessed with many talented professionals who, for two and a half years, helped me build, manage, grow, and finally sell a regional ISP in northeast Wisconsin. This book is also dedicated to all the techies out there who have to continue to make the impossible possible, even when they think management might be crazy.

Of the many dozens of employees who joined me at SparkNET Interactive (my ISP), Christopher Knutson and Bleau Schneider stand out as two senior systems administrators who have taught me many lessons about how an ISP back office can run. Michael Funk, associate editor, who helped edit and improve my prose, and Rick Rodriguez deserve my appreciation for taking my scribbled figures and converting them into plots, graphs, tables, and graphics for this book. For the rest of the SparkNET Interactive family who took great care of the daily duties while I ducked off for multiple months to produce this book, my gratitude. (Funny, the place always runs better when I'm gone. :-))

To Todd, Bill, Brian, and the staff at *Boardwatch*, who take my monthly ISP marketing columns and turn them into much better gold than I send in, my thanks. The exposure I have received through *Boardwatch* has enabled me to get the interviews and create the checklists that I was able to include in this book. While I'm on the *Boardwatch* magazine topic, I'd like to acknowledge Jack Rickard, a man I greatly respect for his contribution to the ISP industry and for being a positive voice of the ISP underdog, for writing the foreword for this book.

To Jason Zigmont, for his contributions to Chapter 6, What to Include in Your ISP Marketing Business Plan, and for allowing us to include his comprehensive *ISP Business Plan* as Appendix A of this book.

I am grateful to the many people who allowed me to interview them for this book and the hundreds who have sent me private e-mails with their ISP insights. And finally, I'd like to thank the industry insiders who shared their research and experience with me.

I would like to thank the staff of John Wiley & Sons, Carol Long and Emilie Herman, who deserve my thanks for their help in bringing this book from raw form to publication. Their editorial guidance has been instrumental.

Acknowledgment must also go to my two business mentors, Mike Upchurch and Ken Melotte, who have guided me in the formation of many of my business philosophies. I also believe in principle-centered leadership, which is taught by Stephen Covey, but many of my business principles have come from the likes of Tony Robbins, Jay Abraham, Wayne Dyer, Jay Conrad Levinson, Zig Ziglar, Larry Chase, and Barney Zick. A large part of my marketing and sales background packed into this book came from real-life experiences shaped by those I've just noted and I'm very grateful for their contribution to my life.

This book was in the works for more than a year. The information you'll find here is a result of my speaking and traveling from coast to coast and three different countries for ISP conferences, conducting dozens of interviews, reading tens of thousands of e-mails, and enduring many nights without sleep working to meet editorial deadlines. I'd like to thank my very loving wife, Roxanne, and son, Cameron, for supporting me in this project, along with my parents, who taught me that all things are possible if one is willing to work hard enough.

About the Author

Christopher Knight (aka "Sparky") is founder and managing editor of the ISP-Lists.com e-mail discussion list community, which was recently acquired by internet.com Corporation. He is also the CEO of an early-stage, high-tech start-up business, called SparkNET Interactive which specializes in high-volume, permission-based opt-in e-mail list hosting, promotion, management, and media planning.

Knight has firsthand inside experience with building, growing, promoting, marketing, and then selling an ISP, having built a successful regional ISP in Wisconsin. He also built a competing ISP business, which was privately labeled, allowing him to sell a premium ISP service under one name brand and a lower-cost, lower-service alternative under a different brand utilizing one dial-up network. This ISP was sold to a regional telco in late 1998 and taught him many lessons on ISP exit strategies, many of which are found in this book.

In addition to writing a monthly ISP-Marketing column for the popular ISP magazine *Boardwatch*, Knight also writes a weekly column on ISP business issues for internet.com's ISP-Planet.com network. To see a link to every article ever written by Knight, visit http://Christopher-Knight.com/.

The ISP-Lists.com network of 50 or more e-mail discussion lists with over 25,000 members is one of Knight's largest accomplishments for the ISP industry. Every day, hundreds of thousands of e-mails are exchanged by the discussion list community, which Knight founded in 1996 and continues to lead for internet.com.

Sparky is also a popular speaker on various ISP marketing and business topics for events such as ISPCon, ISP/C's ISP Forum, ISPBF.com's ISP Business Forum, and the ISP Summit.

xxiv ISP Marketing Survival Guide

Knight holds a degree in marketing and communications, is a Microsoft Certified Professional, is a member of the Internet Service Providers Consortium (ISP/C), was that organization's director of marketing in 1997, and is a member of the Internet Service Providers Business Forum (ISPBF.com).

Why Be an Internet Service Provider and the Benefits of Being One

Internet Service Providers (ISPs) form the basis of one of the Internet's most crucial roles: getting the people of Earth connected to each other by providing access to the Internet. Even though the Internet has been around since the late 1960s, it wasn't until 1991 when the first true Internet Access Provider (IAP) emerged in the commercial sense that we understand it today. Before that, many educational institutions provided either free or low-cost, nongraphical Internet access to students, alumni, and anyone else who would beg them to provide it.

Today it's a totally different story as the entry cost into this business has dramatically declined. Meanwhile, the competition has increased significantly. And, there is still time to get into the game, as poor service providers and high national churn rates tell us that ISP subscribers are not satisfied yet. As long as consumers and business users demand more from their Internet access experience, new ISPs who address the new needs will continue to prosper.

The biggest reason for or advantage of being an ISP varies from person to person. But unlike many business owners who work and slave for years or even decades to find out that no one wants to buy their businesses, ISPs have plenty of interested parties looking to acquire them and their subscriber bases. Many large ISPs have complete acquisition departments that do nothing but focus on setting up deals, identifying new acquisition prospects, and scouting acquisitions to help grow their ISPs.

Years ago I e-mailed Mike McQuary, president of MindSpring (NAS-DAQ: MSPG), and asked him for advice on what I should do as a budding ISP. He said, "Build it very fast." I never forgot that, and Mike was right. It certainly seems as if building an ISP, in terms of the valuation you're able to achieve, is a moving target. For example: Ever since the start of the ISP industry, companies have paid more and more for subscribers when growing through targeted acquisition. Does this then mean that you should keep building your ISP because as each month goes by, your subscriber base is worth more and more? This is not necessarily so because as the threat of free Internet access—advertiser-supported model—rolls along further, the window of opportunity for small to medium-size ISPs is in constant flux.

Advantages and Disadvantages of Being an ISP

If you are an ISP or are considering starting one, here are some of the major *advantages* that you can count on:

- Your subscriber base carries value when or if you decide to sell, which means you are constantly building an asset that appreciates.

- Your revenue model is a recurring revenue model, which means that as you grow, your revenue will continue to climb in a predictable fashion.

- New telecommunications deregulation and increased competition both mean lower-cost services from your telecommunications vendors, which translates into increased profitability for you.

- New services and specialization allow you to seriously consider outsourcing many of the areas of your ISP business in which you do not want to specialize, which frees you to do what you do best.

- High national churn rates mean that your prospects are not happy with some of your competitors, which allows ISPs that really deliver great service to prosper and keep their subscribers longer.

- Equipment costs are going down and PC server power is going up, which allows you to accomplish more for less; meanwhile, ISPs that have been in the marketplace may not have received a return on their relatively new hardware.

- ISP collocation is a serious option to consider. *Collocation* means that you physically locate your ISP within a building that is either a telecommunications provider or one that has other high-tech Internet access providers all sharing high-bandwidth pipes. This option wasn't available just a few short years ago.

- Small ISPs with creative management and a smart marketing team can make a big impact with few employees as new ISP niche markets open up.

Unfortunately, it's not all roses, as any ISP veteran will tell you. During your life as an ISP many industry changes and new customer demands will force you to improve or lose. Some of the major changes include the speed at which users want to access the Internet and the impact the success of the free ISP advertising-based models has on your primary revenue streams.

Here are some of the primary *disadvantages* of being an ISP:

- In the beginning you will fight negative cash flow as if it was one of your worst enemies. Regardless of your profitability or lack thereof, you must maintain some order of positive cash flow or be capitalized while you grow—or perish.

- New technologies obsolete old technologies at least twice as fast as you are allowed by law to depreciate your software and hardware on your financial statements. This results in uneven financial statements as you write off hardware that is often sold at a fraction of what you paid for it just a few years ago.

- Circuit tariffs are constantly changing, depending on the legal weather in Washington, D.C. This means you could be in a contract for an unfavorable tariff as new ones become available. Because of early circuit termination charges in your contracts, you can be forced to pay off your telecommunications provider before the end of a contract just to continue buying from it at a lower rate for the same service. It's weird, but it happens all the time.

- Talented employees who truly care about their work and/or are highly skilled are expensive and move around a lot, leaving your ISP wide open to problems if you're unable to attract and retain them.

- You may not personally be in control of the local telecommunications loop between your customer and your access switches, which means that your customers will be dissatisfied with your service at times and there will be nothing you can do for them.

- Your competitors could have deeper pockets than you, and be able to outspend you in marketing dollars, or be able to buy your competitors before you can.

- The government could threaten new and unfair taxation on the way you do business, creating advantages for some and great disadvantages for others.

- Your ability to stay focused on the niche you have chosen for your ISP will be continually assaulted and you could be enticed daily to leave your niche by the "grass is always greener" syndrome.

Types of ISPs

There are three basic types of ISPs today:

1. *Facilities-based ISPs.* These own their own Internet access servers and equipment. Most small ISPs are facilities-based which is considered the traditional ISP setup.

2. *Non-facilities-based ISPs.* These outsource their access equipment to a third-party wholesale provider. Most national providers use this option in order to provide service in hundreds of cities without costly infrastructure.

3. *Facilities- and non-facilities-based ISPs.* These utilize both options for how their ISPs are structured. This option is becoming more and more common as regional ISPs look to go national without the build-out costs of deploying hundreds of POPs (points of presence) by continuing to use their existing infrastructure.

ISP MARKETING AND INNOVATION TIP

Peter F. Drucker, the famous author and speaker on innovation and entrepreneurship, had this famous thought to share: "Business has only two basic functions—marketing and innovation." With that said, I want to remind you that you are reading a marketing book, even though this can read sometimes like an ISP business basics book. The important distinction is that some of the following ISP business models have a lot to do with being innovative with the way you set up your organization, allowing you to focus on sales and marketing, which is the only way you are going to grow besides the possibility of growth by acquisition (covered in Chapter 9, How to Acquire New Subscribers via Acquisition of Other Internet Service Providers).

Which one is right for you? Let's dig deeper into this topic and look at the advantages and disadvantages of your options. For these examples, assume that we're talking purely about the decision as to whether you should outsource your dial-up, ISDN, or DSL services to a wholesale provider who will private-label them for you.

It should be noted here that there are many other aspects of your ISP business that you can outsource which will allow you to do what you do best. The only functions that I recommend you never outsource are your marketing components. No one will do these better than you can. It's still okay to hire a marketing consultant if you need to, but never hand over your marketing function to some magical company who promises to have your best interest ahead of its own—I have yet to see such a business model.

Facilities-based ISP

First, let's take a look at the facilities-based model shown in Figure 1.1. This is the traditional model for all ISPs who started out in this field in the early days, as it was the *only* way to do it. In this model, the local telecommunications provider provides the ISP with either POTS (plain old telephone service) analog lines or channelized T1 or PRI (primary rate circuit) digital lines, and the ISP's subscribers dial it directly.

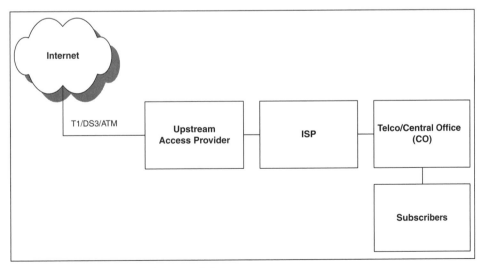

Figure 1.1 Facilities-based ISP model.

Here are many of the advantages of being a facilities-based ISP:

- You own and personally control 100 percent of your dial-up access switches and servers.

- As you hit economies of scale, your costs become lower.

- You're able to maneuver more quickly to meet market demand since your lead time from decision to implementation is totally up to you. You decide how fast you and your team can acquire the right equipment and install it.

- You'll be faster to the market with the latest dial-up speed or quality enhancements since you are in total control of the introduction of new technology instead of hoping or waiting for an outsourced dial-up provider to upgrade its switches.

- You're able to wholesale your network to other ISPs, whereas it might be impossible to cost-effectively wholesale a non-facilities-based ISP.

- You are able to receive additional termination revenues if you have telecommunication ties or have CLEC (Competitive Local Exchange Carrier) status. This option could be cheaper if you are starting out small and wish to grow slowly instead of having to meet the high minimum requirements that wholesale dial-up access providers expect.

- Your users will enjoy faster connectivity when accessing your local e-mail or Web content because they are directly connected to your network. For example, when they check their e-mail while dialed up directly to your service, they are not going through the entire Internet to check it, but rather are accessing it directly, which is a much faster method.

An important distinction is that facilities-based ISPs may no longer be the perfect option for many newcomers to the market, even though they have been the right or only choice for the last five to six years. It really depends on your market and niche focus, and what your core competencies are or will be soon.

Let's take a look at some of the disadvantages of running a pure facilities-based ISP:

- Got cash? Will burn. In the short term, this option can result in negative cash flow where you will spend capital for which you may not get a very high return. You also run the risk of investing in something that could become obsolete.

- You'll either need to be highly skilled in technical issues yourself or have expensive trained experts on staff to manage your network around the clock.

- Your dial-up access servers will depreciate must faster than the government may allow for tax-accounting purposes.

- Flexibility could be limited because you have signed leased line contracts with commitments to your local telecommunications provider. Many of these carry hefty early termination fees if you shut them down in the first three to five years.

- If your POPs (points of presence) are spread out all over the country, it will get expensive to dispatch technicians to maintain your network and troubleshoot problems.

- You may not be able to afford to have *cold spares,* or redundant hardware, standing by to save the day when your primary hardware fails; all electromechanical hardware will fail from time to time.

Non-facilities-based ISP

The non-facilities-based model came into existence compliments of the national tier one providers who needed to find a way to get higher returns on their network infrastructure costs. Here, we must also thank the likes of America Online (AOL), Prodigy, CompuServe, and others. In the mid-1980s these ISPs decided that they would not become backbone or online service providers but would rather outsource the back end of their online networks to specialists in dial-up access. In turn, these large companies would keep their focus on building businesses in the media, publishing, advertising, and community arenas. Most consumers never knew that when they dialed up AOL, it was not always AOL's network that they were dialed into even though their total experience was a fully AOL-branded, seamless service.

You can become a non-facilities-based ISP by using any one or a combination of wholesale dial-up access providers such as UUnet, PSInet, GTE Internetworking, BellAtlantic, MegaPOP, Ziplink, or NaviNet, to name a few. It's important not to confuse wholesale dial-up access providers with services such as iPass.com, Gric.net, or others that provide roaming services on shared networks. There is a strong quality difference between a business that owns its entire network versus one that manages many dozens to hundreds of other networks and is an intermediary provider.

The basic tenet of a non-facilities ISP, as seen in Figure 1.2, is that your subscribers will dial up a third-party wholesale access provider who will authenticate your user base and provide daily or monthly real-time stats on your subscriber usage patterns. Depending on your size, and the economics of your geographic position as it relates to where your wholesale provider is, you may or may not be required to establish a circuit (fractional T1, T1, or greater) between yourself and your wholesale dial-up access provider. This is usually done to save bandwidth on the backbone network and can dramatically improve speed responsiveness for your subscribers.

Here are the advantages of the non-facilities-based ISP model:

- You can spend your available capital on marketing and sales expenses that could have a higher chance of generating new subscribers rather than putting a lot of money into hardware which is less likely to increase sales.

- Flexibility is high. You can start an ISP overnight and private-label it all through any dial-up access switch wholesaler. This is great for those who want to build one of the new vertical ISP concepts now being introduced.

- You don't need high-end skilled technical support. As a result, you could save a lot of money when things go wrong because you can always pick up the phone and call your wholesale provider instead.

And now the disadvantages of running a non-facilities-based ISP:

- Dial-up wholesalers are usually run by very large companies that are

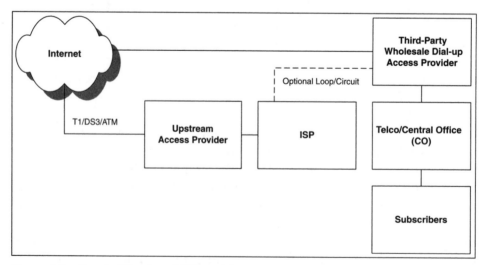

Figure 1.2   Non-facilities-based ISP model.

unable to adopt new technology first, which means that you may not be able to deliver the fastest or latest Internet access service enhancements to your customers.

■ Your reputation could suffer because you are totally reliant on someone else to deliver the access service you sell. No one may ever care about uptime or quality like you do, but as the wholesale dial-up industry evolves, quality of service (QoS) standards will improve and this will become less of a concern.

Which Is Right for Your Business?

There is no easy solution. There are a number of issues that come into play when choosing how your ISP will be set up, such as your available capital, how far you want your geographic reach to be, and the strategic future direction for your ISP.

Your ISP exit strategy, which is how the owners of your ISP will be rewarded for their investment, will also play a major role in determining which setup option you choose. For example: It's easier to sell a non-facilities-based ISP to another non-facilities-based provider who uses the same third-party wholesale dial-up provider. Your customers will be on the same network, which means that even though they may have a new ISP name to get used to, at least their dial-up access experience will be much more stable than if they had to dial up another network.

101 Questions to Ask Before You Begin Your ISP Business

Knowing all the answers is impossible, but knowing which questions to ask can make or break the success of your ISP. The quality of your life and business are in direct proportion to the quality of the questions you ask of yourself and your team. Your brain can only answer the questions you ask of it, which makes it very important to make sure you ask positive and empowering questions, rather than questions which lead you to frustration or the same results that you may already be getting.

DEFINITION OF ISP INSANITY

"Doing the same thing over and over again, and expecting a different result."

What follows is a list of 101 questions that you should ask yourself, to help you evaluate where you are, where you wish to go, and how you'll get there quickly. The questions are divided into seven different categories. It's important to not just read the questions, but to read them and stop to formulate answers in your mind or, better yet, to write the answer down.

ISP Business Basics Questions

1. Why are you building an ISP?
2. Which business or industry are you really in?
3. What are the major critical success indicators for your ISP business?
4. What are the core values of your ISP? How will you behave as a business?
5. What is your ISP mission?
6. What is your ISP vision?
7. When is the last time you wrote a business plan for your ISP, on paper or electronically?
8. Do you have a strategic or market advantage in your target marketplace?
9. What is your anticipated end outcome for your ISP business?
10. What are your most important short-term and long-term goals for your ISP?
11. Are you building an ISP to sell or for an annuity revenue stream?
12. How many years are you going to build it before you look to sell it?
13. How big should you plan on building your ISP? How big could you make it?
14. What guarantees will you offer your clients in writing?
15. What will be your unique selling proposition (USP)?
16. What will be your core price points that will define your position in the marketplace?
17. How will you build your management team?
18. Whom do you need to fire right now? Whom do you need to hire right now?
19. Which billing or accounting management system is best for your ISP?
20. How will you build a strong board of directors?

21. How will you protect your intellectual property, domain names, and trademark or patent rights?

22. Which ISP trade shows will give you the best outside perspective for how to further build your ISP?

23. Where will you strategically locate your corporate headquarters?

ISP Marketing and Sales Questions

1. Who is your target market?

2. How big is that market?

3. Is your ISP focused on business or consumer needs, or both?

4. What qualities do the users in your target market have in common?

5. Where can you find your target prospective customer?

6. How will you communicate your unique selling proposition?

7. Have you included your USP on your Web site, letterhead, envelopes, business cards, trade show displays, and all of your literature?

8. Which media or advertising marketing vehicles will get you the highest prospect of new paying subscriber conversion?

9. How will you track your marketing effectiveness?

10. Which components of your marketing will you test this month?

11. Have you tested new headlines yet? (Note: As much as 95 percent of the effectiveness of an ad is in the headline.)

12. Which of your vendors will give you co-op money for advertising and marketing?

13. What could you do to reduce churn? (How do you stop customers from leaving you?)

14. What will be your sales strategy?

15. Will you have an in-house or external sales force, or both?

16. Will you set up an affiliate, associate, or referral program so your customers can bird-dog sales for you?

17. How much should you give your members for referring their friends?

18. How much should you pay to acquire sales?

19. What is the lowest-cost way to attract new customers?

20. If your ISP is big enough to be a portal, how can you make money with advertising?

21. Are there other advertising revenue opportunities that your larger competitors are pursuing that you are not yet?

22. Can you acquire subscribers cheaper and faster by buying smaller ISPs?

23. Whom should you do joint ventures or co-branding with to grow your ISP?

24. What can you up-sell or cross-sell to your new subscribers at the time of sale in order to increase your average ticket size?

ISP Customer Service Questions

1. What are the minimum service levels that your customers can expect to receive from your ISP?

2. When is the last time you polled your customers to ask them for feedback on your service?

3. How fast will you return e-mails to support and service your subscribers?

4. How can you reduce the number of telephone calls from customers who are asking for support?

5. How good is the quality of your FAQ (Frequently Asked Questions)?

6. Does your FAQ need to be updated, and if so, how often should it be updated?

7. Does your phone system allow you to meet the needs of your clients fast enough and without hassle?

8. On average, how many minutes are your clients on hold (for those who have ISP call centers)?

9. Have you empowered your front-line staff to satisfy and please your subscribers?

10. Are there any tools for which your employees keep asking but you have not given, that will assist you in delivering better service?

11. When is the last time anyone on your staff got a customer testimonial letter?

12. Are you doing things that will increase or decrease the number of happy versus unhappy customer letters to management?

13. Has your Acceptable Use Policy (AUP) been updated recently?

14. How will you handle spammers who abuse your network?

15. How will you protect your clients against spam abuse? (*Spamming* is the sending of unsolicited commercial e-mail and is bad netiquette.)

ISP Investment, Banking, and Capital-Raising Questions

1. How much money do you need to fully execute the vision of your CEO or owners?

2. Which option or capital-raising investment vehicle makes the most sense for your ISP?

3. Does leasing make more sense than buying? Which is right for your ISP?

4. Do any of your vendors offer you vendor-financing options or deferred payment options?

5. Who specifically can help you raise capital for your ISP?

6. Where can you find people who specialize in raising cash for ISPs?

7. Which community forums or industry associations should you join to rub elbows with the decision-makers who can assist you in the pursuit of your goals?

8. Who can take your ISP public? What are the different ways to do that?

9. How much of a credit line with your bank must you have to conduct business?

10. Is your ISP currently in positive or negative cash flow? (*Positive cash flow* is when you have more money coming in than you have money going out.)

11. At what point in your ISP game plan will your ISP be in positive cash flow?

12. What telco (telecommunications) service options or avenues exist beyond those you are offered from your local Bell company? Does it make sense to become a CLEC or merge with one? How can you reduce your telco expenses?

ISP Technology and Network Questions

1. Should you outsource your dial-up POPs, servers, and equipment or do it all in-house?

2. Will you collocate your ISP in a data center or haul T1 and/or T3 pipes out to your current office?

3. How many servers will you need to deliver excellent service?

4. Which platform gives you the highest return—NT or Unix, or both?

5. How will you monitor your network for uptime?

6. Will you use an external third-party monitoring service and, if so, which one specifically?

7. What is your problem-solving or emergency escalation procedure?

8. What will you do for power conditioning, protection, and backup power supplies?

9. Who is in charge of taking daily, weekly, and monthly network inventories of your hardware and software assets?

ISP Human Resource Questions

1. What minimum level of skills must your technical support staff have?

2. How do you ensure that you are able to retain talented staff members?

3. How will you attract key personnel?

4. Will you need the assistance of a recruiter, or can you do this on your own?

5. What level of benefits will be necessary to acquire and retain talented staff members?

6. What can you do to make it fun to work at your ISP? Do you have a fun budget?

7. Have your employees signed noncompete, confidentiality, and invention rights clauses?

8. What about your programmers? Do you own the copyright to the work they are producing while they are working on your company's time?

ISP Exit Strategy Questions

1. What is your ISP exit strategy?
2. When is the right time to exit?
3. How big must your ISP be to get ready for your exit?
4. How will you value your ISP?
5. How does the market value your ISP or ISPs similar to yours?
6. What about telco contract early termination charges? What will it cost you to go out of business?
7. Will you sell your ISP to a regional, local, national, or international ISP?
8. Who are the top three or four best candidates who might want to buy your ISP?
9. How will you ensure that your customers are well taken care of after you are no longer serving them? (Remember that your reputation goes with you to your next adventure!)
10. What are the tax implications of your ISP exit strategy?

Your answers to the preceding questions may not be the same as for someone else or your ISP competitors, but they do need to be the right answers for you, your business, and where you are at this stage of the ISP game.

One last thought for this chapter: It's been said that thinking is one of the hardest things to do on Earth, which is why so few people actually do it. Choose to be different. You'll find that if you do the previously mentioned exercise, you will have joined the few real leaders who do whatever it takes to make their businesses successful.

CHAPTER 2

Planning Your ISP Exit Strategy as Part of Your Start-up

What does your ISP exit strategy have to do with your marketing plans, or for that matter, why is it in an ISP marketing book? A central theme that should become apparent in this book is that your end outcome or end goal is always your first step to determining which strategies will be right for you and your ISP business. Your chosen exit strategy will determine many things including the amount of capital you will need to accomplish your goals, your marketing mix along with budget, your sales focus, and your positioning statement. Just about every part of your ISP future will be based on the daily realization that you are a step closer to your goal. IBM is a great example of a company that started out with its end goals clearly stated before it began, and every day management focused on making up the difference between where they were and where they wanted to end up. You can and must do the same thing or suffer the consequences of being a business that is drifting without purpose.

Your written ISP exit strategy states your business purpose along with a timeline within which you must achieve certain milestones to stay on track. It can be a great reality check for many who find themselves lost and without focus. Some ISPs are built for an annuity, or for the pure purpose of recurring revenues, or for profits alone. While there is nothing wrong with that, the ISP marketplace can be very volatile and could force you at some time to consider what your exit strategy should be so that you don't overspend or underspend while building your business.

There are sure to be many books that specialize in helping you navigate ISP exit strategies and giving ISP valuation/investment advice, but this book gives you a quick overview of the different types of ISP exit models in existence at the time of this writing. When you view the various figures, remember that there are literally hundreds to thousands of different combinations of ISP exit strategies, and what works for you could be different from what worked for me or another ISP. The first example of an ISP exit strategy is shown in Figure 2.1. It is the most popular and is the easiest to maneuver since there are usually many buyers who are larger fish or ISPs than yourself. If your ISP fits into their business model and business cycle timing, you could sell out to a bigger ISP. While it's the norm to sell out to a larger ISP, please note that many deals have been financed by highly creative *smaller* ISPs who have bought much larger ISPs.

The next example, shown in Figure 2.2, is often dreamed about at one time by almost every ISP owner. But only a select few will ever make it into the paper billionaire CEO club by selling an interest in their ISP for equity financing via angels, venture capital firms, and/or eventually the public with an IPO (initial public offering). Paul Stapleton, one of the principals of Rampart & Associates, an ISP investment banker and editor/publisher of the *I$P Report* (a financial newsletter for ISPs), explained that within the ISP industry, there are very few ISPs who think like "billion dollar managers."

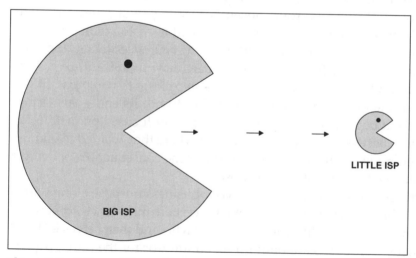

LITTLE ISP

BIG ISP

Figure 2.1   Sell your ISP to a bigger fish.

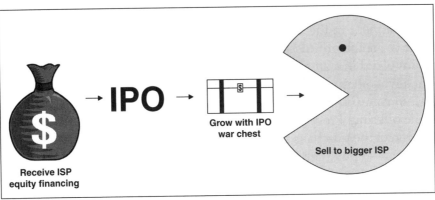

Receive ISP equity financing → IPO → Grow with IPO war chest → Sell to bigger ISP

Figure 2.2   Use minority venture capital, angel investment, or IPO to grow; then sell your ISP to a bigger fish.

Stapleton states that the typical ISP owner/manager could run an excellent ISP shop, but few have management skills of that scale. This creates a ceiling that 90 percent of the ISPs seldom ever break through. *Billion dollar managers* are ISPs who are able to bring the market value of their ISPs to a billion dollars or higher. They also share many or all of the following qualities:

- Strong sales skills
- Financial discipline/basic skill set
- Strong sense of the ISP industry; has the qualities of a visionary
- Focus on positive cash flow and driving earnings
- Technological proficiency; knows the right questions to ask
- Ability to delegate to qualified people
- Sense of confidence; ability to convey this to the customer base
- Focus on improving net quality/reliability

If you're one of the dreamers hoping to be the next billion-dollar ISP, the real question is, are you willing to do whatever it takes to acquire the skills you need to make it to the top?

HOW BIG CAN YOUR ISP BE?

The size of your ISP will be in direct proportion to the exact size you have imagined in your mind. Your ISP cannot ever grow larger in the physical world until you can imagine it as possible in your mental world.

A new model that has evolved purely out of the frenzy of positive investor sentiment in the bull-run stock market, which has been favoring Internet IPOs, is the promissory note, shown in Figure 2.3. This is a way to become involved in a small ISP membership aggregation IPO rollout with other ISPs who all go public together under one name. An example of this is OneMain.com (NASDAQ: ONEM), which raised $215 million in its initial public offering. Proceeds from the sale of shares were used to pay the cash portion of the purchase prices in the acquisitions of 17 Internet Service Providers, to repay certain indebtedness of these Internet Service Providers, and to use for general corporate purposes. Six months later, this ISP had half a million subscribers, and, if you do the math, it appears that each individual ISP received far more value per subscriber than they might have if they just sold out to a larger fish.

What's an ISP Worth?

Determining an ISP's value is one of the most challenging tasks for any ISP CEO, owner, or investor. The following models are based on fee-based ISPs and *not* the free-based advertising-supported ISP models. Remember that there are literally hundreds of factors that could affect the exact price or val-

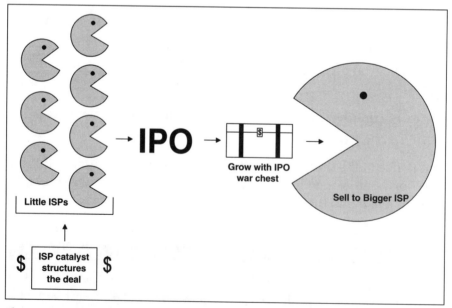

Figure 2.3 Promissory note to become involved in a small ISP membership aggregation IPO rollout.

uation of an ISP. After speaking with many ISP venture capital firms to get a handle on the common denominators of how to determine ISP valuation, Shaun M. Gilley, Vice President of Seruus Advisors (www.seruus.com), said it best in the following way.

There are basically three ways to value any business:

Discounted Cash Flow (DCF) valuation. This type of valuation focuses on the projected cash flows of the business. To develop a DCF model, you take the historical cash flows of the business combined with projected future cash flows and apply a time-value *discount* rate (interest rate) to the future cash flows to translate them to *present* value. Thus, the value of the business is the net present value of expected future cash flows (EBITDA, earnings before interest, taxes, depreciation, and amortization, is the commonly used measure of cash flow in telecom). This model says that a business is worth the cash it will actually generate in the future. There are some private company/public company differences in value due to the fact that a public company has greater access to capital and typically has a proven business model and professional management, and so forth. The more mature a business gets, presumably the more one is able to predict with some certainty what future cash flows will be. *Ceteris paribus,* the less the perceived risk, the greater the value.

Comparable public companies. This type of valuation compares a public company to a private company using a metric such as revenues per subscriber, cash flow per subscriber, and so on to approximate value. The difficulty here is that it is hard to find a public company that closely matches a private company (size is usually quite different, for example, and pure plays are hard to find).

Comparable private transactions (mergers and acquisitions, M&A). This is a valuation technique that relies on knowledge of purchases of similar companies. It is easier to find a private company that matches another private company but often difficult to find out how much someone actually paid in a transaction. Intermediaries (such as ourselves) often have better access (through the deals they do) to actual market-based transactions. This is valuable information since it reflects the real-world price someone was willing to pay for a company.

There is actually a fourth value method—the *Greater Fool Theorem.* There are some people who have an irrational approach to buying a company. They pay too much! It's always nice to have a greater fool around if you are the seller and the greater fool is the buyer.

From a simple perspective, here are a few more ways to calculate ISP valuations:

- Based on a multiple of annualized revenue, which can mean less than one year's sales, or a multiple, such as 1.25 or 2 times annualized sales or even higher. If you receive anything greater than 1 times sales, you're pricing in the right direction.

- Based on a value per subscriber, with the value per subscriber climbing as the total number of subscribers increases. Figure 2.4 shows an overview of this concept. This figure is not meant to be all-inclusive, but rather shows the amount some of the past ISPs have been acquired for over the last year, along with what some of the publicly reporting ISPs have reported in their securities disclosure statements. There are many items that will dramatically affect your valuation, and some of these items include the average price point of your service ($9.95 per month versus $19.95 per month), and your geographic position relative to your potential buyers' needs. The more closely your ISP resembles your ideal acquisition candidates' needs, the higher your potential valuation.

There is a big difference between when an ISP with market momentum is bought versus when an ISP's customer list is acquired. An ISP with mar-

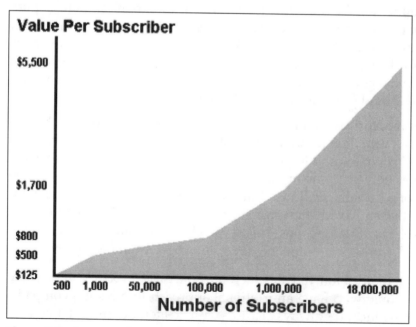

Figure 2.4   Average value per subscriber based on ISP size.

ket momentum is worth considerably more because of its chance for future earnings from previous marketing and brand-building investments.

Why determine the value of your subscribers? If you know how much the market is currently valuing other ISPs that are similar to yours, you can make financial decisions as to how aggressive your marketing budget and growth focus should be. It is *not* true that external forces including the consolidation within the ISP industry, the emerging cable Internet industry, and the free ISP ad-supported model, will bring the value of your subscribers down. The value of ISP subscriber bases has continued to climb every year since the start of this industry; it doesn't look like it will be slowing down anytime soon.

What is an ISP worth? The easy answer is: whatever a buyer is willing to pay for it if a seller is willing to sell it. A key distinction here is that buying an ISP is very different from just buying an ISP subscriber base. An ISP purchase will have a return that keeps on going after the deal is done; whereas a subscriber base purchase only assumes hope of the same thing, but not the same level of expectation. Most privately traded ISPs sell only their assets, not their corporate shell, because most buyers fear (and rightfully so) unknown variables or liabilities, which could sour the value after the fact. Don't be afraid to think outside of the box when setting up or thinking about your deal because every buyer's needs are unique and every seller's needs are also unique, which makes for an infinite number of possible negotiations when seeking the win-win deal.

Lifetime Value of an ISP Subscriber

The lifetime value of your average subscriber is the number of years the average customer of your ISP does business with you times the amount of revenue you receive from such a customer over this period.

For example: Jane Doe is a dial-up subscriber and pays $240 a year for service. She will be with your ISP for 3.5 years, making her worth $840 to you in guaranteed sales revenue. Assuming you have a 30 percent margin, she also represents approximately $200 in gross profit to your ISP over the lifetime of her purchase of service from you. If you know that you will be able to sell this account for 1.2 times annual earnings (for the sake of the example), when you sell this account, assuming it converts to the new ISP, you will get $288 ($240 × 1.2). With these current numbers ($200 in profit over the lifetime, which is conservative because it assumes you did not upsell or cross-sell her anything, plus $288 that you'll get when you sell your accounts), $488 in gross, pretax profit is the lifetime value of this subscriber.

How much can you afford to spend to acquire this customer without losing money? The answer is about $400, assuming unknown variables, cost to acquire the sale, and the fact that a national average of only 80 percent of customers convert when ISP subscriber bases are sold.

Use the *lifetime value of a subscriber* to remind yourself and your team that customers mean much more to you than the measly monthly fee they might pay you for Internet access. It's much easier to justify growth through acquisition when you know the full value of how much cash you could realize from customers over the lifetime of their purchases from you.

Easy Techniques to Increase Market Value

Value perceived is value achieved. Here are some quick as well as some not-so-quick strategies you can do to immediately increase the market value of your ISP business:

Require or encourage your clients who pay less than $100 per month to pay via credit card. Every business has credit cards. Not only does paper invoicing cost more in extra time, postage, and labor, but it's been proven that credit card customers are easier to maintain; they increase your positive cash flow because you bill their cards and get paid on time, rather than always having to wait 30 days or longer to get paid. You may wish to consider charging for paper invoices. Many ISPs have begun charging between $1 and $5 per invoice if they have to send an invoice via snail mail versus e-mail or secure Web access.

Offer electronic checking account draft as a payment option. This is sometimes referred to as ACH (automatic clearinghouse). It will give you the same benefits as credit card billing in that you lower your costs to administer these subscribers and increase your chances of getting paid on time. The downside is that credit card and automatic checking account drafting transactions are not perfect and do bounce, but the benefits still outweigh the disadvantages and greatly simplify your new buyers' ease of conversion. Anything that makes conversion easier and less of a hassle means you get more money when you sell out.

Decide up front how you want to exit from your ISP business. By deciding early on, each day you can focus your energies on maximizing the highest return possible. You do not want to decide your ISP exit strategy a month before you begin to try to figure out *how* you're going to get out—you will be at a disadvantage.

Make a list of potential buyers and learn everything about their values and past ISP behaviors. If you know their value system, you can quietly transform your ISP into being more like the ISP you hope will acquire your business. Just as people prefer people who are like themselves, it's always easier for an ISP to buy another ISP that is just like it or at least is perceived to be just like it. Your ideal goal is to begin identifying potential buyers four to fourteen months before you choose to sell.

Clean up your customer database to ensure you have a firm handle on how many paying subscribers you really have. There are quite a few horror stories about ISPs who found out after the fact that they had several hundred nonpaying subscribers using their systems because of poor RADIUS (Remote Authentication Dial-In User Service) logs or simple database management problems which didn't get a high enough priority. It's best to know now how many true paying subscribers you have than after the deal because you may be losing money that is rightfully yours.

Check with your A/R (accounts receivable) department to make sure your clients are paying on time and that you don't have anyone who owes you more than 90 to 120 days out. This is not about being nice but is strictly a smart business policy that you and your staff may need to implement if you haven't already. Your vendors couldn't care less if your customers pay on time or not at all; they still want to get paid on time regardless of your particular situation.

Simplify your pricing plans. This not only makes it easier for your customers to do business with you, but makes it easier when it's time to size up the value of your subscriber base sorted by price point and to compare it to the price points that your potential ISP buyer is already using.

Check out your early circuit termination charges if you have been in business for three to five years or less. Many DS3, T1, E1, PRI, and other similar circuits came with an agreement you may have signed years ago stating that if you shut down the circuits before the end of the contract, you could be liable for a penalty equal to the cost of the lifetime contract. This penalty can easily creep into thousands of dollars of liability that you may have forgotten about. If you are stuck with a significant early circuit termination charge, you may wish to consider selling to a telco who could repurpose the circuits instead of incurring a huge penalty.

TOP 10 GREAT WAYS TO ENHANCE THE VALUE OF YOUR ISP

When you improve the productivity and profitability of your business, you automatically increase its value. This should be an ongoing process and not just during a merger, divestiture, or at a time when you wish to attract new investors. Here are a few of the many ways to improve your value. There are hundreds of possibilities but here are 10 important points.

10. If you provide complimentary or free services to schools, libraries, radio/TV stations, or churches, don't expect something in return—make it part of the deal. There's no such thing as a free lunch.

9. Keep pricing simple and in the general trend of the industry.

8. Every product is a profit center. In most cases, if a service is not profitable (or not related to the profit of another product), you should delete the item or service. Beware of falling into this trap: "We lose money on every sale . . . but we make it up in volume."

7. It's easier to upgrade on a continuous basis, and *quality* equipment normally pays for itself in the long run.

6. Always be in the marketing mode; continued growth even by one account is in the positive direction. (Don't get stuck in the "radio does not work" mode—TV, radio, newspapers, shoppers, direct mail, and telemarketing work—it's just that every person has a different hot button.)

5. Be able to track subscriber levels, receivables, and prepaid subscriber services to the penny. You need a full-featured billing system.

4. Make automatic check debit or credit card payment the primary way of billing (and have your customer agreement worded so that if you sell the company or accounts these may be transferred to a new owner).

3. Whenever possible, lock in dedicated accounts to long-term contracts.

2. Keep your accounting system up to date, refrain from running nonrelated expense items through the books, and properly capitalize or otherwise break out major capital expenses (there could be a top 20 list for this one alone).

1. Don't provide good customer service—provide excellent customer service.

(Reprinted with permission from Tom Millitzer of New Commerce Communications, www.com-broker.com.)

What about your business continuation strategy? Do you have additional assets that you might wish to sell at the same time as your Internet access subscribers? Can you get more money for your Web hosting/design business, for example, from a different party who would value it higher than your current buyer's offers for your Internet access clients?

Spin your internal processes into a brand name to project a higher perceived value. For example: Let's say that you have a unique or proprietary method of converting your prospective or free-trial customers. Consider this method as a specific name or internal brand, and find out how much more efficient it is than the methods the rest of the marketplace uses. When you can present an internal process that you've put a little extra thought into, along with research that proves your specialized knowledge creates economic impact unlike that of your competitors, your future buyer may perceive that it could implement that process(es) into its ISP to potentially realize a larger gain after the acquisition.

Educate yourself. In this case, not only is knowledge power, but knowledge can create significant additional wealth for your ISP market valuation. Know your numbers, and if you don't, figure them out. What is the lifetime value of a subscriber in terms of revenue to your ISP? Did you know that every major recent ISP acquisition buy/sell transaction is listed by many of the ISP investment bankers? You owe it to yourself to investigate this information so that you know what similar ISPs are fetching in terms of valuation, along with what buyers want and don't want when making an acquisition.

Don't plan on selling out alone. Get help! ISP investment bankers specialize in running a process that forces buyers into a competitive bidding situation thereby optimizing a higher selling price. Their contacts alone could find you a higher valuation than what you could find without them and this often more than makes up for the commission they get paid for structuring the deal. You've worked too hard for too many years to leave extra money lying on the table.

What ISP Buyers Want

There are two basic ISP acquisition buyers: Those who will buy your client base only, and those who want to acquire your whole ISP operation, including your subscriber base, network server, telecommunications hardware/software, internal accounting processes, marketing department, and your employees/talent. It's extremely important that you do not assume that what you think your prospective buyer needs is what it wants to buy. Just like selling any product or service, you must ask, dig, and re-ask questions for clarification to make sure you properly and truly understand what your buyer's obvious and not-so-obvious needs are.

First, let's look at the ISP subscriber-base-only buyer. This is a simple sale, when compared to the ISP buyer who wants the entire company.

A typical profile of needs for such a buyer could be as follows:

- A high raw subscriber count. The more subscribers, the better valuation you will receive.

- Quality of customer service that you've provided along with a positive public reputation.

- Customer base that is within the same geographic area that it serves or can serve with existing POPs (points of presence) or a whole dial-up POP coverage area.

- Low churn and high growth rates.

- Low number of prepaid accounts that will be a liability and possibly an unknown variable for them in the acquisition process.

- Loyal customers who have been with you for more than a few months. The higher the age of the account, the higher the perceived value.

- Great accounting records and history about your client base including technical notes, if you have them, based on customer service calls you've had with your subscribers.

- A subscriber base that closely conforms to its model of the world, including price points, customer or technical support service hours, payment methods, and so on.

The ISP business buyer or investor has a different set of needs and agenda even though it may want some or all of the same things as a client-base buyer.

A typical profile of needs for such a buyer could be as follows:

- Your profitability or your proximity to profitability.

- An experienced management team whose members are comfortable with each other and have a proven success record in other similar or related mature industries. Assurance that this management team can scale as the business grows. Assurance that the team will be able to handle an extremely fast-paced migration of technology as the business climbs.

- A feel for how your ISP will fit into its model, visions of the industry, values, and culture to ensure a chance at success together.

- To study your business processes; to see more documentation than you will probably feel comfortable revealing, including past sales and profit performance figures and your tax returns to verify internal documents, in order to see how well management is maintaining the financial health of the organization.

- Access to your network uptime and reliability records collected by third-party monitoring services.

- To know whether the business has solid contracts or at least a great working relationship with its upstream providers or collocation provider. Do they have a redundancy plan and enough IP addresses and other various network resources to handle needs as the business grows?

- Good written customer contracts, which are also a plus for dedicated Internet access customers of the ISP. Make sure your contracts are assignable to your successor!

- Strong ancilliary revenues such as advertising revenue, affiliate or associate program revenues, and anything that shows you attempted to or are maximizing the leverage you have with your loyal subscriber base.

- To know the morale of your employees; to have private interviews with them (these could be nearly impossible for you to provide because of the conflicts of interest they may cause until you have a deal signed).

- To see a list of praise letters or testimonials that you've received from satisfied clients.

Another general quality that ISP buyers look for when the stakes get higher is whether you are open to stock as a value currency instead of cash, and whether you're open to creative financing. This is where the tables could reverse. Now it's your job to know more about your buyer than you might want to know in order to evaluate which option will provide you with the maximum possible return.

SELLING TIP

Make sure you don't openly disclose internal proprietary or confidential information without a signed NDA (nondisclosure agreement). It may not prevent a worst case scenario but it could help you to sleep a bit easier at night.

10 Things Not to Do When Selling Your ISP

This chapter exists purely from firsthand experience of what it was like to build an ISP for almost three years before selling out to a regional telco. These experiences could save you from making the many mistakes of early ISP pioneers. An exit can be a happy one. Here are the top 10 things not to do when selling out:

1. Don't do it alone. Get help from ISP acquisition, seller, or mergers and acquisitions specialists, your attorney, your accountant (for the tax implications), your business advisors, board, and mentors.

2. Don't forget to do research on the ISP to whom you are considering selling. Just because your potential buyer has deep pockets does not mean it knows how to competently run its business; your reputation could suffer postsale if you don't do your homework.

3. Don't feel forced to finance the deal yourself. The reality is that there are plenty of people out there who can afford to pay you cash up front or can get a loan or line of credit to get you cash up front.

4. Don't forget that you typically will only get paid on your subscribers who will convert to the new ISP. Typically you will lose 10 to 20 percent of your customer base in the conversion. Make sure you factor this in and think very carefully about the transition process.

5. Don't allow the new ISP buyer to dictate how the transition will be. Make sure your contract includes detailed provisions for how the transition will happen. No one knows your customer base better than you do. It's important that you set up 80 percent or more of how the transition process will take place.

6. Don't forget to negotiate a good reseller or affiliate program with your buyer if you are going to continue your ISP operation without your dial-up base, as you will continue to receive new subscriber inquiries which you need to convert to cash or profit for yourself postdeal.

7. Don't do the deal without talking with the CEO of any other ISP that the potential buyer has acquired to find out how their process went and whether they were happy or not about it.

8. Don't sell to the first buyer that offers you a good deal unless it's a serious premium over what other similar ISPs have been acquired for. The perfect setup is when you've positioned yourself to get multiple

> **SELLING YOUR ISP NEGOTIATION TIP**
>
> Selling your business or subscriber base is largely a sales and negotiation process. Make sure you not only talk with CEOs who recently sold out but pick up a couple of audiotape programs on the art of negotiation. A few hundred dollars invested in mastering the science of understanding good negotiation techniques could pay off handsomely when negotiating the sale of your ISP. A good negotiation skills author is Dr. Chester L. Karrass. You can buy his books from any major bookseller or visit him on the Web at www.karrass.com/.

buyers bidding on your ISP or subscriber base or both at the same time, which allows you to not be forced to accept a bid that might not be as attractive as other buyers'.

9. Don't underestimate your value. Everyone who may offer to buy your ISP has a different idea as to what makes or creates more or less value. Your job is to find a buyer who can leverage or give you the highest amount of value per subscriber.

10. Don't be afraid to package, unpackage, or repackage your assets for a single or multiple buyers. You need to evaluate whether you can get more money by selling some of your ISP assets separately versus the whole based on the needs of the potential buyer.

Resources for Selling Your ISP

Even with the highly volatile Internet and ISP industry, many of the following resources and top players in the ISP acquisitions and mergers market have been around since the beginning. If they can't help you, then maybe someone they know will be able to point you in a good direction. Don't be afraid to ask for a referral since many will gladly give one and are well connected. Table 2.1 lists a small handful of investment bankers who focus on the ISP industry. There are literally hundreds of investment bankers who would be more than happy to help ISPs, but there are less than a dozen who make it their business to really understand the ISP market.

Table 2.1 SP Investment Bankers and Mergers and Acquisition Organizations That Specialize in the ISP Market

ORGANIZATION	DESCRIPTION OF SERVICES OFFERED
BIZ-NET Brokers, Inc. Black Canyon Professional Plaza 8611 North Black Canyon Highway Suite 214 Phoenix, Arizona 85021 **Richard Varner** Telephone: (602) 864-5553 Fax: (602) 864-4911 E-mail: biznet@inficad.com Web: http://ISPBuySell.com/	BIZ-NET Brokers is a private mergers and acquisitions firm specializing in Internet-related companies. Its depth of financial experience and network of contacts within the industry is unmatched. BIZ-NET's market knowledge and talented team of professionals guide the seller or buyer through complex negotiations and help them avoid costly and time-consuming mistakes. Its mission is to assist its ISP and Web host clients in the complicated buy-sell process and to maximize their return on investment.
Cheetah Global Financial Group, Inc. 320 East 42nd Street Suite 2409 New York, NY 10017 **William W. Xin** Telephone: (212) 666-4170 Fax: (212) 681-9552 E-mail: xinku@aya.yale.edu	Cheetah Global Financial Group is an investment company with a division on ISP mergers and acquisition services.
Daniels & Associates 3200 Cherry Creek South Drive Suite 500 Denver, Colorado 80209 **Tim David, Bob Allison, Craig Moseley, and Mike Magluilo** Telephone: (303) 778-5555 Fax: (303) 778-5599 E-mail: info@bdaniels.com Web: www.bdaniels.com	Daniels & Associates' Internet Technologies Group provides a full range of investment banking services to ISPs, Web-hosting companies, and systems and network integration firms within the Internet industry. As one of America's most active telecommunications investment banks, it assists clients by structuring and placing debt or equity, gauging the value of Internet companies, and identifying strategic partners to accelerate growth. In addition to obtaining financially attractive transactions for clients, Daniels prides itself on being able to match management teams so that clients fill their personal, as well as corporate, financial goals.
E-Comm Capital Partners, LLC 2 South 457 Bancroft Court Glen Ellyn, IL 60137 **Patrick H. Gaughan, JD, MBA** **Christopher M. Gaughan, CFA** **[Level I completed 1999]** Telephone: (888) 534-9514 Fax: (630) 790-4766 E-mail: info@ecommcap.com Web: www.ecommcap.com	E-Comm Cap does management consulting and venture capital funding/brokering for Internet applications. E-Comm Cap has done work with everything from ISPs to traditional companies implementing innovative Internet technologies. E-Comm Cap has built a successful track record of positioning privately held companies for sustained growth, private placements, and initial public offerings.

Marlin Group, Inc.
117 SW Whitaker St. #1
Portland, OR 97201

David Marlin
Jill Nelson
Telephone: (503) 241-2330
Toll Free (888) 404-8862
Fax: (503) 241-2314
E-mail: info@marlingroup.com
Web: www.marlingroup.com

Marlin Group specializes in the sale of Pacific Northwest ISPs and is in contact with many purchasers and sellers. Companies looking to sell or acquire an ISP in Oregon, Washington, Idaho, Montana, or Northern California are encouraged to contact Marlin Group. Services offered include business sales, acquisitions, valuation, and consulting.

Nations Media Partners
4717 Central
Kansas City, MO 64112

Patrick T. Brock
Telephone: (816) 960-0100
Fax: (816) 960-0113
E-mail: pat@nationsmedia.com
Web: www.nationsmedia.com

Nations Media Partners is a full-service mergers and acquisitions firm dedicated to providing the expertise necessary to successfully complete the sale or acquisition of telecommunications companies, with a dedicated team of professionals focused on the ISP industry. It offers extensive support services before, during, and after each transaction and provides many valuable services including preparing the ISP business for sale, research and analysis of the company, marketing and promoting the business, financial analysis, structuring the transaction including tax consequences, review of legal details, and post-closing assistance.

New Commerce Communications
217 South Main Street
Pardeeville, WI 53954

Tom Millitzer
Telephone: (608) 429-4455
Fax: (608) 429-3430
E-mail: tom@com-broker.com
Web: www.com-broker.com

New Commerce Communications works with ISPs, Internet, Web-hosting, dedicated service, backbone providers, and emerging Internet telecommunications companies. It provides financial consulting services specializing in ISP mergers and acquisitions, ISP financial services, and ISP valuation services. NCC clients fall into two general categories: companies with an entrepreneurial spirit that want to grow, or clients that have obtained their success and want to reap their just rewards.

Rampart Associates, LLC
1600 Wynkoop, Suite 202
Denver, CO 80202

Ted Taylor, Paul Stapleton, Jake Taylor
Telephone: (303) 534-8585
Fax: (303) 534-8686
E-mail: info@rampart.net
Web: www.rampart.net

Rampart Associates is a private investment banking and brokerage firm whose partners have served the Internet and telecommunications industries since 1985. It specializes in seller and buyer representation as well as raising capital for middle-market Internet Service Providers, CLECs, and other telecom networks. It has a depth of financial experience and a network of contacts within the industry, and its goal is to help ISPs and their shareholders prosper through smart mergers, acquisitions or sales, and intelligent financing. Principal Stapleton provides independent industry analysis as editor of *ISP Report,* the Financial Newsletter for Internet Service Providers, and as the financial columnist for *Boardwatch*.

Table 2.1   *(Continued)*

RFC Capital Corporation, a division of Textron Financial Corporation 130 E. Chestnut St. Suite 400 Columbus, OH 43215 **Steven B. Jaffee** Telephone: (614) 229-7979 Toll Free: (888) 732-3863 Fax: (614) 229-4362 E-mail: ptarpey@rfccapital.com Web: www.rfccapital.com	RFC Capital Corporation is a commercial finance organization exclusively serving the needs of telecom, Internet, and related technology companies. While its services do not include straight equity financing, it does provide debt and mezzanine financing solutions. In addition to financing, it also provides consultative services to assist ISPs and related businesses. RFC Capital, based in Columbus, Ohio, is a division of Textron Financial Corporation.
Santa Fe Capital Group, Inc. 142 Lincoln Ave. Suite 500 Santa Fe, NM 87501 **David Silver** Telephone: (505) 984-0001 Fax: (505) 984-0008 E-mail: dsilver@sfcapital.com Web: www.sfcapital.com	Santa Fe Capital Group claims to have raised more capital and has effected more mergers and acquisitions of ISPs and Web hosters for more Internet entrepreneurs than any other similar firm. Following two decades of traditional investment banking—start-up fundings, LBOs, M&A, and workouts and turnarounds—the team at Santa Fe Capital Group entered the Internet industry in March 1995. A quick survey of the Group's Web site reveals that it has served in over 50+ ISP-related deals.
Seruus Advisors, LLC 55 Beattie Place, Suite 1500 Greenville, SC 29601 **Myron J. Goins** Telephone: (864) 233-5517 Fax: (864) 250-0204 E-mail: info@seruus.com Web: *www.seruus.com*	Seruus Advisors does M&A work focused on telecommunications. As telecom is the infrastructure to the information economy, it is involved in more and more Internet transactions, including ISPs. Its sister company, Seruus Ventures, is a venture capital firm also focused on telecommunications.
The Gilley Group, LCC P.O. Box 1936 Greenville, SC 29681-1936 **Sean M. Gilley** Managing Director Telephone: 800-400-8936 E-mail: *Shaun@theGilleyGroup* *.com* Web: *www.thegilleygroup.com*	The Gilley Group does mergers and acquisitions work in telecommunications, ecommerce, and Internet. As telecom is the infrastructure to the information economy, it is involved in more and more Internet transactions, including both buy-side and sell-side ISP engagements.

The ISP-Investor E-mail Discussion List Community

This is a free e-mail discussion list and digest that I started back in 1997. Today, it has over 2,500 list members who include many of the industry's best buyers, sellers, and traders of ISPs. If you are looking to buy, sell, or raise money, or just have a question on anything to do with the ISP-Investor, check this list since it is said to be the largest discussion list of its kind on Earth.

The ISP-Investor list's charter is as follows:

"ISPs buying, selling, trading, investing, mergers and acquisitions are the primary focus of the ISP-Investor list. Industry's leading CEOs and brokers are on this list and lurk for the latest news on who's selling and who's buying ISPs."

You can get your free subscription by sending an e-mail to join-isp-investor@isp-investor.com or you can visit the main homepage for more information at http://ISP-Investor.com/.

CHAPTER

3

Identifying Your Unique Selling Proposition

Building an ISP without clearly defining your Unique Selling Proposition (USP) is like charting a sailboat without a rudder, which leaves your business open to flow with the tides and currents of life instead of what you originally intended. Your USP is what makes you distinct, unique, and is the most attractive quality that will separate your ISP from your competition. It's also a vital component and the first step in designing a marketing strategy that best articulates your benefits to your target audience or core customer profile.

By investing a few hours' work into your USP, you will find that your business will begin to be more focused and less susceptible to distraction by attractive opportunities which may tempt you from time to time. Your team will have a better idea as to where the business is going in order to buy into the vision of your ISP. Your investors and owners will have more confidence in your strategic direction and, best of all, your customers will understand more clearly who it is that you intend to serve first, resulting in a higher-quality and more loyal customer base.

NOTE *Rosser Reeves* is credited as being the creator of the Unique Selling Proposition. USP was deemed one of the greatest advertising creations of the 1950s and lives on today as a tried and true marketing principle.

Your USP is something that more than just defines what your ISP delivers and whom specifically it serves. It should also permeate every single marketing, advertising, pricing, quality, sales, or support function within your business.

Identifying What Makes Your Business Unique

Before you identify what makes your ISP unique, it's more important to identify which needs in the marketplace are unfilled by your competitors or yourself. What gripes or complaints do potential customers in your marketplace have with their current providers?

Here are some typical ISP customer complaints:

- Busy signals are frustrating!

- Slow service or lack of the latest dial-up speed access technology makes it so that I can't connect very fast and this wastes my valuable time.

- Expert technical support is nowhere to be found.

- Technical support talks down to newbie callers; some customers fear calling their ISPs because they feel embarrassed or stupid.

- No one answers the phones or returns e-mails.

- The ISP won't stand behind its services with 100 percent satisfaction guaranteed. Customers are left with 100 percent of the risk of whether or not they have a good experience.

- Lack of selection of different dial-up plans makes it hard to buy from some ISPs who limit the flexibility of what their clients can buy.

- It's hard to do business with ISPs that don't accept every major credit card or illegally charge more to accept them.

USP TIP NO. 1

Your USP should be one crisp and easy-to-articulate sentence that offers a benefit your ISP can clearly deliver, and in a better way than anyone else.

- Lack of maturity of the owners of ISPs, who are possibly running their first businesses ever and don't understand good business behavior and etiquette yet.

- Because many ISPs are undercapitalized, they can't afford the best network hardware/software or talent, which results in bad uptime percentages and is very frustrating for many subscribers.

There are many more complaints, but it's important to think about the many gripes of the marketplace first when deciding which major complaint your USP will answer.

No matter where your ISP is in its development you have many attractive and sometimes hidden assets which can contribute to your USP. It must be believable and it must be something your ISP is able to deliver. There is nothing worse than overpromising and underdelivering, which is quite common in this industry. Don't fall into the same trap as your competitors.

EXPRESSING YOUR USP

Bernard Zick (www.zick.com), one of the best professional speakers I have ever had the pleasure of hearing, had a simple exercise on how to best express your USP. Here is his formula, as I've revised it for the ISP industry:

Say this:

"Do you know how [state the major pain associated with what your target market might experience or feel]?"

"What our ISP does is [state how your ISP relieves this pain.]"

Examples:

"Do you know how most Internet access providers are never there for you on the weekends or nights when you need them most? What we do at [insert ISP name] is provide technical support until midnight during the work week and extended technical support hours on the weekend to make your experience more hassle-free."

"Do you know how many ISPs claim to offer fast access, but then you get on their networks during peak times and it's slow as heck to use? At [insert ISP name], we take speed seriously with our investment in multiple redundant fast T3 lines and have specifically engineered our Cisco-powered network for optimal speed for dial-up client access."

"Do you know how many ISPs seem to be run by two men and a mouse? At [insert ISP name] we have a whole team of Internet experts designed to make your Internet access experience with us a positive and productive one."

Your USP is a promise to solve a specific problem for the potential subscribers in your marketplace. Unfortunately, solving a problem is not the only criterion for choosing the right USP for your ISP. A USP must represent what the marketplace wants in terms of profits, volume, and repeat business in order to meet the financial goals and needs of the business.

Some sample USPs follow:

- The [insert specialty vertical niche market here] ISP
- The Fastest ISP in Texas
- Your Internet, Your Way, or You Don't Pay
- The "No Busies or It's Free, Guaranteed" ISP
- The Friendly ISP—We Make Your Internet Experience Comfortable
- The Linux ISP Specialists
- Death Before Downtime—The 100 percent Uptime ISP
- The First ISP to Provide In-Home Delivery, Training, and Setup Assistance

Your USP also communicates the differentiation among competitors. *Differentiation* refers to a collection of features, benefits, and distinctions that make your ISP services and products better than anyone else's. Your goal is to find out which of your differentiating factors are actually important to your customers.

If you feel lost on the topic of differentiation, remember that delivering truly great customer service is one of the last frontiers that has yet to be mastered by your competition. Many successful ISP owners believe that great service creates differentiation by itself, which in turn creates value for everyone involved.

Excellent *positioning* happens when you have done a great job of creating a meaningful difference in the minds of your prospective buyers in that what they are interested in buying, you are interested in providing.

The meaningful difference can be communicated with your brand packaging of dial-up kits; Web site, tone, and color selection; consistency of advertising and promotional media-related propaganda; design of the benefits statements; marketing; and even word of mouth from each of your employees.

"Positioning is what you do to the mind of the prospect," say Al Ries and Jack Trout, authors of the book, *Marketing Warfare* (McGraw-Hill, 1997). Your key is to make sure everything within your control supports your USP, and does so consistently.

Identifying the Right Niche
for Your Business

Your USP is specifically designed to appeal only to a very select audience, and therefore is not designed to appeal to everybody. The niche for your USP depends on many factors, including the following:

Your current or expected business size. For example: It would be unreasonable to expect a giant ISP such as MindSpring or AOL to be able to offer in-home personal setup service, but it's not that outrageous to expect a small-town ISP with one or two POPs to be able to deliver that kind of personalized attention.

Your available capital. If it's extremely limited, you could consider doing the virtual non-facilities-based solution and invest the difference you save from not building huge infrastructures into sales and marketing avenues.

Your talent. Maybe you've got some expert labor on staff and can leverage it to provide value-added technical support, superior leadership, or sales and marketing advantages for your ISP.

Your network capacity and strength or lack thereof. If you're an existing ISP, then you are likely to have legacy hardware and software. These essentials could be very expensive to replace with the latest technology available, versus a new ISP, who can implement the latest technology for less money without the problems of the original equipment.

Your vendor relationships and alliances with strategic partners. With the unique combination of vendor alliances or partners, you could leverage something that has never been done before, causing a new niche to be created to fill a need which no one has met yet in your marketplace.

Your geographic coverage area. Make sure you know why you have coverage where you do. If your abilities or capital are very limited, it would be better to dominate a local niche than to try to take on nationwide coverage and go bankrupt in 18 months.

Market size and the kind of service or product you want to offer. Ultimately the market decides how cash is spent and whether the product mix you offer is attractive to enough people.

The market's need for the service or products you want to offer. Running a Quake game server could be a lot of fun but how many users

will sign up for it? Make sure your service and product mix is needed
by the market.

"Get Big or Get Out"

Whenever those who have created million-dollar businesses from the
ground up got lost and had to evaluate whether they should stay in a particular business, product, or service line, they often stopped and asked themselves one question: *"Can I get big enough to dominate this market or should I get
out and go find a niche or smaller market where I can either be first or dominate it?"*

The Law of Leadership, according to Al Ries and Jack Trout in their very
popular book, *The 22 Immutable Laws of Marketing* (Harperbusiness, 1994),
states simply that it is better to be first, than it is to be better. In other words,
if you can't be number one in a particular market segment, why not go create a new niche that fills a need that no one has filled yet? You will get to be
first in it, and it will certainly set your ISP apart from competitors who are
not as savvy as you.

You can use Ries and Trout's Law of Leadership in the following ways:

- You can offer a unique combination of ISP services including in-home
  setup, training, and, for a premium, extra or enhanced hand-holding
  services via telephone or on-site visits.

- Few ISPs succeed in follow-up after the sale, but what if your ISP was
  the first to build a branded service that makes you number one at
  follow-up? You'll get a higher prospect-to-customer conversion rate
  and you'll be appreciated by your new soon-to-be-lifelong subscribers.

- You might not be able to be the largest ISP in the world (by the way,
  there is no value to consumers by being the largest unless you can
  communicate a specific benefit or advantage to them that being the
  largest creates), but you could focus on providing the best service
  combination for the city or region through aggressive campaigns or
  growth through targeted acquisition.

- The secret is to get into the prospect's mind first before someone else
  does. Since many people could move into the areas you serve, it's log-

ical to assume they have a need for a new ISP. You'd be wise to position yourself as one of the most friendly and easy-to-use local ISPs for newbies in your neighborhood. You could also consider offering them special online guides to their new home city.

- AOL might own the word *easy* in the mind of the public, but it can't own the words or services the small- to mid-size ISP can actually provide by being the accessible ISP or by being the ISP who is willing to take the extra few minutes to listen to a customer problem. Fulfilling the USP of "friendly ISP" or "caring ISP" must be done through actions, not just words.

Lastly, don't fret if you can't be first. You can always create a new category in which to be first, assuming your target market values it. Marketing has never been about reality but rather the manipulation of perception. Value perceived is valued achieved.

Whom You Do Not Wish to Serve

Another excellent and fun exercise to do when choosing your ISP niche in addition to deciding whom you wish to serve is to decide whom specifically you are *not* going to serve. Sometimes it could seem like 90 percent of the problem calls that you receive are from 10 percent of your client base, or that 80 percent of your most unprofitable clients demonstrate a specific set of definable client traits which you can identify and effect an action plan to change.

There is a recurring theme of advice that comes from seasoned CEO professionals. It is this: "Fire your problem clients or raise the cost of doing business for those who don't conform to your ideal customer profile." These are not easy issues to navigate, but if you want to enhance your bottom line really fast and make going to work more fun again, give this a try.

Based on research from the ISP-Lists community, here are some of the traits of undesirable ISP clients. Remember that one person's undesirable client could be another's core target client, so consider this list as something to just stimulate your thinking.

Traits of undesirable ISP clients include:

- Customers who demand a free trial, even when you don't offer it
- Customers who share their usernames and passwords with their friends and family, who then call to say they can't log in and need your technical assistance—this is fraud unless you allow multiple concurrent connections as part of your pricing packages

- Customers who have a history of signing up for your free trial two or more times and then canceling after the trial period

- Customers who are involved in multilevel marketing, network marketing, scams, pyramid schemes, and anything related to get-rich-quick plans

- Customers who have a history of not paying their bills on time or always making excuses or breaking promises to do so

- Customers who believe their accounts should be extended when they don't use the service during the month. This is an unreasonable expectation—you don't ask your telephone company to credit you for basic service just because you didn't make or receive any calls for a few days. This is usually a customer education issue for your front-line staff.

- Line campers—people who abuse your AUP (Acceptable Use Policy) by treating an unlimited, but not dedicated, account as if it was their personal 24 by 7 dedicated connection to the Internet

- Customers who abuse your service by sending unsolicited bulk e-mail (spamming), hacking into computers on your or someone else's network, abusing USENET, or perpetrating any other system abuse

- Customers who are emotionally or verbally abusive to your employees—life is too short to deal with people who feel they need to use threats and foul language to get what they want

How Your Pricing Strategy Relates to Your USP

There are two basic ISP pricing/service extremes:

- High service/quality, high price
- Low service/quality, low price

Do not try to convince yourself that you can defy these two very basic business pricing model extremes because it cannot be done profitably over the long run. Figure 3.1 shows the four possible price-to-service combinations. The area that is shaded in gray is not *impossible* but is rather not a sustainable business model over the long run.

There is a natural tendency for marketing newcomers to want to deliver high-quality service at very low prices. Perhaps they think that they either don't deserve the prices their competitors are receiving for the same or less of a product or that they can build market share faster by delivering more

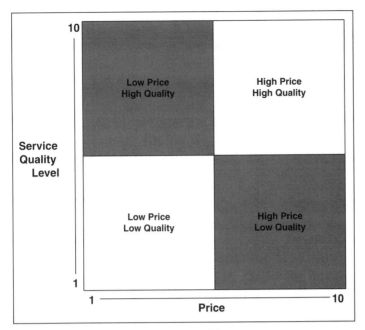

Figure 3.1 ISP pricing business models.

for less. Unfortunately, this model is not sustainable as the ISP will eventually run out of cash and will have to raise prices or find that it has underpriced itself right out of business.

Don't get me wrong. You could achieve significant economies of scale with your ISP in order to offer very attractive prices. While price appears to get a lot of a attention, if you ask your customers what they value most (especially if your service is unreliable because you couldn't afford the best hardware or talent to manage your ISP), they will tell you that price is not as important as uptime, reliability, and use of your service with no hassles.

Deploying Your New USP for Maximum Effectiveness

You've chosen the right USP for your business but does your well-crafted USP work if no one knows about it? Nope. Your USP is the foundation on which your business is built and it should *not* be hidden from public view. Table 3.1 lists the places and ways you can publicize your USP.

In addition, it's important that you have buy-in from the top down, meaning that your ISP CEO walks and talks your USP message, your corporate actions reinforce it (not fight it), and your executive team endorses it.

Table 3.1   Places Where Your USP Belongs

MARKETING MEDIA TYPE	WHERE TO INCLUDE YOUR USP
ISP Web site	On your main page, in your title, in your meta tags, in your "About" section, and throughout your entire site, including order forms and secure payment pages.
Business cards	On front or back.
Letterhead, envelopes, stationery	Always include.
Dial-up kit	On the CD-ROM or diskettes with any manuals or paper stock media included inside.
Direct marketing, coupons, flyers, envelope stuffers, and paper ad media	Always include.
Newspapers, magazines, billboards	Always include on all print media.
Trade shows	On your booth banner, in all of your hand-out materials, in any slide shows you present, on buttons worn by your sales team, and on any giveaways you hand out.
Speeches, presentations, seminars, talks, and lectures	Your presenter should always mention your USP right after he or she says your ISP's name, during, and/or at the close of the talk.
Promotional giveaways	Include on all when possible.
Sales team	Should not only know it by heart but be able to recite it when asked.
Invoices	Include as a tag line or in the notes. Most invoicing systems can do this automatically.
Investor relations documents	Include in any document that is a report from management to owners or investors.
Advertising campaigns	Your USP theme should come through regardless of the media; using the exact words is not always necessary.
Press releases	Include in all of them, usually either in the title or at least toward the end of the release.

A few techniques to get internal buy-in on your chosen USP include the following:

- Get everyone involved in the decision process as to what your USP will be but make sure you, the leader, set the general direction so that your team does not waste time attending lots of meetings where all kinds of interesting but nonrelevant material surfaces.

- Insist that your USP gets included in all the media listed in Table 3.1. Make it a baseline expectation so that eventually everyone uses it without having to be reminded.

- Post the USP in the restrooms where everyone who visits can see it.

- Quiz people in the hallways from time to time and in front of everyone at weekly or monthly staff meetings.

- Develop an internal document that briefly explains why your ISP has chosen your particular USP.

- Include your USP rationale and development in your employee handbook so that new employees get introduced to it in their first week.

Business ISP versus Consumer ISP

The needs of your business clients are radically different from the needs of nonbusiness consumers, and thus, a decision must be made as to whom you will serve as your first priority, and who will be your second. There is a third group that fits right in the middle of these two market segments, the SOHO (small office, home office) subscriber who also has a unique set of needs. By better understanding these market types and their unique sets of needs, you can make informed decisions about which market type you'd like to serve or not serve, as part of your USP.

Typical Needs of Business Clients

Business clients have unique needs:

- High reliability and uptime
- Knowledgeable, accessible, and friendly technical support professionals
- Network performance, speed, and scalability
- No downtime when using your products and services

- Secure commerce: firewalls and appropriate network security services
- High-access bandwidth utilization during the business day and business week—Monday through Friday

Advantages of Serving Business Clients

There are some advantages to serving business clients. These include the following:

- Most valuable client base when you look for high ISP exit valuations per subscriber.
- Most profitable client base possible since businesses are accustomed to paying for the kinds of services they need. While they may negotiate hard on price/performance, they will always find the money to pay for the kinds of services that will help solve their business challenges.
- Typically can be up-sold and cross-sold more additional products than any other type of Internet access client.

Disadvantages of Serving Business Clients

There are also some disadvantages of serving business clients. These include the following:

- Some may expect your ISP to perform as if it were part of the mature telecommunications industry, which it is obviously not.
- Some may ask you to do presentations or make on-site visits when you'd prefer to handle things over the telephone or via e-mail. Extra hand-holding is the norm but is usually worth it when it comes time to invoice the business client.
- Some may be slow to pay at times. Some businesses have people who do nothing but calculate how long they can go without paying you in order to keep their cash as long as possible.

Typical Needs of SOHO Clients

Small Office/Home Office clients have specific needs. These include the following:

- Low cost, reliable service
- Need evening and weekend technical support since they work hours that are sometimes more analogous to those of the consumer

Advantages of Serving SOHO Clients

The following are some advantages to serving SOHO clients:

- Large audience to go after since they all need Internet access
- Typically need and are willing to pay for the higher level of Internet access speed, which means more money per month for you

Disadvantages of Serving SOHO Clients

There are disadvantages to serving SOHO clients. These include the following:

- Subject to emotional swings of new SOHO business owners who have never been on their own before and don't know how to behave professionally when under extreme pressure
- May be slow paying their bills since most don't have built-in accounts payable departments

Typical Needs of Consumer Clients

Consumer clients have different needs. These include the following:

- Nighttime and weekend technical support
- High access and bandwidth resources nights and weekends
- Caring front-line technical support that doesn't speak over their heads and is willing to spend an enormous amount of time providing good Samaritan-like computer and Internet access assistance

Advantages of Serving Consumer Clients

There are some advantages to serving consumer clients. These include the following:

- They are great to sell additional consumer e-commerce items to, and can be an excellent source of targeted advertising revenue for your ISP.

- Most consumers work at businesses; the consumer's business can become your next business client from good word of mouth.

Disadvantages of Serving Consumer Clients

Disadvantages to serving consumer clients include the following:

- Can be verbally abusive as they care less about the relationship than a business or SOHO subscriber; many think of their ISP as a commodity service, resulting in lower loyalty for some

- Worth less than a business client when selling your ISP because of the lower average ticket price

- Low "clue level" of new users results in longer technical support calls during nonbusiness hours, which results in higher labor costs per user

Few ISPs go to the extreme and say that they are only a business ISP or a consumer ISP. However, you need to choose whom you are going to focus on first and build your business decisions around providing answers and solutions for that market instead of being all things to everyone, which we already know is not healthy or always possible.

Four Ways to Ensure You Own Your Market Niche

Once you've chosen the niche on which to focus all of your resources, the first step to ensure that you emerge the winner is to realize who your first and strongest competitor is. Believe it or not, it's you. It's always you and your ability to deliver better and faster speed of service, your ability to be more cunning than your competition in the execution of your worthy goals and business desires. If you start every day by finding one thing to improve, within three months you will have done more to advance your business than your average competitor will have done in a year.

TIP Your goal here is to increase the distance between where your business is and where your closest competitor is. Every day you will focus your actions on taking at least one step to widen the gap, making it harder for your competitors to follow.

Many of your competitors will be reading this book but the difference between who will emerge the winner and who will be the loser all depends on your ability to *execute* your plan faster.

Beyond getting the right mindset, there are proprietary ways that you can lock up your niche:

Domain name registration. Perhaps you already have your domain name but what about the domain name of every brand name you've created, every division within your company, and every misspelling of your name (with an *s*, without an *s*, with a dash, without a dash, and so on)? When the cost is less than $100 to get a domain name, there is nothing worse than knowing your competitor is stealing your traffic because it registered a domain that was similar to your domain and is wrongly capturing some of your traffic.

Trademarks. Filing for a federal or international trademark usually runs into the several-thousand-dollar range. It is a no-brainer if you want to avoid paying huge legal bills in the future when someone challenges your right to your domain or brand name. File for a trademark for your domain name, your primary USP, and your company name. You must first obtain a registered trademark by law before you can begin using the symbol ® as a registered mark. This is not a job for your normal company counsel but rather is best done by intellectual property (IP) attorneys who specialize in Internet business law.

Patents. Maybe you've discovered a unique way to generate subscribers faster than anyone else, or a special way to get users on the Internet. Consult your IP lawyer for which items you should apply for a trademark and which items are worthy of the much more expensive patent process. According to www.patents.com, in the United States there are three kinds of patents—utility patents, design patents, and plant patents. A patent permits its owner to exclude members of the public from making, using, or selling the claimed invention. Most countries of the world have patent systems although the patent terms and types of patents vary.

Copyrights. You can copyright your Web site, your dial-up kit information, your marketing materials, and anything that has a unique set of words or advertising copy that your business uses in commerce. If your copyright is registered, you can legally prevent others from stealing your works for their own public commercial or personal benefit.

Many ISPs have no problem choosing a niche that they feel they can serve. Unfortunately, many don't stop there and try to serve seven or eight

---

NAILING YOUR NICHE

The niche you choose must be substantial enough to generate enough sales revenue to meet your financial goals.

You must be able to measure the size of your niche and what your percentage of it is and who specifically has the other portion of it. Your niche must also be easily reachable within your available ISP resources to attract consumers' attention. For example, it's unreasonable to expect a new ISP with less than $100,000 in seed capital to mass-mail free start-up CD-ROMs to every consumer in its market 25 times a year, like a major ISP competitor might be able to afford easily.

---

niches all at the same time. This is not a long-term, sustainable strategy for most ISPs on a finite business budget and limited access to resources. It would be better to totally dominate one niche than to serve seven to ten of them poorly.

Goal-Setting Strategies

". . . You are searching for the magic key that will unlock the door to the source of power; and yet you have the key in your own hands, and you may use it the moment you learn to control your thoughts. . . ."
Napolean Hill

The good news is that very few of your ISP competitors set goals. The bad news is that if you don't, you're doomed to end up at the end of best-effort street instead of fully realizing the potential of your business and yourself. Be different. Be better. Think.

A goal is a dream with a deadline. In order to make goal setting a worthwhile exercise, here is a list of criteria for effective goal setting:

- The goal must be realistically achievable and believable. For example, it would be unrealistic to believe you could become the number one ISP in the world with less than several billion dollars of capital, but it is realistic to believe that you could be the number one ISP in your market niche or the best at a specific category of services.

- The goal must have a specific deadline or timeline. A goal without a deadline is a goal that will never happen.

- You must be able to clearly specify your goal. The more specific you are, the higher the odds that you will realize the goal faster.

- How is less important than why.

- Your goal should be high enough. If you shoot for the stars and land on the moon, you will be farther than most of your competitors ever imagined. For example, don't shoot for happy customers but rather for delivering excellent service that is considered so highly by your subscribers that you receive 10 to 20 testimonial praise letters every month.

- Goals themselves don't provide the inspiration you may need to complete them. That must come from you.

- Your personal and business goals must be in line with your values and the values of the ownership of your ISP.

- Write your goals as if they have already happened. For example, instead of "We will be the best ISP in our region for Mac support," say this: "We provide the best Mac support in the region."

- Goals cannot contradict other goals. For example, you can't offer a high level of personalized hand-holding service for free or supercheap dial-up prices. In this example, you must choose whether your goal is to deliver outstanding service and charge for it or deliver cheap prices and low to no service-level guarantees.

- Your ISP goals should be stated in a positive way. There is an old saying, "Whatever you are for, strengthens you. Whatever you are against, weakens you." For example, your goal should not be to beat your competitor's uptime performance but rather to reach 100 percent uptime for your personal ISP best.

- Your goals must be written down. Until you write them down on paper or on your computer, they don't count. As Goethe said,

Until one is committed there is always hesitancy, the chance to draw back, always ineffectiveness. Concerning all acts of initiative (and creation), there is one elementary truth—ignorance of which kills countless ideas and splendid plans: That the moment one definitely commits oneself, then Providence moves too. All sorts of things occur to help one that would never otherwise have occurred. A whole stream of events issues from the decision, raising in one's favor all manner of unforeseen incidents and meetings and material assistance, which no man could have dreamed would come his way. Whatever you can do, or dream you can, begin it. Boldness has genius, power, and magic in it. Begin it now.

One last tip for this short course on ISP goal setting: As soon as you have written down one of the goals that you are absolutely committed to achieving, take one action step toward its realization immediately before you go home for the day. There is a universal law that says whatever is in motion, stays in motion and whatever is at rest, stays at rest. Get yourself in action toward the attainment of your most important business and personal goals and worry less about whether the action is perfect or not.

CHAPTER 4

The Only Three Ways to Grow Your ISP

Think about this for a moment: Even if you have failed to educate them as to what is available from your ISP, you do not have the right to deny your clients the benefits of the services that your clients do not know about. Do not assume that your clients know or care about every product or service you can offer them. It's your responsibility to do the educating as to the benefits of the services you can offer them.

The purpose of this chapter is to share with you the foundation upon which your entire ISP marketing arsenal will be based. While there are literally hundreds and thousands of strategies to build and grow your ISP, every single one falls into one of three types of profit and sales growth categories:

1. Increase the number of new subscribers

2. Increase your average ticket price

3. Increase the frequency of repurchase

One goal of this chapter is to help train your brain to think in one of the preceding three modes of business growth so that you can multiply your sales and profits by making incremental advances in each category. Imagine that you're able to find a way—through the strategies listed in this chapter or other techniques that you're already using or would like to be testing—to increase your ISP by 10 percent this year in each of these categories. The end result would be an exponential growth of not only your top line revenues but also your bottom line profit.

You need to be aware that when you get stuck focusing on one of the modes of business growth, you accidentally ignore the other two. Unfortunately, new marketers think that the most important strategy to grow an ISP is to get more customers and the rest will take care of itself. Sorry, not so, even though it is important to add significantly more new customers than you are losing because of churn (which is something that is discussed in depth in Chapter 7, Strategies to Reduce Churn). It's vitally important to optimize the value of the relationship with your existing customers who already trust you. Having established this base almost always allows you to acquire more sales at a lower cost of acquisition than the cost to initially acquire a new ISP subscriber.

Some quick definitions: The first category, *increasing the number of new customers,* is self-explanatory. *Increasing your average ticket price* refers to finding out what your average invoice is in a given time period. You can calculate this by dividing your total sales for a month by how many invoices your ISP sent out that month. The end result will be an average revenue per invoice. You can also do this based on average revenue per customer by dividing the total revenue that you have received from each customer by the total invoices that you've sent them in a given period. Either way, the object is to find your base line and focus your attention on growing it incrementally across your entire operation. The last category, *increasing the frequency of repurchase,* refers to finding ways to get your existing subscribers to buy additional services and products more often than they do now.

Strategies to Increase the Number of New Subscribers

Here are 21 strategies for increasing the number of new subscribers:

1. Buy them. This is my favorite, but not always possible for every ISP. If you really want to grow and grow fast, you'll have to leverage organic growth with nonorganic growth via many ISP acquisitions. (See Chapter 9, How to Acquire New Subscribers via Acquisitions of Other Internet Service Providers.)

2. Word of mouth programs. More than 80 percent of the ISPs surveyed said that *word of mouth* is their number one business builder, but less than 20 percent of them have formal programs in place to reward their loyal customers who are referring their friends and family. Sounds like an opportunity to me.

3. Affiliate programs which encourage your current customers and others to hawk new sales and new customers for your business in return for free service for themselves or, typically, a monthly or quarterly commission check from you.

4. You might spend a lot on external promotions, but try giving incentives to your own employees, along with awards and public recognition for the employee who helped sign up the most new subscribers in a given period. You'd be surprised at how much your customer conversion rate can increase when your employees have a few selfish reasons to care. Remember that praise is the lowest-costing and one of the most powerful motivators known in business.

5. Create a reseller channel to distribute your startup disks in return for a monthly commission check or discounted service. Computer retail stores make some of the best resellers or distribution channels. Relationships with computer retail store channels also become an asset when you sell your ISP.

6. Set up OEM (original equipment manufacturer) deals with which you get your ISP dial-up kit included with new PCs or any other high-tech item with which the customer is likely to benefit from Internet access. Set it up so that you only pay for customers that connect or register with your registration server.

7. Start a monthly newsletter for your existing clients and future potential prospects delivering daily or weekly bits of value to help increase their enjoyment or use of the Internet. Within it, subtly advertise your services by showing them as the solutions to the problems you present.

8. Send out press releases periodically of newsworthy items about your company. Local newspapers or television news teams could pick it up for an incalculable amount of free advertising that is sure to spur new Internet access sales for your ISP. Don't feel discouraged if this doesn't happen the first time. The key is consistency and to come up with a newsworthy release (instead of showboating or showing off) tailored to specific media people in your target market who need this sort of information for their beats.

9. Private-label yourself and create a second brand marketed to the opposite audience that your primary ISP serves now. While not always effective, many ISPs have figured out ways to serve the top and bottom of a particular market this way, resulting in more sales from the same network infrastructure.

10. Lower the risk for new customers by offering a money back guarantee or a 100 percent satisfaction guarantee. This will increase new customer conversion and inspire confidence in your existing customers to stay with you longer.

11. Give additional bonuses to new subscribers who sign up before a certain date, such as a free book, a free Internet guide, or a month of enhanced hand-holding service by your friendly technical support services team.

12. Give away coupons for free Internet access at your local computer training facility.

13. Direct mail people in your target market who either have a history of buying the same kind of service you are selling or have a high likelihood of buying it very soon.

14. Provide *lunch-n-learns* if possible, to encourage Internet enthusiasts and new users to come for free food and to learn about the Internet and the kinds of services your ISP offers. Position this as a 90 percent informational event and 10 percent soft sell. Encourage your existing customers to bring a friend, and if they do, to receive a free gift.

15. Do a few select community services for free, such as hosting a Web site, or providing Internet access for underprivileged children, or whatever cause is important to you. Invite the media to cover the story as a positive community builder event. You can also donate limited accounts for local charity auctions as another way of getting free or very low cost exposure to new clients.

16. Educate your prospective clients as to the reasons *why* they should buy from your ISP versus another one. This simple advice is seldom followed, but it can make a remarkable difference when prospects are choosing an ISP online or viewing literature.

17. Use telemarketing. I'm not a big fan of it myself but if the telephone companies continue to do it, it must be because it's a successful way to add new clients. It won't be long before ISPs en masse will adopt this as another vehicle to reach new subscribers. My only advice is to

do it with taste, targeting, and in your first sentence provide the prospect a great big reason why they should listen to you.

18. Improve the quality of your main home page by updating it daily and providing value or a reason why visitors should return. This will get more of the surfers who are not subscribers to keep coming back and hopefully convert them to subscribers. (For example, within two months of doing this myself, traffic climbed tenfold. Increased sales followed shortly thereafter to more than justify the extra labor involved in the updating process.)

19. Buy unsold advertising on cable TV, or make low-ball offers for any unsold media that targets your ideal client profile. You could also try to develop an infomercial to run on Sundays or after the evening news or whenever your target client is most likely to watch. They cost less to produce than you might think.

20. Attend flea markets and amateur radio (ham) events to sign up new subscribers. Booth space is often $10 to $25 and just one new paying subscriber can pay for the cost to do this marketing concept.

21. Test your headlines. Studies have shown that 95 percent of the effectiveness of your marketing is in the headline. If you test three or four different headlines and find one that pulls higher, you can increase your new subscriber sales at no extra cost except the time to track the tests.

Ways to Increase Your Average Ticket Price

Here's some advice for increasing your average ticket price:

1. At the time of sale, when prospects have basically said, "I trust you, I like you, and I want to buy from you," offer an additional product or service that is related to the item they are buying, one that will give them additional benefits or improve their life or business.

2. Awareness alone can do it. Find out what your baseline is right now, and post it internally for your team to see every day so that they can get daily, weekly, or monthly feedback as to how well they are cross-selling and up-selling additional items.

3. Use point of sale (POS) materials to encourage customers to buy more of the services or items that you sell, ones that they might not have known about without this material in their hands. This includes

using your dial-up kit and every other marketing piece you send out to educate your clients as to the additional benefits you can deliver with enhanced services.

4. Increase your prices. You are probably underpriced anyway. Increasing your prices weeds out your lowest-end clients who are only buying on price alone while simultaneously increasing your margins.

5. Increase the size of your minimum package. For example if you sell your services for $14.99 which includes one e-mail account and five megs of storage space for a personal Web site, why not make $19.95 your minimum dial-up price and offer five e-mail accounts and 10 megs of storage space? Your cost for increasing what you deliver is minimal. Meanwhile you're increasing the ticket size of the average monthly order. Ever wonder why the soda sellers sell 90¢ bottles instead of 50¢ cans? Answer: Bigger package size allows for higher average ticket price resulting in a huge profit increase.

6. Reposition your services as being more *up-scale* or of a higher perceived value so that you can command higher prices for the same product. In the United States, Americans value that which is expensive as being a *better* product or service than that which is cheap. Leverage this simple principle either by actually raising your prices or adding extra education to increase your perceived value.

7. Nurture your client base by communicating frequently. More communication always means more sales or, in the worst case, more referrals and recommendations to their friends because you have top-of-mind awareness.

8. Bundle packages together for a special rate, a value-add over separate purchases. For example, suppose that you are selling advertising on your ISP Web site. Instead of selling at a low rate of $25 CPM (cost per thousand), sell at $50 CPM and tell customers that if they prepay, you will give them double their money, which effectively cuts their cost per thousand in half. At the same time, this offer gets you twice as much as they were going to pay you before, thus increasing your average ticket size.

9. Promote your highest-price, highest-profit products first and your lowball price leaders last when it comes to deciding how to spend your marketing dollars.

10. If you are participating in affiliate programs to add revenue to your aggregated ISP traffic audience, instead of promoting $10 books,

always promote the $14 hard cover. Or, instead of promoting products under $20, seek to promote products that are either the most expensive or are in the hundreds of dollars so that your affiliate program revenue has a chance of being higher than if you promoted lower-priced items.

11. By focusing some energy on growing your dedicated connections and dedicated servers clients, instead of having your full attention on growing single dial-up connection accounts, your average ticket goes up. Dedicated clients always cost a multiple more than your dial-up subscribers.

12. Charge a setup fee if you don't yet. When you set up a new telephone line, the phone company charges you a setup fee. Almost every other similar industry charges a setup fee and so should you. While this only increases one of your average tickets, when you have hundreds and thousands of additional dollars coming in on setup fees, you'll notice the increase in profit to your bottom line. The revenue from setup fees may even pay for better dial-up kits in the process.

13. Require your team to up-sell and cross-sell. It should *not* be an option to up- or cross-sell. This is not about pushing your products or services on people who don't want them. No, it is about suggesting a complementary product or service at the time of sale that other ISP customers have found beneficial for themselves or their businesses.

14. Sell an enhanced membership as an upgrade to the customer's Internet access account. You decide what is included in the *special membership,* but make sure it has a high perceived value, a high real value, and a low cost to produce or distribute. You might also consider selling a lifetime membership or a long-term membership, but navigate this option carefully so that it doesn't become a huge liability if your math is off.

Ideas to Increase the Frequency of Repurchase

Here are some ways to increase the frequency of repurchase:

1. Create special price discounts for existing clients on complementary products and services that they must purchase before a deadline expires on the special price.

2. Create your own ISP loyal customer program that rewards your clients for every dollar that they spend with you. Your objective is to get your customers more engaged and interactive with your company and, in the process, to expose them to more of the services that you can offer to increase the value of their lives or businesses.

3. Take customer communication strategy one step further by making personal calls to every single one of your accounts at least six times per year to find out if everything is okay and to probe for additional needs that you might be able to serve. If your customers spend more than $500 a year with you, contact them monthly to make sure they are satisfied. At the same time, ask if they have any new needs that are unmet.

4. Endorse products or services from other companies and give personal recommendations to your clients to buy from particular companies because you believe in them. The companies could offer products or services that are not competitive with yours. Set it up so you receive a commission from every sale. Affiliate programs such as the revolution that Amazon.com started are the easiest to manage. However, making arrangements with businesses you believe in but don't yet have an established affiliate program with or those with no national or regional name recognition are harder to work; these may not pay off after you consider the time it takes to set up a worthwhile program together.

5. Develop a whole set of back-end products that you can offer your customers every month, via direct marketing. Examples include Internet tutorial books, certification programs, domain name registration, Web site design and hosting, and search engine registration.

6. Create an Internet Newbie Program in which the Internet novice can get Internet access, a workbook, and access to an exclusive e-mail discussion list and chat room in order to interact with other new users and guest experts. In addition, on a monthly basis, send them a newsletter that offers additional products that will help them get a higher return from their Internet experience with you.

7. Use the power of *why* to give your existing base a reason to buy an additional product or service from you. Contact your customers via e-mail or fax, whichever you have found is more effective, and always honor their requests to remove them from your marketing database.

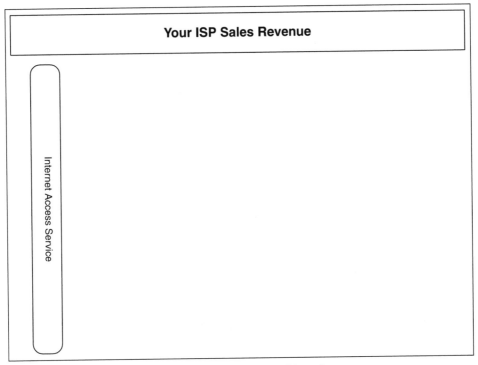

Figure 4.1 Example of what an ISP profit pillar should not be.

Building Your ISP Profit Pillars

This section discusses optimizing your marketing leverage with multiple profit pillars. Before we get into it, imagine a diving board at your local swimming pool that is supported by one large pillar. What happens if 5 or 10 big people jump up and down on the far end of it? Answer: It's going to snap. What happens if the pillar disintegrates over the years? Answer: When the diver jumps, the board is going to break and he or she may get hurt. The analogy is that most businesses base the entire hope for success of their ISP on one primary profit or revenue center, or worse, on a small handful of clients that make up 90 percent of their sales. Both are scary propositions. Figure 4.1 shows an example of what an ISP profit pillar should *not* look like.

Your goal with ISP profit pillars is to stack as many pillars and profit centers as possible to form a solid foundation for your revenue stream. This system ensures that in case any one profit center is weak in a given time

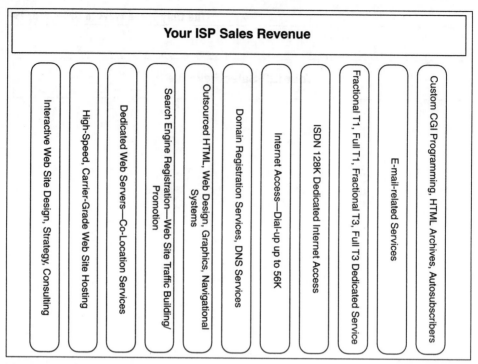

Figure 4.2 Example of what ISP profit pillars should be.

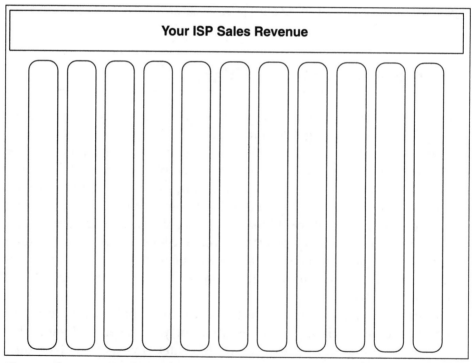

Figure 4.3 ISP profit pillar template.

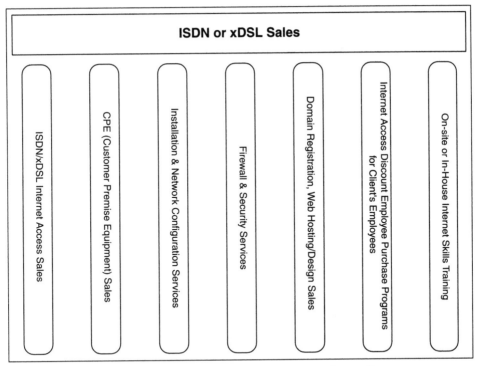

ISDN or xDSL Sales

- ISDN/xDSL Internet Access Sales
- CPE (Customer Premise Equipment) Sales
- Installation & Network Configuration Services
- Firewall & Security Services
- Domain Registration, Web Hosting/Design Sales
- Internet Access Discount Employee Purchase Programs for Client's Employees
- On-site or In-House Internet Skills Training

Figure 4.4   ISP profit pillar: specific product/service cross- and up-selling revenue centers.

period, the others will keep your business flowing smoothing until you can focus attention on enhancing your most profitable revenue streams. Figure 4.2 is an example of what typical and healthy ISP profit pillars might look like.

A quick exercise for you to do right now is to take a look at the template in Figure 4.3. On your computer in a program like Microsoft Publisher, Word, Office, Excel, or any publishing or word processing program, create a similar document and fill in the blanks with the pillars you believe should be your strongest. This exercise is a great way to clarify business priorities visually for you and your team.

You can also use the ISP profit pillar concept whenever you have a visual need for clarifying how you might achieve a marketing objective for a particular profit pillar. For example, Figure 4.4 shows ISDN or xDSL sales as an example of the types of revenue or profit centers associated with the primary product so that you can see the cross sales that go along with this type of client.

One last, but not least, way that you can use the profit pillars concept is to put the profit or revenue center item in the top position and then list

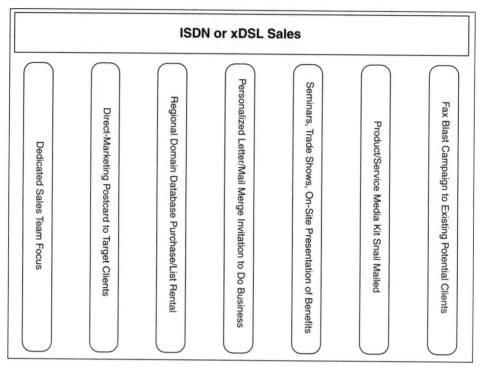

Figure 4.5 ISP profit pillar: marketing and sales avenues to achieve sales.

every known possible way that you can reach or increase sales of that product or service line, as shown in Figure 4.5.

The idea is to not get carried away with line extension and think that your ISP should be serving every niche because that is not the purpose of the profit pillars visuals. The purpose is to maximize the avenues and vehicles that can get you to your end destination the fastest while giving clarity as to what is important within the organization.

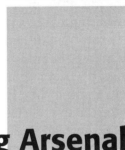

Your ISP Marketing Arsenal

Like any arsenal, the more weapons that you use, the more sales and profit your ISP will crank out.

ISP marketing has three distinct goals:

1. To increase sales
2. To increase profits
3. To increase the market value of your ISP

Marketing is the umbrella term with which we will define everything that you will do within your ISP to drive sales and profits. However, it's important to note that marketing is more than advertising and sales, but rather heavily influences the look and feel of your ISP, your market tone and aggressiveness level, your customer service approach, your promotions, your public relations, and more. The Webster's Revised Unabridged Dictionary defines *marketing* as "the act of selling or of purchasing in, or as in, a market." This chapter contains the tools, weapons, strategies, secrets from the trenches, and real-world techniques that you can implement immediately.

As you read this chapter, think about your business and how the various techniques can be applied to your specific and unique situation. The philosopher and renowned author Kahlil Gibran once said, "The teacher, if indeed wise, does not bid you to enter the house of their wisdom, but leads you to the threshold of your own mind." The goal is to lead you into taking a virtual inventory of your ISP marketing options and to help you select which strategies you should deploy immediately. The final objective is to show you what is possible so that you get a ten- to several hundred-fold return on your investment in this book and the time it takes to read it.

None of what follows matters if you don't at least attempt to implement the ideas and proven strategies found in this book. Great ideas alone don't make a great business, marketing plan, or even ISP, but rather great ideas executed, perfected, and improved daily make a great business and the best hope for a profitable and prosperous future. You should be less worried that your competitors have begun to copy some of the ideas you've developed while building your ISP than you should fear the competitor who can execute faster than you. This is not a business or industry in which you can take five to ten years to figure everything out. The window of opportunity is constantly shifting and, at a minimum, you'll need to start your day running because your success depends on it.

Failure is necessary, but repeating your mistakes can be fatal. You need to learn the art of "fast failing," which is being brave enough to take action toward your greatest end goals without worrying about whether it is the right action. As you identify an action that is not effective, you quickly change your approach until you have the success that you seek before the buzzer sounds and it's the end of your game. Often success in your ISP marketing, sales, and business processes is the result of testing what works, and after identifying what does not work, doing more of what does work.

There is no one magic silver bullet. According to Erika Jolly, vice president of product management and development for MindSpring Enterprises (NASDAQ: MSPG), building a successful ISP has more to do with doing hundreds of small basic things well, and less with doing any one thing right. If you were reading this chapter for the one thing that will turn your luck and ISP around on a dime, while some of you may find that, most will not be so lucky. The most you can hope for is to focus on the basic principles of ISP marketing which are contained in this arsenal of weapons.

This chapter focuses on the basics in six unique categories:

1. ISP marketing
2. ISP advertising
3. ISP public relations
4. ISP promotion and direct marketing/direct response
5. ISP sales force growth and power
6. ISP pricing strategies

ISP Marketing Management by Measurement

"Management by measurement" is a philosophy and a strategy for quantifying your business and marketing goals specifically into numbers and percentages and setting up a game plan to achieve the desired results. It is the force that will help you and your employees follow through to the end.

It's about accountability. Ever have a situation where you didn't want to delegate a marketing task because you knew that no one would ever do it as well as you could, so you didn't delegate it? Yet, by not doing so, you got further and further behind. Maybe you even hampered your own career. Being unable to effectively delegate is a sign of bad leadership or at least a misunderstanding of what good leadership is like. Well, worry no more, because after you fully understand management by measurement, you'll be able to confidently identify the critical success indicators to which your team can be held accountable.

What is a *critical success indicator?* It's a number, ratio, percentage, or outcome that defines whether your ISP has succeeded or failed. Some common ISP business critical success indicators include profit and loss, margin, subscriber-to-modem ratio, subscriber-to-bandwidth ratio, as well as many others. What follows is a list of critical success indicators that may spur your thinking about your specific situation. Every ISP is unique, so some of these may not apply, while others do. Just take what makes sense for your business.

- Prospect to paying subscriber conversion ratio
- Number of new subscribers in a month or given period
- ISP subscriber growth or churn ratio (churn is discussed in depth in Chapter 7, Strategies to Reduce Churn)
- Gross sales revenue, profit, or margin, by your total company, by department, or even by salesperson
- Clickthrough rate (CTR) when doing campaigns to target prospective new customers—the higher the rate, the better
- Public relations, or the number of public media interviews your CEO gives, or the number of magazine or newspapers that pick up your press release
- Number of inquiries per ad campaign
- Average ticket price or average number of days between average purchases (with the goal to increase average ticket prices and decrease the number of days between purchases overall)

- Number of billable hours of your in-house Web, e-mail, or Internet talent

- Number of technical support calls, length of calls, time of each call per day; obtain this information in order to use marketing and expectation setting to reduce technical support labor expense while still delivering superb customer service

There are many more but this list should get you thinking about your ISP and the indicators you want to target. Your corporate values, time lines, and goals will radically affect which critical success indicators you prioritize. The foundation of every great ISP has clearly defined goals, but that is not enough. To be effective, the goals must have a clearly defined time line and critical success indicators needed to achieve the end outcome.

A critical success indicator is also a performance metric that establishes the benchmark target that can be compared with the actual performance. The difference between the benchmark and the actual performance should provide insight into not only what is working, but also what is not working and needs immediate attention. For instance, assume one of your marketing goals is to keep your growth rate of new customers at 10 percent per month, but you are currently only growing at 5 percent per month. With this information, your team evaluates which processes need to be improved or actions taken to increase it to 10 percent, and everyone focuses on improving the number to 10 percent. Figure 5.1 shows an example of what the management by measurement process looks like.

For now, we're more concerned with management by measurement as it relates to your ISP marketing, advertising, PR, sales, profits, and so on, and not how it relates to ISP business management (which could fill the pages of two books this size). With that said, here are the top eight items that you'll have to consider when designing your marketing critical success indicators:

1. Establish baseline data.
2. Identify how the data will be collected for measurement.
3. Define measurement reporting requirements of management.
4. Define the criteria for how you will measure customer satisfaction.
5. Define the variables of the marketing projects that will be evaluated.
6. Identify the resources within your ISP that you'll need.
7. Identify the organization leaders from whom you need *buy in* in order for the implementation of your programs to be successful.

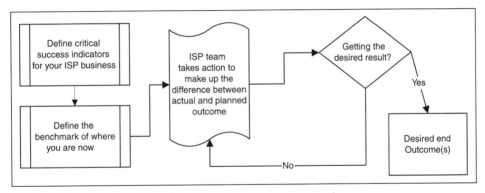

Figure 5.1   ISP management by measurement process overview.

8. Establish realistic outcomes that are achievable with the finite resources at your disposal.

For example, use any of the preceding eight steps that apply. Say that your CEO has determined that to be successful, your ISP team must convert a minimum of 20 percent of all incoming callers with Internet access inquiries into paying subscribers. Management becomes involved and after asking your sales or customer service team to track for a month daily incoming leads versus how many converted into paying customers, you have established that you are currently converting 12 percent of the leads. For the next 30 days, your front line is going to ask the customers who do not sign up why they choose to continue looking, and if possible, handle the objection and complete the sale. If that's too much, at a minimum, the front line will complete an internal report in order to figure out why customers are not converting at as high a rate as your CEO would like. With that information, for the next 30 days after the data collection period, your team will focus on solving the objections which are feasible and work toward the 20 percent conversion goal.

In order for management by measurement to work, your ISP's executive staff needs to have a clear picture of which critical indicators will lead to success. Everyone from the CEO to the front line must understand management's informational needs, along with how the differences can be made up between the plan and the actual results that are achieved. Expectations must be managed in order to make sure that all of the key participants understand and agree on what will be accomplished and by what time line.

Small ISPs may have no problem implementing this simple philosophy. However, larger organizations could run into resistance created by a bureaucracy of people who do not like change, who aren't really committed to extra work, or who won't do whatever it takes to meet what they see as unachievable goals handed down from the pearly gates of the CEO—who has not spoken with a customer in months (which is another problem all by itself). If you are an executive in a large ISP, don't worry about getting everyone to buy into your new management by measurement standards or even the reason why your ISP must focus on them. The key to company-wide adoption is to use the success of a small pilot test as the validator and motivator for fulfilling larger marketing objectives.

In summary, the goal in *any* ISP marketing decision-making process is to determine which indicators are critical to your success; the benchmark of where you are now; the actions necessary to get you from where you are to where you must end up; and a time line that is in line with corporate goals, expectations, and available resources.

Developing a Great Marketing Campaign

All great marketing campaigns have one key element that is crucial to success—a thorough understanding of how the needs of your potential client relate to the services and products that your ISP delivers. It is this simple; however, most business owners and executives look right past this and spend an enormous amount of energy and capital trying to win over new customers. The first step is really about understanding the needs of the target market you have identified and finding a direct, creative way to communicate how your ISP is the perfect answer to your prospects' needs. How can anyone expect to develop a campaign without finding out the desires of the potential customers?

TIP You do not have the right to assume you know what your client or the market wants until you ask your potential client or the market what is important to them. Never assume you know best what the market will respond to; it's your responsibility as a smart marketer to test your marketing strategies. The marketplace will vote with its cash.

There are two basic types of ISP marketing campaigns:

Marketing drive. This is the basic focused marketing push campaign. For this, you design a particular campaign to achieve a specific sales or profit end result. You concentrate that campaign during a very narrow time frame. It can be done for your prospects or existing customers.

Maintenance programs. These types of campaigns are designed to reinforce your marketing drives in order to attract new customers or to provide comfort for existing subscribers. Maintenance programs can be used to retain the market position you've achieved while strengthening repeat business, referrals, and customer satisfaction.

Regardless of which mode you choose, you must specifically define your end goals, including numbers and percentages, before you begin. If you fail to choose the destination for your next marketing campaign, how are you supposed to know whether you have arrived?

Elements to include in a successful ISP marketing campaign include the following:

- A headline that communicates the major benefit in as few words as possible

- The benefits as to why someone should buy from you or from this specific promotion

- Testimonials that prove others trust you and your business

- Your guarantees and anything your ISP offers that removes risk from the customer and keeps pressure on the seller, not the buyer

- A specific offer, along with a price point. A review of many Web logs will show you that average prospective customers want to know quickly how much something costs so they can qualify or disqualify your offer. The higher the price point, the more you'll need to educate and lead the customer to understanding why your ISP charges more than your competitors might charge for what looks like the same product.

- A call to action—if you are going to forget about including a call to action, you might as well not do the campaign at all

TIP Never fear running multiple marketing strategies during a campaign. For example, if you're running a promo to increase your prepaid subscribers because you need some positive cash flow to pay for new equipment, you might want to deploy three to ten different media. These can be postcards, personalized letters, telephone calls, fax blasting if you have customers' permission, personalized e-mail invitations to do business, giveaways of some of your product to a local charity, press releases, and so forth. There is no rule that says you must use only *one* medium at a time. Use as many as possible to get your end result.

Increasing Your Marketing Return on Investment

Your goal is not so much to save money on marketing or find a way to get your ISP marketing done cheaply, but rather to optimize the return so that every marketing investment pays off handsomely. Before you say that marketing costs money, here's some news. Half of the items listed in this ISP marketing arsenal do not cost a dime, except for your time. If you're willing to be creative and innovative, with or without a huge marketing budget, there are always strategies that you can implement to grow your business.

A common mistake that new ISP marketers make is that they focus 100 percent of their limited budget on acquiring new customers and completely ignore their existing customers who can become a huge source of increased sales and profits for your business. Every sale has a cost. New customers cost as much as five times or more than the cost of acquiring repeat business and increased sales via up-selling and cross-selling new products and services to your existing subscribers.

Referring back to management by measurement, you need to know what your current return on investment (ROI) is on your existing campaigns so that you're able to allocate your money into the campaigns producing the highest results at the lowest cost, and decrease or eliminate campaigns which do not produce acceptable returns.

An example of an ROI on an ISP marketing campaign could look like this:

Goal: Increase dedicated business Internet access accounts from the existing client base of 3,000 subscribers by sending a personalized letter with a specific offer to the 1,200 business customers within your subscriber base. Cost of letter, postage, envelope, labor, and telephone follow-up equals $2,400. Within 30 days from the start of the campaign you have received 12 customers interested in switching to a dedicated feed. Six have signed up as new dedicated customers, which is a lead conversion of 1 percent, a paying client conversion of 0.5 percent, and each of those six new accounts cost you $400 to acquire. Your goal with future campaigns for this same product line is to continue acquiring new dedicated Internet access subscribers for $400 or less to increase your lead conversion from 1 percent to a higher return and to increase your conversion from lead to paying subscriber of the new dedicated plan.

Profit Maximization Strategy versus Growth Maximization Strategy

Your marketing investment aggressiveness is in direct proportion to one of these two strategies.

A *profit maximization* strategy is when you are focused on maximizing profit from your existing accounts and maximizing profits with all new accounts that your ISP could attract. This is common in older ISPs who manage to make a profit, have established a growth rate that they are comfortable with, and who need to maximize profits for their shareholders. Only a small minority of ISPs operates under a profit maximization strategy for the obvious reason that the window of opportunity is very small and you must grow and grow quickly in order to survive in many markets.

A typical ISP profit maximization marketing budget could be between 5 to 15 percent and the average dial-up subscriber may be acquired for $20 to $70 per subscriber. Dedicated Internet access accounts would, of course, fetch higher numbers. Selling your subscriber base to an ISP who is focused on a profit maximization strategy will not get you a premium for your base.

A *growth maximization* strategy is when the need for business growth exceeds the need for short-term profits. This is called a *high-burn-rate* ISP marketing strategy, meaning you burn cash extremely fast while attempting to acquire sales and marketshare growth without going out of business in the process. When using this strategy, it's important to know your cash burn rate, available credit lines, access to capital, and the date by which you will have exhausted available cash. You really need to do these things so that while you're playing with fire, you don't get burned and have to consider a "fire sale" (when you sell your ISP because you are forced to, which usually means unfavorable terms for you).

A typical ISP growth maximization marketing budget could be between 15 and 30 percent and the average dial-up subscriber may be acquired for $70 to $350 per subscriber. Dedicated Internet access accounts would, of course, fetch higher numbers. If you are planning on selling your subscriber base to another ISP, make sure you find one that is currently focused on a personal growth maximization strategy, as these are the premium payers in the marketplace.

The profit maximization and growth maximization strategies are compared in Figure 5.2.

TIP When deciding which of the two marketing strategies (profit maximization or growth maximization) to choose for your marketing budget, realize that most ISPs float in and out of these two strategies from time to time, and few run only one strategy for the entire life cycle of their ISP business.

Your goal in marketing is to make a profit. The accepted view is that you must write your ISP business plan so that you are making a profit by the

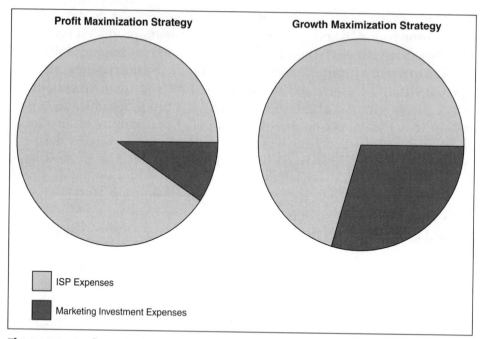

Figure 5.2 Profit maximization versus growth maximization marketing budget.

third year. Some ISPs, however, plan on hypergrowth for less than two years with the expectation that they will sell before they even reach the end of their third year. This is definitely not a business strategy for the weak, timid, or new marketer or entrepreneur. A superfast grow/sell plan requires laser-fast execution of hundreds of marketing strategies, a serious chunk of available capital, a clear understanding of what other businesses are being acquired for currently, and the vision to be able to accurately predict what the ISP buyer's market will look like at the end of this short-fuse ISP concept.

Example 1: You believe, based on research, that in two years an ISP the size yours will be could be able to command $250 per subscriber, so you do everything in your power to acquire subscribers for less than that amount.

Example 2: You believe, based on research, that in order to raise pre-IPO equity financing capital, you need to own a certain significant percentage of the niche on which you are currently focusing, because your business valuation will be significantly enhanced, thus allowing you to give up smaller amounts of equity for cash. In this case, sometimes paying more than the market for subscribers can pay off handsomely, but this is a high-risk strategy, so be warned.

TIP Don't let the hope that you can raise capital be the reason why it's okay to run an ISP unprofitably for a long period of time. Ultimately, if your plan to sell fails, you'll be left to consider plan B, which is managing to a profit anyway. Long term, which can be as short as three to six years in this business, requires a profit focus.

Developing the Personality of an ISP Marketer That Gets Results

As the saying goes, "nothing happens until someone sells something." Marketing is salesmanship regardless of media, whether it is print, electronic, or personally delivered via a human. Because it is salesmanship, it requires the mind of a salesperson first and the mindset of a marketer second. The difference is the function each role plays. Typically a marketer is not sales-oriented and is trained to create demand, study market statistics, and get the phone to ring so that a sales-oriented person or team can convert the lead into a bona fide sale for your ISP. Marketing people within your ISP organization should never be allowed to hold any marketing role until they have had at least some experience as a pure salesperson in order to fully appreciate the results of their actions as a successful marketer and understand their true role.

The key distinctions of a successful ISP marketing personality are as follows:

- Realizes that marketing is only one step in the ISP sales process and that the successful ISP marketer must not only pull off the flawless execution of marketing campaigns, but must also get the buy in of the ISP technicians and the customer service and billing/accounting departments, which make up the total Internet access experience for your subscribers.

- Keeps a huge collection of the best ISP marketing ads published by competitors and other industries for future personal use or to spur idea creation.

- Strongly believes in testing every marketing variable, always seeking what will get the highest results with each targeted campaign.

- Is detached from his or her ego enough to realize that great advertising is not about telling everyone how great your ISP, your offer, or your service is, but rather is more interested in uncovering your prospects' deepest desires and working to find ways to show them how your ISP can solve their problems or be the solution to their wants and needs.

- Is numbers focused. Whether it's cost per lead, cost per subscriber, or conversion ratios, he or she knows if a marketing campaign is on or off purpose and adjusts during the campaign instead of making excuses at the end of a bad campaign.

- Realizes that a market never gets tired of a marketing campaign that produces results. Refuses to bow to internal pressures to update or "fix" a campaign that is producing great results, even if everyone in the office hates it because it's boring or old.

- Has studied copyrighting secrets in order to produce irresistible, benefit-oriented attractive copy that compels the target market to take action.

- Is never satisfied and always seeks to increase ways to get a higher return on every marketing ad dollar invested.

- Is positive, has an upbeat personality, and smiles a lot. Personal enthusiasm gets communicated in the work, and while the marketer is not a perfectionist, he or she ensures that every marketing piece is as consistent and demonstrates the same quality as the entire organization.

- Is always open to new strategies which might be weird, wild, or even a bit silly; if they produce positive results, a good ISP marketer has an open mind to new possibilities.

- Has a competitive spirit. Tracks every marketing result, follows your marketing calendar closely, and works to improve every campaign involving as many marketing weapons as possible simultaneously and effectively.

- Believes there is no such thing as failure. Every ISP marketing campaign produces a result, and sometimes you learn ways not to do things. But as long as you are learning and improving, failure is only a stepping stone to greater success.

- Knows that nothing matters except for intelligent action directed toward the realization of the highest ISP priorities.

If you want to be an ISP marketer that gets results, the simple solution is to become a results-focused person, which means that you work to get achievable results regardless of the obstacles that undoubtedly will get in your way. Never confuse efficiency with results, as being efficient is not half as important as getting the desired results first. After you achieve the desired marketing result, you can focus on increasing the efficiency of your marketing effectiveness.

TIP The best ISP marketers do not march to the beat of the same drum as competitors but rather force their competitors to improve or perish. One of your biggest competitors is you and your team's ability to follow up and provide the best service possible today, which is better than it was yesterday. When you compete against yourself, you unleash a power that the market will only be able to combat with the same level of intent.

What to Test as Part of Your ISP Marketing Strategies

The simple concept of testing your different marketing strategies can be one of the most profitable leverages you receive from this book. The majority of your ISP competitors do *not* test their marketing, and therefore are doomed to run unprofitable campaigns or campaigns that do not return as high a conversion or sales rate as one that is optimized with feedback from the target marketplace.

Items you can test within your ISP include the following:

- The quality of your offering, such as your ISP uptime performance, hours of service, ease of dial-up connection (percentage of successful connects), and speed of service
- As many concepts, offers, proposals, big promises, and guarantees as possible
- Which media pulls the highest return and sales conversion
- Which part of your Web site pulls the most new signups or interest so that you can move items around based on customer surfing behavior
- Ad copy, headlines, color, paper, and packaging of the marketing pieces
- Your sales approaches, scripts, and follow-up intervals
- Your ISP price points and prepayment plans or discount choices

There are only two basic rules in the art of testing. They are:

1. Test everything.
2. Test only one variable at a time.

If you test only one aspect, you will fail to uncover some of the best strategies that you will never know about until you test. If you test two or more variables at a time, you'll never know which one led to the real reason you had success or failure in a given campaign.

Why Most ISP Marketing Programs Fail and What to Do About It

You already know everything you need to know to make your ISP a success. This section serves to remind you of what you already know, so that you can revisit a particular strategy and its implementation.

Reasons why most ISP marketing programs fail include the following:

- Failure to clearly define your marketing program's end goals. If you don't know what the end will look like, how will you know if you've arrived?

- Failure to measure the performance of every marketing campaign. Every campaign must improve upon the performance of the previous campaign, and that can only happen when you know your baseline performance and have set realistic targets for improvement the next time around.

- Failure to realize that success depends on doing the basics, day in and day out, and that when you go fishing for new, creative, and sometimes esoteric marketing ideas, you often end up with not-so-fantastic results. It's best to stay focused on the proven basic principles of ISP marketing.

- Failure to test every aspect of your marketing actions in order to improve response, profits, and sales.

- Failure to keep abreast of the changes happening in the marketplace. Participating in a few ISP marketing forums and e-mail discussion lists is not an option but rather a requirement if you want to lead in the marketplace.

- Failure to define and understand your target market. You must do research. Do not be afraid to ask the market what it wants. The market never lies. When was the last time you conducted a study to find out what the marketplace wants?

ISP Marketing Myths Debunked

Just because your competitor is doing it, doesn't mean that it knows what is right or best for your ISP business, or its own business for that matter. There is nothing worse than watching the blind lead the blind, when one ISP follows another ISP's lead, even when it may be the wrong lead for both of them. Be better and keep a keen eye on what your competitors do, but always march to the beat of your own drum. Here are some other common myths that may trap beginner ISP marketing people:

"Word of mouth marketing is enough, and I don't need any other kind of marketing to build my subscriber base." While it is true that many successful ISPs report that the highest number of new subscribers come from word-of-mouth advertising, you will remain a small ISP if you don't use any of the additional ISP marketing weapons contained in this ISP marketing arsenal.

"I can just open up a new POP (point of presence) and new customers will flock to me without very much marketing" or worse, **"I have to open a POP in this market because my competitor is there also."** No. You should only open a POP in a marketplace after you have determined through intelligent market research that there is enough of a market to support and exceed the costs of establishing a new POP.

"Each new market our ISP services will react the same way as our primary markets." Sure they will, and every market has the same needs. Wrong. Every market has unique subscribers with a unique set of needs. Some will need more hand-holding, others will need strong Mac support, some will need advanced technical support, while others will need every technical support word communicated in ultralay terms.

"I can just wait till the end of the month and spend what is left over as my marketing budget." If you do this, you could find that you have nothing left over to spend on marketing. Mentally, you must budget a percentage of sales to reinvest in marketing; otherwise you could find that your well dried up rather quickly.

"We can market like the big companies and get the same results. Carpet bombing startup disks to the masses is an effective strategy that we'll use for our target market." Carpet bombing disks is an effective way to go broke fast for most ISPs. A better strategy is to spend the same money you would have spent on mass mailing startup disks on improving the quality of the kit you are able to send out. Charge a setup fee and give a few informational bonuses to new subscribers which delivers extra perceived value.

"Because we do so well at Internet access (dial-up), we naturally will be good at Web site design, hosting, search engine registration, Web site promotion, e-mail list hosting, dedicated servers, collocation services, and anything related to the Internet experience." This is called *line extension* and it's very dangerous. Marketing is all perception, not a product or reality. The more you extend your brand into new product categories, the more your ISP brand becomes diluted and less effective.

TIP *People who have a history of recently buying a similar service have a much higher chance of becoming your next customer than someone who has never bought your product before.* **There are two sides of the coin to this thought: one is that if you are the first ISP to serve the inexperienced customer, you could win loyalty for the long haul. The other side of the coin is that it may be easier to convert existing customers who are currently dissatisfied with their current ISP provider.**

ISP Branding Basics Explained

Whether you are a small ISP with two employees or a behemoth of an ISP with several hundred, thousands, or even millions of subscribers, branding matters. *Brand,* according to Webster's, is "to burn a distinctive mark into or upon with a hot iron, to indicate quality, ownership, etc." You don't want to burn anyone physically, even if you do want to burn the best qualities of your ISP into the minds of your market niche. Branding is not to be confused with your unique selling proposition (USP), which is a benefit that is distinct from your competitors. Your ISP brand is the feeling that your target market has toward your business.

So, if branding is the sense the marketplace has about your ISP, how can you ensure that those feelings are positive?

To get an answer to that question, look at the top three things that people wish to buy from you:

1. Confidence

2. Quality product

3. Excellent service

The order here is important because a great product and great service mean nothing if the subscriber or customer doesn't have the trust and confidence that your ISP will deliver. *Confidence* is delivered when your ISP acts consistently, respects the privacy of its members, is dependable and reliable, delivers what is promised, and does what the CEO of the ISP says will get done. The *quality of the product* is actually more important than the level of service you provide because there is no shortage of ISPs with good caring people who deliver excellent customer service, but don't have their acts together when it comes to running a dial-up network. Great service can keep a dissatisfied subscriber from leaving for a while, but ultimately, he or she is going to seek an ISP who has a stable network and competent people to run it. *Excellent service* is the differentiating variable that sets your ISP apart from your competitors and is the key that leads to value.

Your ISP brand is influenced by every action you take in the marketplace, from the tone your people have with customers or prospects, your aggressiveness level, the quality of your marketing, the uptime and speed of your network, and the way you handle complaints to the way you make it easy for people to do business with you. Branding is not something you do only to attract new customers or convert prospects to switch to your ISP, but rather it is something that is vitally important to your existing customer base and recurring revenue stream if you hope to increase your sales from existing members.

One way to find out if you're strong or courageous enough to handle the truth is to attend your community's next business expo or trade show and informally poll people about your ISP—whether they have heard of it and, for the ones that have, what their opinion of it is? Many of the decisions as to whom to choose when it comes to commodity items such as dial-up Internet access come down to the unconscious decision as to who is better. Considering it's this important, it's best that you find out how the market feels about you so that you either continue what you are doing (if market reaction is positive) or take actions that could lead to a more favorable impression of your ISP.

TIP You stand behind your ISP, right? Then don't hide from the public. Put your name, picture, and a brief personal introduction on your Web site and in marketing vehicles so that people can get a feeling for what type of person is in charge. People buy from people who are like them. If you'll risk a bit by telling people about yourself, your ISP, and why you personally guarantee that they will have a 100 percent satisfying experience or will get their money back, you'll create confidence. Go all the way and advertise your e-mail address and direct phone line to your office. When the volume of inquiries directed to you gets too big, delegate this to your VP or executive assistant who will be empowered to solve 99 percent of the issues on your behalf.

Strategies to profit from your ISP brand personality include the following:

- The name of your ISP must be easy to remember, easy to spell, easy to not misspell, easy to pronounce, and not be offensive to your market niche. If it's not, consider changing it now, immediately, because each day that goes forward, it will cost more and more to change.

- You must own your domain name and brand name and every variation of it. That includes owning it in the .com, .net, and .org spaces, and in singular and plural forms, and common misspellings of it. You may also wish to register the domain names of any new brand or sub-brand that you launch.

- Give first. This is the Internet way, anyway, isn't it? That includes writing a weekly or monthly column for your local newspaper or magazine, speaking on a weekend radio talk show giving Internet tips, and speaking at the local library, trade shows, roundtables, and the like.

- Create exclusivity that only your paid members receive. Membership has its benefits, American Express says, and so should you deliver special benefits for your paid members. Make sure you deny non-paying members the special benefit so as to keep the value real. Exclusive benefits can include information or articles you've written, a newsletter, a special telephone number for priority support, a secret e-mail address for faster support, a free seminar, or anything to help them get more out of their Internet experience and feel special.

- Make your dial-up kit feel more like a welcome kit for new subscribers. Include a letter from the CEO congratulating and thanking them on their wise decision to choose your ISP, along with reminding them of the benefits they now have access to as a paying member. It's also a great time to ask for referrals and tell them about any referral program you might have in place to reward them for sending their friends to you.

TIP If you own all of the suggested variations of your domain name, it's important to metarefresh all of the variations to your core domain, instead of DNS resolving. For example: Your business is called MyISPInteractive.com, but you also own MyISPInteractive.net, so whenever users go to MyISPInteractive.net, they are automatically pushed or forwarded to MyISPInteractive.com in order to keep the integrity of the domain brand intact. If you just CNAME or DNS resolve, there is no forwarding, which dilutes your branding.

Making It Easier for New Customers to Buy from You

AOL has proved by its size (millions of dial-up customers) that ISP customers want their Internet experience to be easy. Even though your company might not be the next AOL, there are many quick and inexpensive strategies that you can employ to make it easier for potential customers to buy from your ISP. It's your responsibility to make it easier for your potential and existing customers to be able to buy and buy more from you. The end result is that the easier you make it for people to buy from your business, the higher your sales will be and the quicker you'll reach your business goals.

There are seven ways to make it easier to do business with your subscribers:

Accept all major credit cards, including MasterCard, Visa, Discover, and American Express. Some of these cards cost you as much as 3–4 percent of the gross sale to accept, but the additional convenience for the customer, along with the facts that you get your money faster, and the customers who pay with credit cards are worth more in terms of ISP valuations, make this a must. Normally, your local bank can help you get your merchant accounts set up within a few weeks.

Make your team and technical support services available during the hours your target client needs you the most. For business-focused ISPs, that means from 8 A.M. until 6 P.M. Monday through Friday; for SOHO (small office, home office) and consumer-focused ISPs, it means being available until 10 P.M. and on weekends. This is not to suggest that you operate your ISP service 24 hours a day, although many of your customers may wish that you did, but your available hours must make financial sense. You need to decide whether your extended hours bring in more sales, reduce churn, and keep your customers happier longer.

Your subscribers don't care about your business problems, or the personal problems of your employees. Make sure subscribers are free from having to listen to any employee on your ISP team complaining so that there are less real and perceived hassles. Excuses coming from you or your people do not make your ISP easy to buy from.

Offer on-site delivery and installation for a fee or include it in a package deal that covers the cost. There is a certain percentage of new and potential loyal ISP subscribers that would love for you to come to their house or business to set up Internet access.

Is your marketing contradicting, confusing, or cluttered with too much information? Does it lack a theme or focus? Simplify, simplify, simplify. The quicker and easier it is to be understood, the more you'll increase your sales. Make sure that your marketing programs, literature, and people don't contradict one another. Regularly compare your copy so that you are sure you are sending the same message with every marketing vehicle.

How many people will call you today and hang up before their call is handled? How many minutes are people on hold today? How many calls came in and went unanswered? Do you even know how many calls are getting dropped on a daily basis? There is software that you can buy that will integrate with your phone system to tell you this information in real time and usually pays for itself in a few months in improved customer service.

Your Web site must pass the two-second rule which states that customers with a problem need to be able get a name, number, or e-mail address to resolve their issue in two seconds. Most people hide their identity, as if to dodge personal responsibility. If you want to win and lead with your ISP, get your name and your contact e-mail addresses and telephone numbers somewhere where people can find them very quickly.

Ask yourself often: *"In which areas of our business are we making it difficult for customers to buy from us? What changes can we make to improve the problem areas?"* If you want a real wake up call, try calling the phone number for your ISP's sales or customer service line and pretend you are a potential customer.

What to Include in Your ISP Dial-up Kit

If you want to make your new customers' experience easier and increase your conversion ratio from prospect to paying subscriber, what you include in your dial-up kit is critical. Your goal is to make getting connected on the Internet with your ISP the most painless thing that your new customer-to-be has done today. This, of course, is easier said than done, because software versions and operating systems keep changing, making it harder to control the customer's experience with your dial-up service.

Following are eight things to include in your dial-up kit:

1. CD-ROM or diskette containing everything customers need to get on the Net.

2. One-page "Quick-Guide" for the impatient who want to get on the Internet as fast as possible without reading a book.

3. An in-depth guide to installation, including tips, suggestions, known bugs or problems along with the workaround or patch.

4. Your technical support phone number, e-mail address, and a brief overview of your hours and the kind of technical support services your ISP offers. This is your chance to teach the customers self-sufficiency so that they don't call you for problems that they could solve themselves.

5. If you provide an e-mail-based, chat-based, or Web-based technical support forum for all of your members, this is the place to tell them about it.

6. More information about the services your ISP offers including a coupon or discount for an Internet training class and cost breakdowns for enhanced services such as more e-mail accounts, additional storage space for the personal Web pages, a personal domain name, and so forth. Make sure you include your sales phone number and e-mail address along with business hours so the customer can reach someone to sign up for the service upgrades.

7. A list of all of your dial-up POP (points of presence) access numbers along with the URL where you update the list from time to time. In this way, you make it easy for your customer to access dial-up numbers when they travel or move.

8. *Optional:* An Internet glossary or a basic book about the Internet for novices. Many booksellers offer great quantity discounts for ISPs who are looking to bundle these types of books in with their dial-up kits. By providing some basics, you may also reduce your support labor by empowering your customers to solve their own problems.

Here are two items *not* to include in your dial-up kit:

1. Forty disks including all of the latest versions of different freeware or shareware applications. Your customers don't want to spend time setting up their Internet connection. It would be easier for the customer to download this information from online after they're set up (and if they're interested). This also saves you valuable disk costs.

2. An untested dial-up kit. It is critical that you or someone on your staff tests the dial-up kit on all the major platforms (Windows, Mac, UNIX, Linux) that you support.

There are also many businesses now that produce Internet dial-up kits for ISPs. These outsourced kits can be privately labeled and branded with your ISP name and logo.

One last word on the topic of dial-up kits: Get them in the mail the same day that the customer asks for them. It's important to reel in the new customer and get them connected as fast as possible, before you lose them.

ISP Marketing Strategies That Produce Instant Results

There are a number of things you can do that produce results within a week to 10 days. With each of these suggestions, you'll need to assess the impact of its effectiveness or lack thereof.

- Price inducements almost always create a surge of new subscribers but be careful—never give a new customer a better deal than you've offered your existing loyal customers.

- Up-sell or cross-sell an additional item that is related to the service your new customer just bought at the time of sale. You could find yourself adding a 10 to 30 percent increase in sales immediately.

- Teach your techies how to handle sales leads, basic pricing, and sign up new customers. At a very minimum, you should train your techies to forward all leads to your sales team so that opportunities don't get lost in the shuffle.

- Make your Web site sign-up form easier to use if you haven't already. Test it. Add testimonials to it to see if this increases new customer sign-ups. In many cases, it can and will increase sales.

- Give your customers a big enough incentive or reason why they should refer their friends to you. The reason why should include what's in it for them.

- It is not the responsibility of your new subscribers to figure out how to use your service. It is your responsibility to help them maximize their return from using your network. Do a follow-up call within the first seven to ten days of every new customer's experience with your ISP to make sure they are getting what they expected.

Shoestring and Grassroots Marketing

Many ISPs are bootstrapping their marketing without any influx of capital. Following that trend, some successful grass roots tactics for you to try are

ISP ADVERTISING INSIGHT

"Advertising is . . . merely a substitute for a personal sales force."

—*Rosser Reeves, from "Reality in Advertising"*

listed here. Earlier in this book, I said that the more weapons you use, the more your sales will increase. In this case, the more *effective* weapons you use, the higher your sales will be. All of these ideas have been implemented at one time or another by an ISP. Some of these tactics are wild, and many of them work. However, be aware that what works for one ISP in one region of the country might not work for another, and vice versa. Why not try them all and find out which ones work for your ISP, and then do more of those.

Your ISP grassroots marketing arsenal could include the following:

- Place ads in restrooms, above the stalls and on the walls. Many local restaurants have policies for handling this, so check with the management first.

- Swap ads on a one-to-one basis with other businesses in your coverage area. A one-third-page coupon works best for envelope stuffing when you send out your monthly invoices.

- At the end of a voting season, there are thousands of political *vote for me* signs that are discarded. What if you had them relabeled with *Choose [insert your ISP name]* and gave a free month of service to the first 1,000 customers who agreed to display them on their lawns for 45 to 90 days? (Check with local ordinances which may prohibit this.)

- Improve the value of your main ISP startup home page so that it's worth visiting daily. At the same time, you're able to sneak in special offers for the audience whose attention you have grabbed by delivering fresh content daily.

- Fax blast every customer in your database who has agreed to be on your fax mailing list. A typical fax blast (which should not be done more than once per month) would include special offers, domain registration service, Web hosting or Web design options, and so on.

- Visit your competitor's directory of customers and create a database of potential customers to snail mail an offer with a follow-up phone call two weeks after.

- Sign up resellers, dealers, or affiliates to bring you new subscribers and pay them on a commission basis. The beauty is that they are not on your payroll and only get paid when they deliver new sales to you.

- Got a local business expo coming up soon? Why not offer to speak as an Internet expert representing your ISP and delivering valuable information that the audience can use?

- Try gas pump toppers in your local POP calling area. If you focus on consumers, this is one place to find them.

- Try ads on parking meters or park benches. Again, get permission first or find a business that offers this service.

- Give away free access coupons to every student of your local Microsoft, Cisco, Novell, or other related authorized educational computer training facilities.

- Donate access coupons or Web site hosting coupons to local charity auctions or as giveaways during fund-raisers. Chances are that you will always get the repeat business after the term of the coupon expires.

- Get a few people together to be *positive picketers* who march in front of businesses with signs that say how good your business is. Call your local media to cover this. Though this may sound very strange, it could be powerful if you are able to find a dozen customers who will do this in exchange for a free month or two of service.

- Educate your front line to be able to handle objections, so that they can convert more prospects into paying subscribers.

- Try ads on videocassette boxes at your local video store.

- Make up 3 by 4 inch window decals of your ISP's name and logo and give them to your employees to place on their cars. You could also do this with your customers by creating a *Win with a Sticker and Stick with a Winner* campaign. What you do is provide bumper stickers emblazoned with your ISP name and logo and 800 number. Set up a call-in line so that when they are spotted, the caller can qualify for a prize, such as a free month of service, which you'll give away each month.

- Test ads on local shopping carts or register receipts. Use direct-response coupon tags so that you can track where the leads come from.

- Why not put your logo on a bunch of helium balloons if you've got a retail store where people can sign up? Anything that creates excitement or interest can only lead to more attention for your ISP and ultimately more customers.

Creating Effective ISP Press Releases

Press releases and the role of your ISP's public relations director or department can make a positive economic impact on the success of your business.

However, it's important to understand what makes a good press release and what they will and won't do for you. Do not count on a press release to bring you instant sales response and cash into your business even though they sometimes can lead to that end. However, they can lead to increasing the buzz and exposure about your ISP at the same time you are positioning yourself to attract new investors or the attention of the media to cover your business. Another positive role of press releases is that they do sell confidence.

> **TIP** Set up an e-mail announcement list server so that those who surf your press releases section on your Web site can sign up to receive an update whenever you have a new press release to share with them. Every public ISP should have this already, and every savvy private ISP should consider this low-cost, high-return buzz and nearly free exposure vehicle.

There are three levels of press releases that you might release throughout your life as an ISP. Following, they are listed from lowest-cost to highest-cost:

1. Internal press releases, for which you create the release, post it on your Web site, and send it to your press release e-mail announcement list only.

2. Internet press releases for which you do no. 1, plus pay for services such as the Internet News Bureau or Internet Wire to distribute your release to a targeted audience all via e-mail, and with no hard copies.

3. Regional or national press releases, for which you do no. 2, plus send the release through one of the targeted newswire services such as BusinessWire or PR Newswire for regional distribution to either select cities, select markets, select types of industries, or any other highly localized regional or national distribution. Often you also get e-mail distribution as part of this service. This level of service, which is the most expensive, has the highest impact of available media outlets today.

Your choice of press release distribution will vary based on your budget and expected outcomes. A typical ISP with 2,000 subscribers might invest $2,000 to $5,000 per year on PR distribution, whereas an ISP with 10,000 to 100,000 subscribers may invest a very high multiple of that number based on whether it intends to go public or stay private.

Here are seven tips to create effective ISP press releases:

Must be sent to the right people. Create a database of people that you have either met, heard of, or know to whom you need to send the release. Oftentimes you can call the various local or regional media firms and ask for the technology or Internet news media contact. Do not send it out to a large spam list of various publications that are not targeted on your industry, as you are just wasting your time and theirs.

Must be newsworthy. Press releases that are self-indulgent are hard to sell to the news outlets, so make sure your release has a newsworthy component or at least a tie-in with a current news event. For example: A local TV station is covering how blind people are able to start and run businesses over the Internet and you know that your ISP has special capabilities for helping blind people to get on the Internet. This is a perfect tie-in and adds value to the TV station's news story and at the same time builds word of mouth for your ISP.

Publications have editorial deadlines. That means that the Internet or technology publication that you wish to get your release covered in is often planned months or a year in advance. Most ISPs release news when they have a new product or a new relationship or something new that just happened to them. One way to get yourself covered in a feature is to find out what the publication's schedule is and create special releases that speak to those editorial features.

Format it correctly. There are many unwritten rules as to the format of press releases; the more you follow industry trends, the better off you'll be. This includes your PR contact information, corporate contact information, headline, body, and the established format to indicate the end of your release.

Ninety-five percent of the effectiveness of your release will be the headline. Editors are flooded with hundreds, if not thousands of press releases a day, and the headline is what most of them scan for key words that fit their current needs. Put some serious thought into the headline, as it will determine the lion's share of your shot at additional exposure.

Keep your copy crisp and to the point. Don't be verbose or include extra words that you don't need. When you pay to distribute your release, it's usually by the word, so the fewer words, the lower the cost. Most people don't have all day to read your release, so keep it short, brief, and to the point. If they want more information, they will visit you on the Web or call you.

Tell, don't sell. Make sure your release speaks in terms of benefits and answers the question of the potential customer: "What's in this for me?"

Producing Results with Word-of-Mouth Campaigns

Word-of-mouth campaigns are often cited as the vehicle that can deliver from 10 percent to as high as 100 percent of the new subscribers that you will sign up this year. Undoubtedly, new subscribers find out about your ISP more often than not by talking with your current subscribers. What is shocking is that many ISPs say that word-of-mouth advertising is their most powerful advertising vehicle, yet 90 percent and more of them have no formal program in place to ensure that positive things are being said about their ISP by others. If you know that word-of-mouth advertising is effective, why not throw some fuel onto the fire and see how high you can burn your new subscriber sign-up rate flames by implementing a formal word-of-mouth awareness campaign?

Word-of-mouth campaigns are not something that you do for a very short while, but rather they are made from the way that your ISP behaves, handles problems, rewards contribution, and delivers service at key moments during the sales process. Positive word of mouth only happens when your subscribers' level of expectation has been exceeded. What have you done lately to improve the perceived value of your services?

Negative word of mouth occurs when your subscribers' level of expectation is not met, or worse, when you don't deliver on promised benefits.

Your goal is to leverage positive word-of-mouth advertising while minimizing the power of negative word of mouth, which can destroy your ISP much faster. It is important to handle customer service issues even when it appears in the short term that you are losing money by providing so much service. Consider it this way: What is the true cost of a new subscriber from a word-of-mouth referral? Many times on the surface, your cost to acquire the customer looks to be nothing or near nothing. However, that's a narrow perspective because every sale has a cost of acquisition. When you are faced with a problem you brought on, you know the right thing to do is to give a customer a partial or full refund or extend the customer's service. It's just this expense that becomes the true cost of a future sale which may come to you from word-of-mouth advertising. The reality is that when you focus on pleasing your present customers, you are actually investing in future sales.

Here is a short course on making positive ISP word of mouth work for you:

- Put your brightest and most customer-friendly, positive people on the front line, and slowly weed out or fire anyone who does not meet your standards. Every time an employee interacts with a customer, you want the best chance that expectations are not only met but exceeded.

- Sit down right now with your team and brainstorm ways that you can either manage customer expectations so that you can exceed them or find honest, true ways that you can do little things that mean a big difference for your customers.

- Find ways to go above and beyond the call of duty. For example, answer requests for tech support faster than any competitor. Be available 15 to 30 minutes past the time you advertise that you close, to provide after-hours support; make sure to let your subscribers know that you're closed but will attempt to help them anyhow. Watch your error logs to anticipate those who might be having a login problem and call them to see if there is anything you can do to help.

- Create an e-mail list where your customers can request an update on your business, the latest specials, new services, or special deals. This is a great way to connect weekly or monthly with your customers and maintain awareness, which is one of the keys to creating referrals.

- Use public recognition on your Web site in order to thank the top three to ten people who sign up new subscribers or friends. Have a contest and give away something of value or cash to whoever sends you the most new referrals.

- Remember to ask for referrals and others to help you build your ISP. "Ask and you shall receive" still applies to life and business today, but you've got to ask for it.

- How many e-mails do your technical support send in response to subscriber inquires? Why not include a link to an ad in the SIG (special interest group) list of your technical support personnel, which encourages people to sign up for your referral program?

How to Get More Testimonials Than You Can Shake a Stick At

Testimonial marketing is powerful. It costs very little to use this advertising vehicle while creating incredible leverage for your ISP. There are two basic goals for testimonial marketing: how to get them and what to do with them.
Strategies to get great testimonials include the following:

- Ask for them.
- Program customers to write them for you by saying these simple words right after you have delivered great service or are being

thanked by your client: "Thanks. Could I ask you for a favor? Could you write me a letter on your company letterhead stating the kind of service you received from me? I'm creating a portfolio for myself and would really appreciate it."

- Make it easy by providing a testimonial or feedback submission form on your Web site. Make sure you add a permission button to reprint any customer comments without having to ask them for further permission.

- Provide a feedback form in your dial-up kit with space for comments that can be filled out and returned to you in the prepaid postage envelope you provided.

- Provide a $20 bill for each testimonial written on company letterhead that any staff member gets during a given period.

Following is a list of how to leverage testimonials to drive your ISP sales through the roof:

- Include them on the order page of your secure sign-up form. Many ISPs report that their surfer-to-new-subscriber conversion doubles with this tactic. You can also integrate them into your Web site and off-line marketing in order to improve customer confidence.

- If you are selling Web site hosting or design-related consulting services, make sure that in addition to samples of what you have produced, you also include copies of testimonials you have received.

- When sifting through all of the testimonials that you have received, make sure you send prospective customers targeted testimonials, ones that will be the most meaningful to them. Examples of these are testimonials from a competitor or someone the prospect knows and trusts.

TIP If you haven't received a testimonial in the last six months, it's time to check out why. Lack of praise for your ISP can be a sign that customer expectation is not being met or that something is wrong and needs attention.

Using Direct Response to Drive Subscribers to Sign Up Now

One of the biggest mistakes ISP marketers make is that they engage in non-targeted mass marketing. Worse, many who do market to their target niche send institutional-type brand advertising instead of direct response marketing. From now on, you are only going to invest your limited marketing budget on acquiring customers from your target market using direct response advertising vehicles that will be outlined in this chapter.

Direct response advertising is when you get a target customer to buy from you by presenting factual information, a compelling story, and why your ISP is better than others or what your USP is along with a call to action. It differs from *institutional advertising* in that it is designed to speak directly to the prospective customer's needs, desires, and wants, rather than self-indulgent advertising.

Example of a direct response advertisement. You identify that people who are new to your community need to set up a new Internet service, assuming they don't carry over national access from a previous provider. You then send them a targeted, personalized letter welcoming them to your community along with why your ISP is the best, the services you can offer them, a price or value inducement to get them to buy now, and a call to action. This is direct response marketing because you attempted to get a response from a highly targeted potential new buyer.

Example of an institutional advertisement. You identify that people who are new to your community need to set up a new Internet service, assuming they don't carry over national access from a previous provider. You have learned that these new people to your area often sign up for cable, you then call your local cable carrier and you buy 30- and 60-second ads that extol the benefits of your ISP, why your service is superior to any one else's, why you are number one, how long you've been in business, and possibly who your founder is or why you started your ISP. This is an institutional ad because there is no call to action. Actually, there is a bunch of fluff in institutional advertising that doesn't even address the needs of the intended audiences, such as needing a friendly local ISP, nor does this kind of ad tell how someone could contact your ISP if he or she wanted to sign up.

Direct response goes beyond direct mail, because any ad, including a TV ad campaign, can be converted to direct response by simply talking directly to the audience, telling them how and why they should buy from you, along with how they can become an instant customer.

> **TIP** When ISP salespeople are out selling to prospective customers, their closure rate may be between 2 and 30 percent. However, if they were to use direct response advertising to attract only qualified customers who already want what they sell, their closure rate can easily double to 4 to 60 percent. Direct response marketing is this powerful and should be used to decrease the time of your sales cycle and increase your productive selling time.

Effective Direct Mail Formats

While direct mail formats come in almost every flavor, there are four that are very effective and deserve to be tested. They include the following:

1. 8 × 5 inch postcard, shown in Figure 5.3, with your compelling offer or emotional appeal on the front and the specific call to action on the back. The beauty of postcards is that they are one of the lowest-cost forms of direct mail and still produce sales results. They are also great for when you want to reinforce other types of direct mail, such as sending a successive set of four postcards in a row, each selling a different set of reasons why the customer should buy from you.

2. 8½ × 11 personalized letter, shown in Figure 5.4, along with a 8½ × 7½ inch folded brochure which extols the benefits and further compelling reasons why they should buy your service all stuffed into a #10 envelope. You can also test hand writing the envelopes, or include a tag line, or test a benefit statement on the envelope in the front or back. Your primary goal is to get the envelope opened up, because without that, your offer will not get a chance to be received by your target audience.

3. Same as no. 2, but the letter is 8½ × 14 inches and contains a coupon at the bottom along with perforation which allows the customer to fill it out and either fax it to you, include it with a future invoice payment, or snail mail it back because you put a postage prepaid BRM (Business Reply Mail) stamp on the back side of the coupon. This example is shown in Figure 5.5. Contact your local post office for more information on setting up a BRM account.

4. A self-mailer, shown in Figure 5.6. This is great for when you want a low-cost mailing done, but you don't have the time to develop a perfect

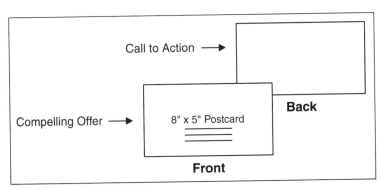

Figure 5.3 8 × 5 inch postcard.

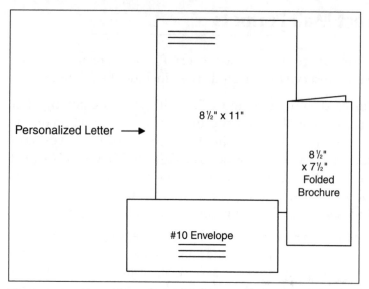

Figure 5.4 8½ × 11 letter/brochure with a #10 envelope.

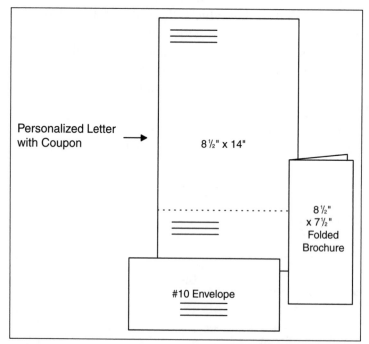

Figure 5.5 8½ × 14 inch letter with coupon/brochure and a #10 envelope.

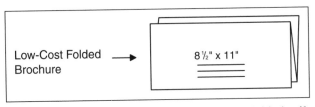

Figure 5.6   An 8½ × 11 or 14 inch letter-size folded self-mailer.

marketing piece. In this case, just take a piece of paper (heavier weight than normal, such as 60- to 80-pound paper, so that it doesn't get destroyed through the mail) and fold or trifold it with the addresses applied by an ink-jet printer (cheaper than a laser printer) onto one side of the mailer. However, don't use this one for your premium services; it's a better vehicle for lower-end sales. Many times your local print shop cannot only produce all of these for you but it can also get them in the mail for you using its bulk mail account. This saves you the expense and time of setting up a bulk mail account of your own.

ISP Direct Mail Tips, Tricks, and Secrets

Many ISPs waste an incredible amount of marketing money on ineffective direct mail. Here are nine strategies that will help increase the cost-effectiveness of your marketing:

Does your mailing look like junk? If your mail gives the impression that it is junk mail, it will probably be perceived as junk mail. Make sure that you take into consideration the type of customer, price point, and market objective when you select the direct mail vehicle. For example: If you are courting Fortune 1000 firms to buy dedicated direct access from you, you will *not* want to use a 20-lb 8½ × 11 piece of paper folded in half with a stamp, but rather a highly targeted, personalized, and professional approach would be much better.

Did you tell a story? It's hard to write good ad copy. A story is an effective way to engage readers and helps them understand how your ISP solves problems, saves them time, and provides reliable service. These can be case studies from current, satisfied customers (make sure you get the customer's permission to tell his or her story).

Did you use testimonials to reinforce that others in the community also agree that you provide great service? This is your proof that your offer is approved by others.

Did you address "what's in it for me" for your reader? How many times did you use the words "you" in your writing? Make sure you try to think like the customers, knowing that they don't particularly care about your product and only care about how your ISP will improve their life, save them time, and solve their problems.

Did you use first-class postage? Research has proven that a first-class stamp, while costing more than bulk, can give the impression that this mail isn't junk mail and that it should be opened.

Did you tell the reader what to do? Your copy *must* lead to action, which drives readers to wanting the benefit of your service immediately. You can provide specifications such as calling, e-mailing, or faxing their order in. You can even tell them how you don't want them to contact you so that you control the sales process a bit more while still giving the customer what they wanted.

Did you enclose a response form or order form that they can fill out, fax back, or return to you via snail mail, or a secure URL, allowing them to sign up with a special offer code? In addition to asking for the order and including a call to action, you also need to include a way for them to take action, such as a response form to fill out and send in. Research has also proven that if you already have the customer's information on the preprinted form, response increases, even though your costs increase for this form of personalization.

Is your mailing targeted to people whom you have identified as likely buyers of your kind of ISP services? You do not have enough money to market to people who are not your target client, so make sure you only send to prequalified potential buyers. For example: You sell Web hosting services so it's safe to assume that anyone who has a domain name within your service region is a targeted prospect for a letter from you. On the other hand, sending a letter to everyone in your service region with an offer for Web hosting will not be as effective and will result in lower return.

Did you include a powerful P.S.? The post script at the end of your letter is the second-most read part of your letter, right after your headline. Make sure your P.S. restates the offer and gives another call for a specific action by the reader.

As with all of the ISP marketing tips in this chapter, remember to test your marketing. Do more of what you have found that works and stop doing marketing that has proved ineffective. This does require, of course, that you measure each marketing campaign in terms of results which is a minimum requirement of any marketing plan.

TIP In order to save money and improve your response rates, after each direct mailing, be sure to update your database based on the undeliverables. Remove people you are no longer able to reach and update forwarding addresses.

ISP Drip Marketing Revealed

ISP drip marketing is when you leverage the *guerilla marketing law of 29* (from Jay Conrad Levinson, more than 26 books on guerilla marketing), which states that in order for anyone new to buy from you, he or she needs to hear, see, think, be told, and feel good about buying from you about 29 times. Use this law of marketing to find unique ways to increase the chances that your message is being heard, seen, thought of, and referred to, to get your potential client to become a paying subscriber faster.

This is also a great strategy for new sales reps at your ISP company, who are unsure of what to do to increase their sales. When in doubt, call, letter, e-mail, fax, call, letter, e-mail, fax, call, letter, e-mail, fax, call, letter, e-mail, fax, and call until you either are told or discover that the client has no need or you get the sale.

When you consider drip marketing, instead of just planning for a single media use for an ISP marketing campaign, plan for three to seven media pushes in successive order in order to leverage the law of 29 and close a higher percentage of possible sales. For example: Your goal is to increase Web design revenue, so you identify 2,000 domain owners, your dial-up customers, who might need Web design services. You then send a personalized letter to each one, but you don't stop there. A week later, you send them a postcard restating a benefit and three more reasons why they should buy from you. A week to 10 days later, you send another postcard, offering them another three reasons why they should choose your company. Another week later, you send them another postcard with a specific offer related to the original, but one which absolutely ends by Friday, so they must hurry. On the Wednesday before the offer expires, you send a fax blast to the 2,000 members (assuming you have their fax numbers), again giving them the ability to opt out. From Thursday through Friday night, you and your team call until your fingers are so tired that you can't dial any longer or you reach all 2,000 in this marketing drive. Do you think this sort of campaign might produce higher results than just one letter or one media and no follow-up call? You bet it does. [I know from personal experience.]

Finding and Reaching Your Target Customers

Before you can find your target or ideal client, you must define who they are. To say that your target market is everyone within your geographic coverage area is too wide. You probably don't have the budget, and shouldn't spend it even if you do, to reach a mass audience. Your target is to only spend marketing dollars to acquire customers who have a high chance of needing or already using similar services as that which your ISP company offers.

A key guideline is that subscribers of another ISP (that is, your competitor) are two to five times more likely to become your next customers than a potential subscriber who has never been on the Internet. There are two arguments to this thought process:

1. If it's true that it costs less to acquire a subscriber who is already somewhat Internet savvy, then why would anyone want to ever focus on potential Internet newbies? As for these experienced subscribers, if they converted to your ISP so easily because of their dissatisfaction with their current ISP, will they leave your ISP also just as quickly?

2. An alternative viewpoint says that going after new customers who have never been on the Internet outweighs the additional cost it may take to educate and acquire their business because they may be with you longer than a "switcher." You'll have to decide which is more important for your marketing focus.

Take out a piece of paper, call everyone together, and write down in exacting detail what your "ideal" subscriber looks like. Here are some questions that you may wish to ask yourself when coming up with your ideal client profile along with where you might be able to find them:

- Are we going to focus on converting new users or are we going to focus on converting "switchers" who hop from ISP to ISP when they are not satisfied?

- Are we going after high-price, high-service, upscale clientele or are we after low-price, low-service, economy-type customers?

- Who are the customers we do not want, and should we make sure that we don't attract their attention?

- Who are the customers that can best benefit from our Unique Selling Proposition?

- Where can we find these people? Which media vehicles are the best to reach this profile? Where does our ideal client hang out?

- What are their friends like? What do they value most in life?

- How much money do they earn annually, and what else should we know about the lifestyle of our ideal clients?

- What are some of our clients' pet peeves? What really bugs them about the whole Internet experience?

TIP Today, go out and secure three new customers that meet your ideal criteria.

The Greatest Asset Your ISP Owns and How to Exploit It

It's your *customer list* that can have the greatest amount of marketing leverage, if properly applied. You may have heard this before, but it costs less to make an additional sale to an existing subscriber than it does to acquire a new subscriber. Because of this, exploiting your customer database can be very profitable, but you *must* also consider the privacy of your clients. Selling customer e-mail addresses is one of the biggest sins an ISP or any business can commit against their clients because of the trust that is lost.

From your customer list, you have a list of subscribers, both business and residential, who have a recent history of buying your Internet access products. Any customer who has just bought something should be considered part of a *live* list. A live list is the best to leverage.

Here are a few examples of how you can exploit your customer database:

- You have a list of customers who buy Internet access but have not registered their own domain name yet, so you send them a targeted direct response.

- You have a list of customers who buy a high-usage, but not dedicated account, so you send them a direct response offer to upgrade their account to a full 24 by 7 dedicated premium account.

- You have a list of customers who have bought Web site hosting accounts, but they are not buying Web site design service from you yet, so you send them all a direct response offer for your Web design packages.

■ You have a list of customers who buy ISDN service currently, and you send them a direct response offer to sign up for a fraction or full T1, for improved speed and circuit reliability and stability.

■ You have a list of dial-up customers who have bought Web site design service from you, but have not yet set up e-mail list servers for their Web sites, and this is a service you offer. So you send them a direct response offer to set up an e-mail list or two for their corporate Web site projects.

The applications are endless, but you can see how easy it is to leverage your existing customer database. Because they already trust you and are doing business with you, your chances of closing more deals is higher versus selling to someone who has never heard of you.

When your ISP grows beyond 10,000 members or so, you think about renting your customer snail mailing list to professional list brokers who manage the mailings. These brokers ensure that no one ever actually gets your customer list, even though they sell it to others who want to reach your customers for noncompeting offers or products. Be sure to seed your list with multiple personal addresses so that you ensure your list does not get abused. Check your list broker's references for integrity.

Coupon insert swapping is another way you can leverage your customer list and monthly invoicing. Try this: Find another business, such as a dry cleaner, and offer to swap a one-third-sheet coupon of theirs that you will stuff in your monthly invoices and, in turn, they will do the same for you. This kind of shared lead seeding gives each of you access to people who may have never heard of either of you, and at a very low cost.

TIP When was the last time you made a backup of your customer list? This should be done monthly at a minimum, and as your ISP grows, it should be done weekly and eventually daily. Don't wait to learn the lesson that many have learned the hard way when a hard drive fails and their customer database is unrecoverable.

The second most valuable part of your ISP database is the names of people who either were past customers, are free trial users who did not convert, or are potential prospects who entered one of your contests or sweepstakes. These are people and businesses who know about you and should never be ignored. This group should continually be enticed to do business with you via direct response offers.

Copywriting Your Way to ISP Profits

Small ISPs already know who is in charge of writing all the marketing copy within their organizations. You are or your boss is or the owner is. It's seldom or never delegated out to any big ad agency who makes its money by making sure you spend as large a media budget as possible. Why is it that senior executives and CEOs of big ISPs are not encouraged to write their own ad copy, but rather are encouraged to outsource the ad copy to an ad agency? Large or small, every principal of every ISP should be involved in reviewing all copy. No one can sell in print like the principals of an ISP can. Unless your ad agency can prove that its ad copy has generated lots of new revenue for ISPs in the past, write your own copy for all ads. Let your ad agency, if you use one, deal with the placement of the ads in the proper media while you write at least the starter copy.

When it comes to copywriting, if you want the short cut, it's this: 95 percent of the effectiveness of your ad copy is always your headline. This is the first item that you test when trying to improve on the response rate to your marketing. Realize that your headline is not only something that you put in print, but it's also the first words you speak during your radio or TV commercial. It is also the first words that your sales reps say when they attempt to get the attention of a client or prospective client. It's the primary benefit-oriented statement that helps the reader decide whether they wish to read on or listen further to your pitch.

Words That Sell

Your	Free	Secure	Guaranteed	High-speed
Reliable	Fast	You	Results	New
Discover	Introducing	Save	Safe	Sale
Trustworthy	Right	Powerful	Comfortable	Happy
Healthy	Good-looking	Fun	Exciting	Value
Win	Wanted	Alternative	Benefits	Easy
Love	Money	Gain	Now	Because
Proud	Performance	Competitor	Good	Great
Excellent	Solution	Fresh	Energetic	Quick
Secret	Perfect	Complete	Dependable	Proven

The two that are the most powerful are *your* and *free*, because you are always writing to get the attention of *your* reader and address his or her unique needs. It should come as no surprise that the word *free* is also just as powerful, as everyone likes getting something for nothing or at least a bonus to help make the deal more attractive. Refer back to the preceding list the next time you write the headline or any copy for your next ad piece. See if you can punch the copy up a bit by using adverbs and more of the sell words.

Also remember to keep your copy crisp, brief, and to the point.

The following are three quick copywriting tips:

1. Establish your objective before you write one word. Is this a thank-you letter, a letter to an existing member to whom you are pitching a higher level of account, or a prospect who has never heard of you? Your job is to break down the barrier and get the reader to call for a free trial kit.

2. Grab your readers' attention and hold it by writing to them, for them, about them, and not about you, your ego, or anything unrelated to the benefit the customers will receive if they respond to your offer.

3. Always include a *call to action*, which encourages the reader to pick up the phone and call 1-800-your phone number, or e-mail for more information, or sign up securely on the Web at your URL. Whatever your call to action is, you must spell it out clearly, telling the readers exactly what they should do to take advantage of it.

Seminars, Lunch-n-Learn Customer Education Programs

Customer education programs or seminars are great low-cost/high-return vehicles which you can use to sell more of your services, especially your higher-level premium services, such as Web site design, promotion, consulting, or dedicated Internet access accounts for businesses.

If your ISP is under 10,000 subscribers, and they all come from a relatively close geographic region, then *lunch-n-learns* are something that you could consider. Typically, this type of event lasts for 45 to 60 minutes and is over lunch. [I discovered the power of this concept by accident after I created what we called *Sparky's Lunch N Learn* for our ISP, which was designed to share our expertise for free over lunch. It cost us about $700 to produce, and within 2 to 6 weeks after each of these lunchtime events, we earned $5,000 to $7,000 in additional sales that we would have not received without the event. As you can guess, we then ran them every single month until my ISP was sold.]

The following are some strategies to make your lunch-n-learns effective:

- Schedule a yearful of them in advance so that when you market the events, if people can't make this month's event, they might be able to attend or schedule themselves for a future event.

- At each event, create a different theme or primary topic that is of interest to your community. Include handouts and anything that complements your short presentation.

- Test which time of day and month is best for your community. [For us, the third Thursday of the month from 11:30 A.M. until 1 P.M. was perfect. Avoid doing them during any typical business crunch time, such as the beginning of a month.

- Have door prizes, in order to collect business cards to build your marketing database and follow-up list. Typical giveaways should include coupons for samples of your services, such as two dial-up accounts free for a month, two coupons you can give to your friends for a free month of service, a Web design discount or $200 off a $2,000 package, a free Web hosting setup fee waived, or free hosting for the first two months of any new account.

- Get your whole ISP involved so that someone greets people at the door, gives everyone name badges, prepares the food, assists with beverages, and makes sure everyone is comfortable.

- Have PCs set up, so that people who want to see whether their domain name is available can look it up on the spot and sign up before they leave.

- Use drip marketing to promote the event, including an announcement in your monthly e-mail newsletter; an e-mail to your entire database inviting everyone for free food, fun, and a brief Internet education; a fax blast; a postcard; a personal invitation to attend; or include a one-third-sheet coupon in your monthly invoices about these special events.

- Make sure you include an ice breaker exercise at the beginning during which you have everyone introduce themselves to everyone else. This is a business networking event and it could result in your visitors doing business with each other; they'll thank you for bringing them all together.

- This is not a sell-hard event. This is a customer-giving event where you also make yourself available to answer specific questions about their business and Internet needs.

- Set up balloons, additional signage, and go the extra step to let everyone know that this is a special event, not just something you whipped together at the last minute.

- If you can't do it at your facility, consider doing it at a local conference hotel or center. They can often handle all of the food and beverages, allowing you to concentrate on the event itself.

- Make sure your team dresses up. This is a dress-to-impress event for which the minimum dress code should be your company polo shirt up to appropriate business attire.

- *Optional:* Put a dollar value on the event, and make it RSVP. Have your sales team provide tickets for the event throughout the month to their customers and prospects. The more you make people feel that this is an exclusive event, the higher your response may be.

Another low-cost strategy is to give a monthly seminar at the local library in your biggest POP region. This can include libraries at the local colleges as well. Some ISPs have gotten big results at local community colleges and adult education programs where the age of the average student is five to ten years older than at a four-year university.

You could also offer to speak at community and nonprofit events such as rotary or chamber of commerce events in your area. Many of these opportunities can lead to your reaching hundreds if not thousands of people who will regard you as the expert in the community for ISPs. In addition, you may be able to convert them into paying subscribers at a cost lower than normal advertising.

In addition to the nonprofit speaking opportunities, don't forget the opportunity to speak to a business or a specific department of a business as your way of introducing your ISP to them. Create a training package that you can give for free, along with a value-added Internet training package that has a premium price if they want more, and offer this to local businesses. You can also bundle each of the training packages with different deals.

TIP As with all of your marketing, keep track of your expenses and the sales or leads which result so that you can determine your effectiveness. If the event is successful, pour more of your money into creating additional exposure for each event so that you continue to reach more new potential subscribers. If the event is failing, consider lowering your costs to produce it and use only e-mail to notify your subscriber base about the event. [In our early days, this was all we could afford, and we'd typically pull 30 people per 1,000 people we contacted.]

Ambush Strategies for Rollouts in New Cities

So, you're in an expansion mode, planning to roll out POPs in areas where you've had no previous presence. Here's a POP deployment marketing guide that will help you ambush your competitors and give you the greatest leverage in your new markets.

Start with a question: When is a good time to begin to plan the marketing campaign for your new POP deployment? The answer is as soon as you know you're going to be opening a new POP. The wrong time to plan your marketing strategy is the week before—or worse, the week or month after—you launch. Some ISPs believe it's better to get into a market, get your server bugs worked out, and then introduce yourself, so you don't stumble. An opposing philosophy, however, is that it's much more profitable to charge forward first and figure out the back end second—assuming you have quality technical talent who are committed to doing whatever it takes to make the back end smooth.

In warfare, *ambush*—hiding, waiting to attack an unsuspecting enemy—has a slightly dishonorable connotation. But in business (as in war), the element of surprise is a powerful advantage. If you can keep your plans secret up until the day you introduce your new POP to the public, you can win as much as a 30-day cushion before your new local competitors can react and mount a counteroffensive to your marketing blitz.

And a marketing blitz is what you'll need to jump-start a market where customers may not have heard of your ISP before. A *blitz* is when you pour it on hard and strong for a brief period of time, and then wrap back around for future blitzes or maintenance marketing.

Your goal is to impact target prospects 29 times during your blitz (Levinson's guerilla marketing General Law), so that you not only expose yourself to your new target market, but you get a high frequency of exposure to the same people whom you are hoping to convert into paying subscribers.

Here is a creative idea list for your marketing department. Try as many of these as you can.

- Join the local chamber of commerce in the communities you'll be entering.

- Get a list of the local media—newspapers, radio, TV, and others—and make sure they are notified of your arrival via a press release at least two weeks in advance.

- Give something away to charity through a contest, or build a Web site for two or three local nonprofit organizations. Then talk this up in your press release.

- Send a promo postcard to every business in the new POP area just before launch, either offering the business a free trial (if you focus on the business market) or offering their employees a discount program (if you focus on the consumer market).

- Enter a float in the local parade and distribute free sign-up disks and candy. (Don't laugh—this unconventional strategy can clean up in small communities.)

- Contact local computer and PC service shops and offer them free accounts for the first six months to introduce yourself. Talk to them to see if they are happy with their current ISP. Perhaps, they might be interested in earning money for referrals.

- Offer free, one-hour Internet seminars in the local libraries and promote them in the schools, local colleges, and local newspapers. Give two month's free access to the first 60 people who show up as well as rewarding your new customers for referring their friends.

- Buy a snail mail list of everyone in your new POP area who has bought a PC in the last six months and send them something special in the mail. Call them if you can. Introduce yourself and offer to help them with their Internet experience.

- Are there any local talk radio shows on which you could get yourself booked? Call around and find out. Becoming the town expert on the radio is a great way to gain publicity—even if you do the show by telephone from another state.

- Contact local media outlets and look for organizations that either don't have an ISP yet or aren't satisfied with their current one. The object here is to barter access service for billboards, air time, or other valuable exposure, thus lowering your cash marketing cost. Again, don't stop when you hear that the organization already has an ISP because, typically, there's going to be some level of dissatisfaction. This is a great opportunity for you to be their number 2 choice which can lead to you becoming their number 1 choice if their current provider slips up.

- Make sure your Web site speaks to any new community in which you're opening a POP. Providing local content is a great way to connect with a new community.

- Notify your existing customers with an e-mail so that they can refer their friends who might live in the new POP coverage area to sign up with you.

If you are a more aggressive ISP marketing guerrilla, consider these ideas:

- Send out a probe (code word for VP of business development) to your new POP area 45 to 60 days in advance and try to buy the smaller ISPs who are out of cash or ready for a clean exit. It's great fun to start up in a new POP community with hundreds or thousands of ready-made customers instead of having to grow it all organically.

- Consider buying new subscribers. Hey, if your new subscribers are worth $100 to $500 each, what is wrong with paying them up to $100 to join your service? The telcos do this all the time with the $5 to $50 check they send out that entices you to convert your long distance to them. One hundred dollars might be a bit extreme, but it sure would get my attention and there's little question that it would cause a lot of people to switch to you. Not a bad investment when you're going to get at least $200 or more from the new subscriber annually.

- Consider not putting your capital into POP costs; lease the POP instead. This allows you to pour more available capital into buying market share instead of infrastructure.

If you're a facilities-based ISP and your POP costs you $25,000 to implement, make sure you can spend $25,000 in marketing it or don't open the POP. A lot of ISPs get a POP opened up with zero cash left to market their service. You can guess which way the business runs . . . down. Another way to figure it: Budget $20 to $50 per new subscriber you want to attract. If it ends up costing you less than that, consider the difference a bonus in return for your marketing savvy.

Making Local Trade Shows Produce New Subscribers

One of the first rules of trade show success is always to select the trade shows that attract the same audience as your target client. For the ISP industry, this would include any business expo, computer or IT show, ham fests (amateur radio), discount PC expos, and any niche shows which also attract your ISP client profile.

To make the trade show more powerful for your business, ask if you can be a seminar leader for any concurrent educational classes that often go along with trade shows. This can give you a great chance for additional exposure and your only cost is your time and materials for the presentation.

Profitable trade shows are based on the 80 percent you do *before* the show and your ability to draw your ideal client to your booth and ultimately make that person a subscriber. Most trade show attendees have a specific agenda. The reasons you give them as to why they should attend your booth can help get your booth on their must-visit list.

Here are some creative strategies that you can use to get your target audience to stop by your booth:

- Advertise in local ham radio or computer users' newsletters.

- Add a tag line to your envelopes, your postage meter, your invoices, your faxes, indicating your booth and a special prize that they can enter to win if they stop by.

- Provide complimentary trade show passes to your best customers and best prospective new customers.

- Direct mail a postcard to your existing base stating that if any current subscriber gets a friend to sign up when they visit your booth, the offer on the postcard is redeemable for two months of free service for both of them.

- Issue a press release at the same time as the expo announcing a new product or service, such as a speed increase, affiliate or new reseller program, or any new enhanced services that your ISP is now offering.

- Include information about the expo in your e-mail newsletter or in a special notice to your existing client base and describe the special deals you'll be offering at the expo.

- List upcoming trade shows and conferences in which you will be exhibiting on your Web site so that a potential new customer can plan on the most convenient time to visit your exhibit.

Though you probably have very responsible salespeople, make sure you have a sales manager, VP, or someone in a leadership position supervising your entire trade show exhibit to ensure that this concentrated exposure is well received and your standards are being adhered to. Your sales team should be trained to work the crowd. They should be friendly, ask clarifying and qualifying questions, get the prospect's card, and take notes on the hottest prospects for future follow-up. They should invite every prospect to register to win prizes in your fish bowl giveaway (if you have one) and they should not spend too much time with any one person so they can move more prospects through your trade show pipeline.

> **TIP** It's important to not only be able to have great conversational openers for the passers-by but you must be able to communicate, in 30 seconds or less, what makes your ISP unique versus your top two competitors. If they want to hear more, you should at least be able to recite the top seven reasons why your ISP delivers what the client wants most as you ask your qualifying questions.

Sponsorship Swaps, Bartering, and Ad-Trading Made Easy

One of the rules of grassroots marketing or guerilla marketing is to find ways to get additional exposure for your ISP at a zero cash cost. This can be done by sponsorship, swapping ads, or bartering items that you can deliver value for in exchange for items you need to grow the business or increase your sales. A *sponsorship swap* is anytime someone else, who has access to an audience that is attractive or similar to your ideal client profile, and you swap ads to each other's customers based on a 1:1 proportion.

You have two types of services at your ISP: those with a high margin and those with a low margin. Your goal is to aggregate the majority of your trade barter with your highest-margin products, so you get maximum value for the lowest cost of goods. Typical high-margin items include anything that you'd normally bill as labor which could include Web site design, Web site promotion, search engine optimization, CGI or Perl programming, or

---

TRADE SHOW DON'TS

While working your booth, don't: eat, drink, smoke, talk on the phone, leave your booth empty during trade show hours, ignore attendees, think you know prospective customers' needs before you talk with them and ask them questions, hand out dial-up kits freely (these should be reserved only for serious potential buyers), or read (your attention should be on prospects, not your personal reading pleasure). Don't be a border guard or put a table between you and your prospects, which means don't block interested prospects from coming inside your booth (stand to the side making your booth inviting and friendly to visit).

system administration services. Your dial-up accounts are low-margin items, so avoid using them as part of any barter unless they are part of a larger deal that allows you to use some of your higher-margin services.

Typical advertising barters include the following:

- Envelope invoicing stuffers. Typically a one-third-sheet coupon that each of you stuffs in your monthly invoices.

- E-mail or print newsletter text or classified ad swap. This is usually a 5 to 7 line by 60 character e-mail text ad that you swap with another local business's newsletter.

- Strike a deal with the local radio station and offer to buy any canceled or unsold spot ads it has for a third or a quarter of its posted rate. Your form of payment is Web site design, hosting, and promotion services only.

- In his self-published workbook *25 Ways to Bring Cash Into Your ISP,* David Silver, of Santa Fe Capital Group, suggests that you give away free products or services to any student in your community that maintains a 3.5 GPA. The local TV evening news will run that story for sure and may barter back to your ISP a free video news release slot.

The ISP Yellow Page Ad: How to Get the Highest Return

The goal with your ISP's yellow page ad in the local phone book of your target market(s) is to acquire new sales that exceed the cost of the ad. Most ISPs pay $50 to $1,000 per month for their yellow page ads, which means that if you are paying $500 a month for a yellow page ad, you must acquire 20 new accounts at a minimum of $25 per account to break even.

One little guerilla marketing secret is to take a lunch break for 2 to 3 hours at your local library along with your marketing director and sales manager. The library will have every yellow page of every MSA (metropolitan statistical area). Your objective is to page through about 50 of them

BARTER KEY DISTINCTION

You must barter only the services or products that you know will have a low cost of goods and make sure your dollar-for-dollar barter arrangement is based on your retail prices, not any volume discount or promotion.

looking for the ad design that pops out and makes you want to call for Internet service. After you and your team have identified your top 10 favorite examples, make photocopies and bring the design ideas back to your creative services staff to use as the basis for a new ad of your own.

Elements to include in your ad for best results are your USP, bullet point reasons why the prospect should buy from you, your phone number, price points if applicable, your URL and e-mail address, and your hours of operation.

Make sure that your order-entry system is tracking the origin of every single new Internet service sale. At the end of the year, when you are getting ready to evaluate whether you're going to renew your yellow page ad, get a report from your customer database system which shows how many new accounts can be attributed to your yellow page ad over the last year. Renewing the yellow page ad then becomes a simple math game based on whether it was an investment or expense for the previous year.

TIP Bigger ads don't always produce bigger sales or more of them. Your goal is not a bigger ad, but an ad that gets bigger results.

Proven Ways to Build a Powerful ISP Sales Force

The first distinction is that everyone is in sales, from your customer service team to your technicians, from top management all the way down to the front line. Everyone at your organization is in sales and that means that every employee who has a moment of truth (which is every time they interact with a customer) either sells confidence or sells a lack of confidence. Many ISP CEOs begin their day randomly asking everyone from top to bottom within their organization, "What did you sell today?" This action sends the message that your ISP values sales and that anyone who contributes to increasing sales will be appreciated.

Sales is absolutely the most powerful role within your ISP business. From the sales team and its function comes the lion's share of your ISP revenue stream and control of the margin. Your profit report card has a lot to do with the performance of your sales team. Sales is also the best place to train someone who you hope to eventually lead your ISP. It's likely that every future ISP CEO will come from a strong sales and marketing background. Instead of covering the basics of sales, which is already well done in hundreds of books, this section discusses sales as it specifically relates to your ISP. If you want some sales basics, read books by Zig Ziglar, Brian

Tracy, Tom Hopkins, and the many fine authors who have focused their careers on teaching successful sales strategies.

Before I discuss specific strategies to help you increase your ISP sales numbers, first focus on closing the holes and stopping the damage of any known or unknown self-defeating behaviors within your ISP. Whether your team is committed to you is not relevant, because most people will rise to the level of expectation that you set as long as it's realistic and you're willing to live by the same standards that you're asking of your team. With that said, accept nothing less than 100 percent commitment from your sales team and the rest of your staff.

The following are some common ISP ailments:

- A front line that lacks a caring attitude or is burnt out by the same repetitive, seemingly silly questions novice users ask. No, it is not okay to talk badly about your subscribers in the office nor is it cool to call them "lusers," which is ISP speak for low-end user. Every day, ISPs are losing valued customers due to an attitude of indifference by some employees. Worse, if you let this continue to happen, you are at fault also.

- Technicians who don't know how to handle sales leads or sales situations and consequently lose the sale. This can be remedied easily through daily and weekly education; an incentive program could be a good idea as well. Many times, your ISP techies are in the best position to influence customer purchase decision making because most customers don't believe that your techies are on commission and therefore have nothing to gain by their honest recommendations.

- Speaking of your most influential group (techies), when it comes to swinging customer opinion, a common challenge in the ISP industry, ISPs maintain billable hours to achieve the swing. However, there can be confusion as to what your Internet service includes versus what your sales rep sold the client. The sell may have implied service that will require tech hours above and beyond the call of duty. Make sure you focus on eliminating unpaid consulting or unpaid service work that was not part of the service offer. This can happen when your subscribers play your tech off the sales rep. Good internal communication can solve this. You could even consider tracking billable hours per technician and give small prizes or recognition to whomever has the highest percentages this week or month.

- A sales or customer service team who does not follow up with new subscribers to make sure they are doing okay is the number one reason why new Internet access trial customers don't become paying subscribers. To lead in this field, you and your team need to be the ISP king of follow-up.

TIP There is not enough time in a day, in this fast-paced industry, to teach a person who cannot sell to sell. Therefore, resist the temptation to hire a computer or Internet geek who has perfect Internet terminology that has just asked for a sales job but has never held a sales position in his or her life. You can always teach Internet skills and terminology faster to someone who is a salesperson at heart than teach salesmanship to a geek.

Dial-up Internet Access Sales Strategies

The following are some strategies you can use to better your dial-up Internet access sales:

- Pay close attention to your incoming lead to sales conversion, and create contests internally to reward whoever has the highest closure ratio. Your marketing dollars have been heavily invested to get your phone to ring, and your inside sales team's primary job is to close 100 percent of every possible lead.
- Bag large dial-up deals by organizing an outside ISP sales force to call on the local schools and nonprofit organizations, or to set up employee dial-up discount programs for the largest employers in your area, preferably starting with the ones that are already buying from you.

Leased Line, Dedicated Circuit Sales

Sales of this sort include ISDN, DSL, T1 and DS3. The following is a list of ways to better sales in this area.

- Do not assume that just because someone can sign up a simple Internet access account that they can close dedicated bandwidth deals without a significant amount of training.
- A dedicated bandwidth deal is best done by a sales engineer (a glorified name for your best customer-friendly technician) who understands enough of the basics of the ISP industry to sell dedicated access solutions from the circuit, bandwidth size, CPE (customer premise equipment) to the routers and proper servers based on client demand.

- If you've got great technicians who can't sell, pair them up with a sales rep dedicated to organizing the sales function. Your technician can help inspire enough confidence in the customer that your ISP knows what it is doing while your sales rep manages the customer relationship and closes the deal.

- Search your RADIUS logs (authentication) to identify who your highest business users are and send them literature, prompting them to contact you for pricing for a customized dedicated connection. You may want to convert as many of your highest unlimited dial-up users to dedicated circuits in order to improve your customer-to-dial-up port ratios, not to mention your profit margin.

- If you can't be number 1, be number 2. Seek out every business within your coverage area, and figure out who is currently providing them bandwidth and Internet access services. Even if they are happy with their current provider, plant the seed that if they are ever not satisfied, to keep you in mind.

Web Site Hosting and Design, Search Engine Registration, and Domain Services

The following are some strategies for boosting your Web site hosting and design, search engine registration, and domain services sales:

- Identify every business within your coverage area in which you can physically shake the hands of your customer and potential customers. Yellow pages can help, or local directories or even chamber of commerce mailing lists. Your goal is to send them a one-page invitation to register their domain name, if they have not yet. Every great Web sale begins after a business chooses their domain name, and there are still millions of businesses without a domain name. Get busy.

- These are perfect products and services for up-selling and cross-selling. Include a one-third-sheet coupon in monthly invoices inviting current customers to sample your additional Web services.

- Offer free Web samples. In this case, businesses send you their logo, information, and marketing brochure, and you send them a quick sample of what their Web site could look like. The short time it takes you to whip together a sample is often worth the effort if you make the sale.

What to Include and Not Include in Your ISP Proposal

Your ISP proposal is one of the most important documents to a prospective customer. It not only communicates the benefits of why the person should buy from you, but it shows how the proposal can be customized to meet individual needs and describes how to buy from you.

An ISP proposal should not be

- Sent via snail mail if you can avoid it—hand deliver it if it's important, or at least send it using priority overnight to indicate its importance

- A one-page price quote only (unless the customer asks for this)

- More than five pages long, unless absolutely necessary

- A form letter or a fill-in-the-blanks form (nothing could be less personal)

- Sloppy, inaccurate, or untyped

An ISP proposal should include the following:

- An executive summary, outlining in one paragraph what is included in it

- Customer input restated reaffirming why you are presenting this particular proposal

- Benefits and key applications as they relate to customer's needs

- Comparisons to your competitor or your other more expensive products or services

- References or testimonials that you've received from similar product or service sales

- Details on service and support systems available and costs

- Recommendations and exact costs, broken down multiple ways

- A call to action to lead your prospect to the next step

ISP Telephone Selling Basics

A large percentage of your sales is going to be done with the telephone so it's important to master some of the basics of telephone etiquette. Here are four key points to keep in mind:

Presence. When your clients close their eyes, do they see you as a strong leader or a clump of Silly Putty? Smile when speaking and stand up, in order to deliver maximum impact.

Rapport. With the depersonalization of the Internet, it's more important than ever to start and maintain a positive rapport with the human at the other end. You can get this by speaking slowly at first and then quickly moving up to the same speed as the other person, or you can soften your voice or speak louder. It all depends on the other person.

Articulate. Your prospects must be able to understand what you are saying and it must make sense to them. Don't talk over their head using Internet lingo, but if you sense that they are Internet savvy, talk at their level so you don't insult their intelligence.

Warmth. Make your voice nonthreatening, sincere, and nice.

TIP Get a mirror and put it in your desk so that when you are talking with your client you can cause yourself to smile and look pleasant. Even though they can't see you, the human at the other end can always sense your emotion.

Increasing Your Customer Conversion Rate

Every day your ISP receives new subscriber leads, free trial requests, referrals, dealer or reseller and affiliate sales leads, but they all don't convert. For those who don't convert, you've just lost money based on the cost to acquire the lead (yes, every lead has a cost to acquire by itself), you've lost the profits on the sale and the recurring revenue stream that customer would have represented, and you also have lost any chance at referrals from these potential customers.

Your customer conversion rate is the number of prospects who become paying clients divided by the total inquiries you received in a given period of time. For example: You received 800 leads this month, of which 160 signed up and became paying subscribers of your service, which means you converted 20 percent of your leads.

Your goal is to have the highest possible conversion rate. What if you already have a 100 percent conversion rate? Does that mean you have nothing to learn here and that you've mastered ISP prospect-to-customer conversion? Not likely, because if you are closing 100 percent of every sale, that says that you are not getting enough leads because 100 percent conversion, in practical experience, can only happen if you do not have enough leads coming in. That means while you can congratulate yourself for your cunning salesmanship to convert 100 percent of your leads into paying customers, you now should create a new challenge for yourself—increase the number of leads that you generate.

If you received one lead and you didn't close it on the spot, does that mean that your conversion rate is zero? Not yet. Your conversion rate in this example is zero only if you don't follow up and pursue that client. It doesn't matter if it's a simple dial-up sale, a dedicated Internet access account, or a Web design, hosting, or promotion sale. Research has shown that 8 percent of sales are closed on the first call, and that as high as 58 percent of all sales are made after the fourteenth contact or follow-up. Now, obviously you are not going to call a residential customer 14 times to sell him or her a dial-up account, but it's not unreasonable to assume that you could call a business account at least that many times in order to secure its business.

Some quick strategies to increase your ISP conversion rate are as follows:

Remove the risk from the customer and place 100 percent of the risk to do business with your ISP on your own shoulders. This means giving a 100 percent satisfaction guarantee, a money back if not satisfied guarantee, a free trial for some, a no busies or it's free guarantee, or a "you'll love us or it won't cost you a dime" guarantee.

Make it a better than risk-free offer. You can do this by giving customers a free gift that is theirs to keep, even if they discontinue service with you. Items to consider include an Internet tips book, an online Internet guide or CD-ROM, or an Internet training certificate.

Give something extra or include a value-add item in exchange for buying now. This is an inducement to make the sale more attractive to the buyers so that they can correctly assume that the amount of value they are receiving far outweighs their current cost to do business with you. Include a free bonus to encourage them to buy before a certain deadline.

Invest the time to educate your client. A client who knows how to use your Internet services is a lower-cost client to support and also leads to increased referrals. You can also use your Web site or marketing materials to shorten your sales cycle by allowing them to do some of the education for you. You may consider giving an Internet basics training class for a promotion to increase conversion.

Make your ISP easier to buy from. This includes accepting every major form of credit card or direct checking draft, customer-friendly hours, expert technical support, and a phone system that allows callers to reach a human quickly without trapping them in auto-attendant or voice mail jail.

Focus on making your ISP irresistible to buy from. Go above and beyond the call of duty, establish a leadership position in your community, give your prospective clients extra tools in order to grow their businesses while they are using your service.

Repackage your Internet access services to suit different buyers' needs. Packaging refers to what you include for what price point. For example: Create a family ISP dial-up package which includes enough e-mail accounts for the kids and the tools that a family might need. Try to create a few different business packages with varying levels of service to more closely match the need of the potential buyer.

Forget Cold Calling—Get Them to Call You via Sales by Attraction

Cold calling is a waste of time. After hiring 200 salespeople over the past ten years, I have learned that less than 12 percent of all salespeople have an "engager" sales personality. They are people who love cold calling or the challenge of the sale. That means 88 percent of the rest of the sales force hates cold calling or engaging new customers who have never heard of them. So, as long as you know that a great majority of salespeople are going to be ineffective off the bat at increasing their sales using cold calling, look at some of the alternatives.

Sales via attraction is my term for learning how to attract sales or generate demand for yourself, your ISP, and your business. It's not only an art, but a necessity, if you want to have more sales than you can ever imagine without cold calling. It's almost as if cold calling is the result of salespeople who didn't care enough to find out something about the potential customers, because if you know anything about potential customers and their anticipated needs, they are no longer a cold-call prospect, but rather a warm lead.

Eight proven techniques for generating demand for yourself and/or your ISP follow:

- Building the brand called *you* creates demand by itself and this includes making your name easy to remember, communicating a consistent message in the marketplace, and not shifting focus every other month. Be clear and very careful, as you can only hope to leave one or two important words in the mind of your prospects and customers.

- Add your personality and caring attitude to your sales approach whether it's face to face, on the Web, through e-mail, or over the telephone. Connect with your audience on a human level.

- Let your prospects and customers know that they will get a speedy response from you on any issue. Time is money today and anyone who responds faster to customer needs is in strong demand.

- Explain the reasons why someone should choose your ISP and then overdeliver. When you make your promises, make them realistic. Sometimes you can even share a reason why someone should not buy from you, as a tool to gain their confidence. Honesty is always attractive and will enhance the demand for your services.

- Be proactive in showing your prospect and existing customers how to save money while using your services.

- Offer to speak for local business trade shows, rotary events, chamber of commerce conferences, or any opportunity to be the expert, and share some of your knowledge with your prospective customer base in a non-direct sales situation which often lead to soft-selling opportunities thereafter.

- Author a newsletter, book, guide, tutorial, or anything in print, whether it be on paper, in a magazine, newspaper, or on the Web. The published word has power and it builds credibility for you and your ISP.

- Create a club, membership, or anything which promotes exclusivity and specialness, but only if your prospect qualifies. This little technique, which is not only attractive, also encourages interest and speculation as to how a customer can become qualified to join the special services your ISP offers. Give your existing special customers a secret password to give their friends so that when they call in as a referral, you can ask for the secret password in order to qualify them for membership. Some people may assume that because it's harder to get an account with your ISP, there must be a reason why you don't just accept anyone off the street and that can be attractive to some prospects. This technique is sometimes called "business by invitation only." Another method is when every customer needs to be sponsored by someone else to be eligible to become a paying customer. Now, you don't have to do this for your entire ISP operation, but what if you did it for an elite gold club package of extended or enhanced services?

Tracking Your Competitors and Their Customers

Some of you are going to hate me for sharing what were once protected secrets for only the extra-savvy entrepreneurs, but now they are fair game for everyone to pursue. Tracking competitors is actually easier than tracking their customers, whom you also hope to woo over to your service without breaking the rules of a fair ISP war. The number one rule in this game of ISP competitor war etiquette is *never* spam or send mass e-mails to your competitors' customers inviting them to your ISP. This is cheating. This is a great way to get a bad reputation in the community and loss of respect by your competitors.

To track your competitors, start with the two biggest resources: The List (www.thelist.com) and Boardwatch's ISP Directory (www.boardwatch.com) along with yellow pages for tracking the most up-to-date list of who is in the same markets as your POPs. Your purpose for tracking your competitors is to determine your competitiveness, do pricing and value studies, anticipate trends, and make sure your business is on track and able to respond to any competitive external threat before it happens.

This next strategy is more suited to local or regional ISPs who have less than a dozen POPs and have a sales team in each market or within reach of the market. If you'd like to know the domain names of the customers your competitors are hosting, you'll need three things:

1. A program that can walk a class C IP block, such as WS_Ping ProPack (*www.wsping.com*)

2. Your competitor's primary and secondary DNS service IP addresses (which are available by doing a WHOIS lookup of their primary domain)

3. A directory of your competitor's customers, which can usually be found off its home page, or by using a service such as Yahoo's local directories

To get the domain names, start by scanning the IP block from 1 to 254 of your competitor's primary DNS server; then do Nslookups of random domains of known sites that are hosted by your competitor as found in its external directory; and walk the rest of the other 253 IP addresses in that block. Put all of this information into a spreadsheet. Then take your findings and do WHOIS lookups on each one, which will then give you information to build a lead database of contacts for snail mail.

You can get the snail mail address of your competitor's dial-up customers by fingering (a Unix term) each of them if your competitor has the Finger server option turned on and not secured. If it has it turned on, but you have to be a dial-up member to get it, pay the $20 to get an account and get the information. Sometimes ISPs will list their customers' personal Web pages which are also in the same name as their username and can be fingered for more information, or you can have an assistant surf each page for contact information if it's provided. Another strategy is to visit any Web or e-mail discussion lists or boards that your competitors have set up to read client gripes or complaints and to watch trends. The end result is that you are creating a database of potential customers to snail mail a series of invitations that can entice them to switch to your ISP instead.

Another dirty little secret, unknown to many, is that some ISPs are running Majordomo, which is a list server, in order to send their customers a monthly e-mail newsletter. If you get lucky enough and the competitor is running v1.93 or v.194 which comes standard with a minor bug (which can be fixed) that allows you to send an e-mail to the majordomo@yourcompetitorsISPname.net with the command: which @ in the body of your e-mail, it will then return every e-mail address on every list on that server. Pretty scary stuff, eh? If you are running either of these versions, well, stop reading this book, and go find the switch within Majordomo to close this security hole. Majordomo's home is www.greatcircle.com.

Your ISP Pricing Strategy

The price points you choose will determine the market's perception of your ISP, your quality, along with your profits, margins or lack thereof, as well as the number of subscribers and customers you will be able to sign up. We've already discussed that you cannot be a very low priced ISP while delivering premium service levels because of the true costs associated with delivering a high level of service. Nor can you sustain premium service for a long period of time charging dirt cheap prices before your accountant tells you *game over.*

Factors to consider when determining your pricing include the following:

The true cost of the goods sold and the value or worth of your time to deliver them. If you're pricing your dial-up service, then your cost is based on what the wholesale dial-up provider charges you. If you are a facilities-based ISP, then it's based on how many ports you have, your user-to-port ratio (8 to 14 users per port is good, assuming no busy signals are being given), your server, bandwidth, labor, tracking, support, and operating costs.

Where your competitors are priced. On a quarterly basis, have someone on your staff do competitive research on the markets that you currently serve and then plot where the competition stands relative to your pricing.

The needs of your target audience. Pricing yourself too low may not give you the profit margin you need to do an adequate job, which basically prices you right out of the market all together. Pricing too high could scare away too high a percentage of your target market.

Regardless of what your customers tell you, price is not the primary decision maker. Most research studies have found that 14 percent of your customers on average buy based on price alone, which leaves 86 percent buying for other reasons. Real value is the name of the game. Finding new and creative ways to communicate to the customer that the value you are delivering exceeds the price that they are paying. You must also continue to educate even after you have them as paying subscribers because every month they will be enticed by your competitors. It's your job to remind them why they are staying with you.

As your ISP prices climb, the level of customer education climbs proportionately. This means that if you are priced above the market, you must expend more energy and marketing dollars to educate the market as to the reasons *why* your price still gives the customer more value than it costs them to subscribe.

The market can be very price sensitive when buying dial-up Internet access because it is often viewed as a commodity item. This means that you can influence and increase subscriber sign-up rates with price. However, this is a very dangerous game. You can run into negative cash flow problems very quickly if you're unable to up-sell or cross-sell your new subscribers enough to pay for the true cost of delivering service to them.

Assuming that you started out in a lower price range than you would have liked, a great many of you reading this book are faced with the challenge of raising rates because either you've underpriced yourself or you just feel it's time to raise them for any number of reasons. Did you know that major telecommunications companies have staffs of people who do nothing but calculate how many people will leave if they raise rates by a dollar? Raising your rates to at least the industry standard is the minimum that you should do for the niche or marketplace that you serve.

The following are the five right ways to tell your customers that you're raising your rates:

1. Give them some new perceived value that costs you very little at the same time you are announcing the rate hike. This could include something that you were already going to do for them anyway such as extending your technical support hours, providing a guarantee of faster e-mail support turnaround, or decreasing the amount of time they might have to be on hold by hiring more people.

2. Always give them a 30-day written notice. It's the courteous thing to do and anything else could lead to resentment and potentially lost confidence and lost subscribers.

3. Share the benefits first, as it relates to them, before sharing the rate hike. The more expensive your product or services are, the more you'll need to educate the customer as to why it costs what it costs.

4. While prepaid Internet access accounts are not always a good thing (because they are a liability), this is a perfect time to encourage everyone to sign up by Friday at the old rate for six to twelve months. This tactic will give you a quick boost in positive cash flow for the month.

5. Only deliver a rate increase at the peak of the best service your ISP has been delivering. If you know that you've been underdelivering and have been providing bad service, expect that your rate hike will be met with subscriber exodus.

Here are five wrong ways to tell your customers that you're raising your rates:

1. "We couldn't make enough money, so we're going to hit you up for it." Remember that your customer does not care about your cash flow problems.

2. "Our employees wanted more money or they threatened to quit, so in order to keep them happy, we're going to raise your rate." Beyond the fact that saying this would be highly unprofessional, your customers don't care about your employees, your expenses, or your problems.

3. "Because our competitors charge more, we're going to also." This is a lame excuse and your subscribers are buying from you, not your competitors, but don't blame them when they want to leave if an ISP really uses this excuse.

4. "We're your only choice in town, so it's pay more or leave." Don't let your minimonopoly, if you have one, go to your head. Stay humble, appreciative, and thankful for the subscribers you do have.

5. "Prices are just going up. They just are. I don't know why." Educate your front line so that they know specifically why prices are going up and how to handle some of the common objections customers may have.

In the next chapter, "How to Write Your ISP Marketing Business Plan," one of the industry experts on ISP business plans, Jason Zigmont of How-ToSell.net, is the guest author.

What to Include in Your ISP Marketing Business Plan

Success occurs when opportunity meets preparation.

—Zig Ziglar

Your ISP business plan is one of the most critical steps to ensure your success as a profitable ISP. To give you an overview of what's in an effective ISP business plan, I'm going to turn you over to Jason Zigmont of How-ToSell.net. Jason authored several ISP business plans and will give you his take on what to include in your business plan and why. At the end of this book in Appendix A, I've included an actual sample ISP business plan that you can use as your template. Take it away, Jason. . . .

The ISP Business Plan Introduction

Your destiny and your company's destiny are in your hands. Not only do you choose your own destiny, but you also write the manual on how to get there. This manual is called a business plan.

A well-designed business plan will not only give you the guidebook for your company, but also help you express to your investors, bank, employees, and anyone else interested in your company, exactly what your company is about. Your business plan is not something you write once, and never look at again, but rather is a document everyone on your team should be involved in writing, with your CEO or investors leading the general focus of your ISP's end outcome.

Whether you are writing your business plan for internal or external uses, the first step is to start writing. While it may seem like a daunting task, once you have it written, your business plan will save you hours every day by keeping you and your team focused on your most important goals. Many people complain about a lack of time but what they really have a problem with is a lack of focus.

This chapter will give you a guideline of what to put into your business plan and what to focus on for internal and external use. Also included in the appendix is a sample ISP business plan from HowToSell.net that will assist you in writing your own business plan.

The Essential Parts of an ISP Business Plan

Business plans should have similar segments and formatting. Each segment contains subsections that we will discuss later within this chapter. Formats can vary, but the general layout is what banks, venture capitalists, and investors are looking for. The essential segments of a complete business plan are as follows:

- Executive summary
- Financing proposal
- Business description
- Industry analysis
- Market analysis and sales forecast
- Marketing plan
- Operating plan
- Organization plan
- Financial plan
- Appendix

Throughout this chapter, you will find references to this list of essential components of a business plan. If there are certain sections you need help on, or that you are focusing on, you may skip to that section for more detail.

Writing Your ISP Business Plan

When you are using the business plan for internal uses, you will spend less time on the summaries and situational reviews. Conversely, if your business plan is for external use, summaries and situational reviews are essential as they may be the only thing outsiders read.

Business plans do not have to be written in formal language but clear, good English will help your readers understand what you are writing about. Do not use jargon, and use abbreviations only when you have explained them elsewhere in the business plan. Remember that the readers may know nothing about your business and technology. You need to explain to them your business and technology, while keeping it short and simple.

Following are some tips for writing your ISP business plan:

Write summaries and situational reviews last. These sections summarize the segments that follow them, and therefore are easier to write if you do them last.

Do your research. Your business plan will show the depth of your research, or lack thereof. Reports, surveys, and information gathering are worth their weight in gold. Remember that information about publicly traded ISPs is available at http://edgar.sec.gov/. Read through the filings as they often contain the information you need.

Be honest and realistic. Everyone has competitors and weaknesses. Readers are looking for your weaknesses and how you plan to overcome them. Saying you do not have any competition is the surest way to get your business plan ignored.

Get everyone involved. Your employees are interacting directly with your customers. They could have information that may help you address existing issues. Your employees also have to believe in your vision and business plan if it is to be executed correctly.

Get help. Before you show your business plan to banks, investors, or the public, get someone else's advice on it. Preferably you would like to show it to someone who is representative of the market to whom you will be shopping your plan. For example, if you are looking for a loan, have a banker, or an ex-banker for that matter, look at your plan and give you comments.

Present it professionally. Have your business plan bound and formatted in a professional manner. Unfortunately, books are sometimes judged by their covers and your business plan could be overlooked if it does not look professional.

A good business plan describes in greater detail each segment as you progress through it. The business plan starts off with summaries of summaries, which are mostly used for outside readers, and then details follow. It is the details you will use to run your business on a day-to-day basis.

Executive Summary

The *executive summary* is your first, and in some cases only, chance to make an impression on your reader. Banks and investors receive many business plans every day. If your executive summary does not catch them, chances are your business plan will be overlooked.

The executive summary contains four sections:

1. Business concept and mission statement
2. Operating plan summary
3. Marketing plan summary
4. Financial plan summary

While many people may joke about mission statements being meaningless, your *business concept* and *mission statement* should be your best-crafted explanation of your vision, background, and target market in less than four paragraphs.

The *operating plan, marketing plan,* and *financial plan summaries* are one- to two-paragraph summaries of the summaries of the operating, marketing, and financial plans.

A sample marketing plan summary can look like this:

QEI.net's product will be marketed to middle- and upper-income residential users and small office or home office users. The company's sales will be sufficient to break even and gain a market share of 5,000 users in the first planning year. This plan includes intensive customer interaction to foster additional word-of-mouth sales, which is the largest source of sales for ISPs, and bring down the cost to acquire customers.

Financing Proposal

In many cases, your business plan can be used to inform investors and banks about your company and your financial needs. The *financial proposal* describes the proposal you are making for funding of your company.

The financial proposal should be a one-page description of your monetary needs, repayment terms, and risk factors. You should write your financial proposal after you compile your financial numbers, sales forecast, and financial plan. You should explain what type of funds you are looking for, what they are going to be used for, and what possible collateral you can offer to secure the loan, or in the case of an equity investment, what percentage of equity you are willing to give up for what amount of money.

For example: You decided that based on relative valuations of other ISPs your size that your ISP is worth $30 million, and you are going to ask for $6 million in equity financing in exchange for a 20 percent share of your ISP for the investor.

Business Description

The *business description* segment of your business plan is a guide to your overall business. Readers of your business plan will use the business description segment as a quick reference about your company.

The business description contains six sections:

1. Firm identification

2. Business history

3. Business concept and mission statement

4. Market and target customer group

5. Description of operations

6. Management profile and needs assessment

Firm identification covers your business name, location, and contact information. *Business history* covers what you are, how you were founded, and when and where you were incorporated or organized. *Business concept and mission statement* is a slightly more detailed form of the similar segment of the *executive summary.*

The *market and target customer group* section describes your company, your market, and your target customers. This section is a high-level view of what is included in the *industry analysis* and *market analysis* segments of the business plan.

The description of operations is a high-level view of the operations plan. The management profile and needs assessment is a high-level view of your organizational plan.

Industry Analysis

The *industry analysis* provides an overall view of the competitive market and forces within the industry. In this segment, you have a chance to show your understanding of the market and to paint a picture of what should be expected of the overall industry. It is crucial to be realistic in this section and explain growth factors and possible negative factors in the industry.

The Industry Analysis contains three sections:

1. Industry description
2. Industry competition
3. Industry growth and sales projections

The *industry description* section describes what type of industry you are talking about. The best way to classify your industry is with Standard Industry Classification (SIC) codes which give the reader a point of reference. For ISPs, use SIC code 7375, information retrieval services. You may also reference http://weber.u.washington.edu/~dev/sic.html for a complete list of SIC codes. Within the *industry description*, you should also discuss the future of the ISP industry and the impact such changes may have on it.

The *industry competition* section describes direct and indirect competitors. Direct competitors such as national, regional, and local ISPs are easy to name, and you should give a brief analysis of each. Indirect competitors consist of other options for Internet access such as cable or methods other than ISPs such as a dial-up telecommuter to a corporate server.

The *industry growth and sales projections* section provides numerical representations of the growth of the industry and industry analysts' projections.

Good resources for ISP industry growth and sales projections include the following:

- Forrester Research (www.forrester.com/)
- Gartner Group (www.gartner.com/)
- NUA Internet Surveys (www.nua.ie/surveys/)
- Cahners In-Stat Group (www.instat.com/)

Market Analysis

The *market analysis* segment describes the market you will be targeting and the factors controlling that market. In this segment you will describe your market from a local level, your niche, and your direct competitors and their strengths and weaknesses. You will also discuss your sales forecast and its impact on your bottom line.

The market analysis contains four sections:

1. Market area and market sales potential
2. Target market description
3. Market competition
4. Sales forecast

The *market area and market sales potential* section includes a description of your target market and your target market's overall sales potential. Within this section, you may want to use numbers from your state or national census to determine the number of households or businesses in your target market. From there, you can use the industry average numbers to determine your total target market. U.S. residents can use the U.S. Census at (www.census.gov) for the number of households and residents on a county, state, or national level.

The *target market description* section explains your niche market and its buying characteristics. This section is the start of your marketing plan, and therefore you should touch on how you plan to reach your target market and how you plan to be the best in your niche.

The *market competition* section discusses your direct competitors and their strengths and weaknesses. The more information you can gather on your competitors, the better. Information such as positioning, number of users, growth rates, and churn are invaluable to your business plan reader and to you when positioning yourself against your competitors.

The *sales forecast* section is often the hardest section to do out of the market analysis segment. If you are an established provider, you can use your past sales, in addition to seasonal changes and any marketing push you may make to determine your sales forecast. If you are a start-up provider, you are going to have to base your sales forecast on your projections and other information you may be able to gather. Within the sales forecast section of your market analysis, you want to describe your sales forecast in the aggregate and reference a detailed sales forecast in the appendix to the business plan.

Marketing Plan

The *marketing plan* is often one of the largest and most detailed sections of your business plan. Your marketing plan should cover your strengths, weaknesses, opportunities, and threats (SWOTs). Your business plan should tell you and your reader exactly what users you are going after and how you plan to reach them. In the high-tech life we live in, it is too true that it is not the technology, but actually the marketing that makes a company successful. Readers of your business plan are going to look through your marketing plan to determine whether you are going to be successful, and therefore you should dedicate quite a bit of time to it.

The marketing plan contains seven sections:

1. Marketing plan summary
2. Situational review
3. Strategic opportunities and threats
4. Marketing goals
5. Marketing strategy
6. Marketing budget
7. Marketing controls

The *marketing plan summary* and *situational review* sections are high-level overviews of your marketing plan. Within the situational review, you should cover three subsections: The market, user sign-up, and the competition.

The *strategic opportunities and threats* section is a strengths, weaknesses, opportunities, and threats analysis of you and your competitors. This section is where you analyze your business versus your competitors in depth. The easiest way to write this section is to do a SWOTs analysis and then take the data from that analysis and put it into this section. For example, if you provide quality service at a premium price, that would be a strength. The weakness in your positioning would be that cheap or free providers would be able to use their lower prices against you.

The *marketing goals* section discusses your goals, whatever they may be. Within marketing goals, you will often see three main goals: number of users, gross profit, and market share. Other goals include increasing growth rate, lowering churn, brand awareness, product awareness, and many others.

Marketing strategy is a discussion of your overall strategy and contains the following subsections:

- Target market
- Positioning
- Product
- Service

- Price
- Promotion
- Advertising

Target market discusses your niche and its buying characteristics. *Positioning* describes how your product fits within your target market.

Product describes your product, in detail, as your reader may not be familiar with it. *Service* describes the level of service and any guarantees you may give to your users such as no busy signals or less than seven-minute hold times for support.

The *price* subsection describes your pricing model. You should take the time to describe any impacts your pricing can have on your marketing and any clauses in your Acceptable Use Policies (AUP) that will affect pricing.

Promotion is how you plan to promote your product, while *advertising* is where you plan on promoting your product. These two subsections will help to determine the next section, marketing budget.

The *marketing budget* section is a snapshot of your overall marketing budget that you include in your appendix. Your marketing budget should be broken down by month and by type of marketing. Your marketing budget section should also cover how you determined your budget, such as percentage of sales, average acquisition cost, or whatever other models you may have used. Following is an example.

Marketing Budget

TYPE	TOTAL
Flyers and give-a-ways	$8,000
Seminars and trade shows	$12,000
Print advertising (display)	$28,000
Print Internet directory line ads	$12,000
Radio advertisement	$30,500
TV advertisement	$36,000
CD-ROMs	$15,000
Direct mail	$15,500
Reseller program and co-op marketing	$12,000
Total marketing budget	$170,000

This represents a total $170,000 spent on marketing, or 22 percent of sales. The entire monthly marketing budget is represented in Appendix A in Table A.2.

Marketing controls is the last section of the marketing plan segment. Readers of your marketing plan are looking for how you are going to track the success of your marketing plan and assure you are on budget. You should include how you are going to track your results and how often you are going to analyze the information you track.

Operating Plan

The *operating plan* covers the details of how your ISP is actually going to be run. If it is a virtual ISP (VISP), an ISP which outsources all core functions, there are less details to be included than a facilities-based ISP. If you are a facilities-based ISP you are going to have to describe in detail how your ISP works. You should describe how you provide access and what systems are in place to provide access.

The operating plan contains four sections:

1. Operating plan summary
2. Situational review
3. Operations
4. Quality control and customer service

The *operating plan summary* and *situational review* sections are a high-level overview of the operating plan. Within the situation review, you should state where your base of operations would be, as it will serve as a reference point for your reader.

Operations covers all aspects of your business and how it operates. The essential issues to cover in the operations section include the following:

- Customer service
- Technical support
- Internet access provision

The operations section should contain enough detail so that the reader, no matter what his or her level of experience is, can understand how you provide Internet access and support your users. Diagrams, which should be included in the appendix of your business plan, can be useful to explain what might otherwise be difficult to understand.

The *quality control and customer service* section describes the metrics that you are using to measure quality of service and customer opinions. You should also discuss how often you plan on looking at the metrics and what you plan to do to assure a high level of service.

Organizational Plan

The *organizational plan* gives your reader an insight into who is behind the company and whether you know your strengths and weaknesses. You can have the best marketing plan and operations plan, but if you cannot execute the plans, you are dead in the water.

The organizational plan contains five sections:

1. Organizational plan summary

2. Situational review

3. Management philosophy

4. Key-personnel assessments

5. Compensation and incentives

The *organizational plan summary* and *situational review* sections provide an overall high-level view of the organizational plan. Within the situational review, you should reference the organizational chart in the appendix.

The *management philosophy* section is your chance to explain your way of doing business, your ethics, and how you plan to interact with each other within the company and your customers. Readers will use this segment to judge you and whether you are capable of executing the plan. Readers are also looking for your history and whether you have had successes or failures. If you have a history of failures, stress what you learned from each failure.

The *key-personnel assessments* section puts you and your other key employees in the spotlight. You should explain your personal strengths and weaknesses and how key personnel make up for those weaknesses. Also, if you are missing important hires, state what kinds of people you need and how you are looking for them. Sometimes your bankers or investors may be able to help you find the people you are lacking. In addition, if you have outside board members, list them and their titles and company affiliation in this section while describing their key contribution to your ISP business.

The *compensation and incentives* section is where you explain what your employees are paid and how much you are paid. Be aware that investors will look for salaries or benefits which seem high and will have no problem pointing to them as out of line. Investors and banks are looking to see whether you have made sacrifices and whether you have invested your own time and money in the business. The reason is simple. If you have not put your money or time into it, why should they?

Financial Plan

The *financial plan* provides the actual numbers to back up your presentation. Besides your marketing plan, the financial plan is probably the most important section of your business plan. If you cannot balance the numbers, then you are sure to go out of business.

The financial plan contains six sections:

1. Financial plan summary
2. Situational review
3. Financial goals
4. Cash flow planning
5. Financial controls

The *financial plan summary* and *situational review* sections provide an overall high-level view of your financial plan. The financial plan summary and situational review should include bottom-line numbers such as profit, net loss, gross profit margin, and others.

The *financial goals* section should cover your overall financial goals and how you plan to reach them. Possible goals include higher monthly recurring revenue, lower costs, and positive cash flow.

The *cash flow planning* section is an overview of the cash flow budget which should be included in the appendix.

The *financial controls* section describes the checks and balances in place to assure that you reach your goals and stay within budget. You should also include how often you will look at the budget and what corrective actions will be taken should those targets be missed.

ISP Business Plan Resources

Following are some research resources:

- Forrester Research (www.forrester.com/)
- Gartner Group (www.gartner.com/)

- NUA Internet Surveys (www.nua.ie/surveys/)
- Cahners In-Stat Group (www.instat.com/)
- US Census (www.census.gov/)

Business resources include the following:

- Service Corps of Retired Executives (www.score.org/)
- Small Business Association (www.sba.gov/)
- HowToSell.net (www.howtosell.net/)
- ISP-Lists (www.isp-lists.com/)

A sample ISP business plan is in Appendix A of this book.

Summary

Your business plan's primary purposes are to lay out how you will reach your goals and help communicate those plans to potential investors. Your executive summaries are crucial as outsiders will use your summaries to decide whether your plan is worthy of reading in detail. Investors look to see your level of knowledge, research, vision, and how big of a return they might be able to expect if they invest in your ISP. They are also interested in your time line for implementation and first-level goal attainment. Finally, those who read your business plan are looking for a plan grounded in reality, written in plain language, and clearly defining what is unique about your company.

Strategies to Reduce Churn

Your churn ratio is one of the most critical success indicators for your ISP. It defines the number of clients or subscribers that leave you in a given time period. Because it always costs less to continue to acquire business from your existing clients than it costs to acquire new clients, knowing your churn rate and finding strategies to reduce the number of subscribers who leave you will result in an immediately improved bottom line. It's also a competitive advantage. If your ISP and a local competitor both acquire 2,000 new subscribers this quarter, but you are able to keep 90 percent of them while your competitor is only able to retain 70 percent of them, the result is that the more efficient ISP who proactively looks for ways to reduce churn is able to retain 400 more subscribers. Now that is a serious market advantage.

Because of the relative newness of the ISP industry, the marketplace is shifting and it's not uncommon for a typical ISP to experience annual churn of 24 to 33 percent. Having a third of your customers leave you in a given year is unheard of in many other industries, but in the ISP industry it's a given at this point. Your only hope is that you can provide the best possible service so that you can delay or at least significantly reduce the number of subscribers leaving you until the industry matures.

Here's an example: You are a typical ISP with 4,000 subscribers, and you have 2.5 percent monthly churn (30 percent annualized). That means that during the year you will lose approximately 1,200 subscribers who will never be paying customers again. If the average value of a subscriber is $400, this churn ratio just reduced your true market value by $480,000 (1,200 × $400). Even if you cut this in half, it's still a very scary number when you realize how much you actually lose when a paying subscriber leaves, both in recurring revenues and market capitalization.

Why do your subscribers leave you? Do you know? Tracking this information is as important as tracking who your customers are. Most ISP invoicing systems have the ability to track the exact reason a customer canceled service, and if yours doesn't, consider adding this feature or upgrading to a system that allows you to track churn. Typical reasons for subscriber exodus include the following:

- Poor service–dissatisfied customer (big three reasons could include busy signals, slow download time, and long hold times for customer service).

- You failed to meet expectations, or customer expectations exceed reality of the level of service they can afford or will spend.

- They are satisfied with service, but having poor telecommunication problems, so they leave you for reasons beyond your control.

- Service is generally okay, but when problems are experienced, they are dissatisfied with incompetence or attitude of support staff.

- They switched to a cheaper ISP.

- They switched to one of the free ISPs (who are supported by ads creating banner blitz for the subscriber).

- Service is too difficult to use or subscriber is frustrated with his or her own incompetence.

- They moved out of the area, beyond your geographic coverage area.

- The customer upgraded his or her connection and didn't know you offered the needed service.

- The customer got cable, wireless, satellite access, or some other form of access and no longer needs your service.

- Child left for college and took PC.

- Their computer broke, so they don't need service for a while.

- You disconnected them for nonpayment.

- You disconnected them for abuse or violation of your terms of service (TOS).
- They purchased a new computer, fell for <insert online service> three-year contract computer rebate offer.
- All their friends are on AOL, EarthLink, or MindSpring, so they wanted to switch to the perceived better brand in order to communicate better, or so they believe.
- They can have their payment added to their phone bill, so they leave you because it's more convenient for paying their bills.
- Serious illness or death of customer.
- Your ISP was just acquired and the new owners messed it all up, so they left you.
- Newsfeed is incomplete; tools offered do not meet expectations or are poor when compared to the tools their friends get with your competitors.

You cannot rely on your gut instinct as to why a customer leaves you but you need to track the frequency of the same reason and be willing to add new ones. You need to be able to spot and correct trends that you *do* have control over.

Don't confuse your churn rate with your growth rate. Your growth rate is the opposite of your churn rate. Your growth rate is the number of new subscribers you receive in a given period of time, divided by the number of subscribers you had at the beginning of the period. Your goal is to have your growth rate double your churn rate. If you notice that your churn rate is higher than your growth rate, a bell should sound indicating that it's time to investigate why you're losing subscribers faster than gaining new ones.

Conversion rates are how many prospects converted and became paying subscribers. When computing your churn ratio you must not include customers that you lost because they didn't become paying subscribers because this is your conversion rate, not your churn rate. You must only include paying subscribers who cancel in order to compute your true churn rate. For example: This month, you have 200 subscribers who are getting a free trial, 100 of them don't convert into paying subscribers, and you lost 50 paying subscribers for various reasons. Your churn rate is *only* based on the 50 paying subscribers that you lost.

Churn-reducing strategies are divided into three categories:

1. Things over which you have no control
2. Things over which you have direct control

3. Things over which you have direct control but may need to be altered inside your ISP operation to reduce your churn ratio

For instance, you may need to offer nationwide access to stop losing people who leave you because you don't have a wide enough coverage area. This chapter gives you information on how you can minimize the impact on the items that are out of your control (such as the local loop between your subscribers and their telephone company) and directly improve your churn ratio by focusing on simple things that make a big difference for your subscriber base.

What Is Churn and How Do I Compute Mine?

Your *churn* is the number of subscribers who leave you in a given time period. Your *churn ratio* is the number of subscribers who leave you in a given time period divided by the number of subscribers you had at the beginning of the period. Here are the three most popular ways to compute churn. Choose the one that makes the most sense to you and stick with it.

The basic churn formula looks like this:

$$\text{Churn} = \frac{\text{Subscribers Who Cancel Service in This Period}}{\text{Beginning Subscriber Base Size} + \text{New Subscribers in This Period}}$$

For example: Your ISP has lost 100 subscribers this month. In the beginning of the month you had 2,000 subscribers and you added 200 new subscribers. (100 / (2000 + 200)) = 4.5 percent churn for this month.

This is another possible way to compute your churn ratio:

$$\text{Churn} = \frac{\text{Subscribers Who Cancel Service in This Period} \times 2}{\text{Beginning Subscriber Base Size} + \text{Ending Subscriber Base Size}}$$

For example: Your ISP has lost 100 subscribers this month. In the beginning of the month you had 2,000 subscribers and at the end you had 2,200 subscribers. (100 × 2 / (2000 + 2200)) = 4.8 percent churn for this month.

One more possible way to compute your churn ratio is as follows:

$$\text{Churn} = \frac{\text{Subscribers Who Cancel Service in This Period}}{\text{Beginning Subscriber Base Size}}$$

For example: Your ISP has lost 100 subscribers this month. In the beginning of the month you had 2,000 subscribers. (100 / 2000) = 5 percent churn for this month.

There does not seem to be consensus among the ISP community as to which way is the correct way to compute churn rates (and there are literally at least another half dozen ways to compute it), but the objective is to stick to the same formula so that you're able to monitor the net difference. There is consensus that calculating your churn ratio is something that needs to be done monthly as well as annually, so that you're able to respond immediately to service issues.

Your churn ratio is a direct reflection on your customer retention abilities, how satisfied your subscriber base is with your service, and how loyal your subscribers really are.

Case Study: What ISPs Can Do to Lower Churn Ratios

The secret to getting a feel for what industry churn ratios are includes these two primary resources:

1. Publicly traded ISPs report their churn rate in their shareholder reports.

2. The ISP e-mail discussion lists have over 20,000 members who discuss churn all the time and are a great resource to tap into (*www.isp-lists.com*).

If you can afford the $2,000 to $3,000 it costs for sophisticated market analysis reports, this is also another great way to get relatively accurate churn information so that you can see how your ISP compares to your competitors.

Realizing that the ability to earn a low churn ratio can turn into shareholder value, one ISP's approach (EarthLink Network, NASDAQ: ELNK) was to create a *churn-reducing tool*. It even gave it a brand name: *Fast Lane*. It believes that it could help reduce its less than 4 percent churn rate by as much as 10 to 15 percent. At the time, when you consider EarthLink had more than a million subscribers, you can see that a small 10 to 15 percent reduction in churn can retain an additional 4,000 to 5,000 subscribers in a given time period, which really adds up. EarthLink's Fast Lane product is an application that is designed to optimize each member's connection to the Internet by collecting connection data. This proactive tool gives EarthLink the ability to identify members who are experiencing busy signals or connection failures. Once it knows who's in trouble, it is able to contact the subscriber to assist or fix the problem. The tool goes one step further by putting each customer's connection information in his or her client file so front-line technicians are more informed as to what the particular subscriber's experience has been like in order to assist the person more effectively.

Reducing churn leads to not only improved bottom line revenue and profit growth, but also improves the value of your ISP when you look to exit. An ISP with a high churn ratio is usually worth less than an ISP with a very low churn ratio. Investors or buyers of ISPs today are more savvy than earlier years and demand low churn rates. Churn rates reflect how well you've serviced your members and the likelihood they will continue as subscribers if a new ISP takes over.

Your churn rate also can be affected by any acquisition of a subscriber base where you lose 20 to 25 percent of your newly acquired paying subscribers (the average ISP buyer is able to convert 75 to 85 percent of any typical subscriber base). The point is that you may have stable churn rates that could get thrown off because of acquisitions you may have just made.

Local competition is also known to impact your churn rate as new providers enter into your coverage area and attempt to woo your subscribers into switching. As in sports, a good offense is always the best defense against your competitors. The best time to start is months or years before your competitors arrive. In many cases, your most-feared competitors haven't even arrived on the scene yet, but don't let that stop you from doing everything you can to widen the gap by increasing your marketshare.

In marketing, it's important to differentiate churn from conversion rate when referring to new marketing campaigns you deploy. For example: You kick off a marketing program which draws in 100 new subscribers, but only 50 of them convert to paying subscribers. Your conversion ratio is 50 percent, but none of these numbers have anything to do with churn or your churn ratio until a paying subscriber leaves your service.

Different marketing channels have higher or lower churn rates. For example: Cable Internet access providers will have significantly less churn because along with their basic Internet service, they also could be packaging television-programming content. The subscriber may discontinue the Internet access service, but may keep the cable TV service. In this case, the subscriber would have been included in the churn ratio of the cable provider's Internet access division, but technically the cable provider did not lose the customer. This is the opposite of how a typical ISP would compute churn because the ISP usually loses the entire revenue stream when a customer leaves.

Last, free ISPs or ad-supported ISPs can experience lower churn than a typical fee-based ISP because there is a significantly lower chance that the subscribers will spend any time canceling free basic. This forces the ad-supported ISP to only count active subscribers as their true subscriber count and makes it more difficult to track their churn ratio. Perhaps a better strategy for this type of ISP is to track growth of unique users logging on in a given month and whether that rate is going up or down in a given time period.

> **TIP** It's not what happens, it's what you do that counts. You have the power to dramatically shape your churn rate and can lower it by as much as 20 percent immediately by measuring it, taking many of the actions suggested in this chapter, and get everyone on your staff involved in saving the customers you worked so hard to attract in the first place.

Inexpensive Ways to Reduce Your Churn

First, break out your total churn into four separate categories, shown in Figure 7.1:

1. Items over which you have absolutely no control and cannot prevent, such as death of a customer, customer goes bankrupt, customer decides he or she has no need, customer computer broke and he or she has no intention of fixing it, or the telco provider between your customer and you is poor, which causes a bad service experience. Typically this makes up 7 to 12 percent of your churn.

2. Subscribers whom you must disconnect for nonpayment, bounced checks, or credit cards that consistently come up invalid or rejected

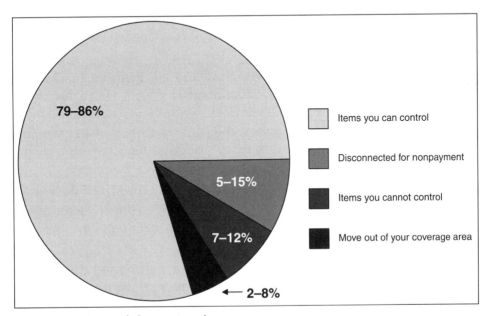

Figure 7.1 Dissected churn categories.

and those who violate your acceptable use policy or were abusive to your people, and you let them go. This makes up approximately 5 to 15 percent of your total churn.

3. Subscribers who move out of your coverage area. Two to 8 percent move annually, and if you do not have a nationwide footprint, you may lose these subscribers.

4. Subscribers who leave for any other reason that is within your control account for the lion's share of your total churn ratio which is typically 79 to 86 percent.

Strategies for Reducing Bad Credit Disconnects

It's a fact of life that a certain percentage of your subscribers and clients will not pay you or will not pay you on time. This will cause negative cash flow for you along with additional labor or collection fees associated with attempting to get paid. The good news is that there are quite a few things that you can do to reduce your exposure to these risks; they include the following:

- Head them off at the pass by creating a solid payment policy up front, such as all sales under $50 must be credit card; establish a fee for checks or credit cards that bounce; and make sure you charge the maximum interest allowed by law on all past due balances (typically 1.5 or 18 percent annually).

- The more on the ball your accounting and ISP invoicing staff is, the less your customers will take advantage of you. If your subscribers know that if they are 35 to 45 days late with their payment, you will definitely disconnect them, they will be more prompt. Compare this policy to many ISPs who don't stay on top of their past-due clients until they are 45 to 90 days in arrears and it's too late.

- If you're selling a high-end Internet access product, such as a T1/DS3/ATM circuit, do a credit check or get business references on your clients so that you don't acquire clients that don't have the ability to pay.

- Work out a payment plan (if it's a dedicated client and the average monthly invoice is over $500) if they are having short-term cash problems. Sometimes instead of paying six or 12 months in advance, many clients can better afford your services if they paid monthly or biweekly. It's always better to work something out than lose their revenue stream altogether.

- When it comes time for a disconnect notice, attempt human-to-human personal contact versus a cold form letter or no letter at all. Sometimes a mistake could have happened or they really did lose the last invoice and you can correct the problem together instead of turning them into a churn statistic.

You can't force your clients to always pay on time, but you can teach them by your actions and proactive policies how to get the most from your ISP without abusing their privileges.

Strategies for Reducing Churn from Subscribers Who Move

It's a sad day when you lose a subscriber because he or she is moving. It's an even sadder day when customers move to an area where you actually have another POP, but they have no idea because you failed to educate them as to your total coverage area. Make sure that your front line is able to ask every canceling subscriber where they are moving so that you can check to see if you can continue servicing them. Here are some additional strategies to save these clients:

- Increase your coverage area by supplementing your existing facilities-based POPs with virtual POPs owned by the dozens of wholesale Internet access port providers. Many now offer low minimum monthly requirements, such as less than $2,000 per month, which makes it very affordable for the average to midsize ISP to expand nationwide, overnight.

- Increase your coverage area by adding a third-party roaming service partner to cover areas that your national providers don't reach.

- Increase your local coverage area by swapping dial-up port banks with your competitors, giving each other access to each other's backyard, and reducing your true build-out costs to put in a full POP. Whoever is the better marketer is going to win anyway, so why not leverage your competitors?

- Increase your coverage area by partnering with an aggressive local telco that may be able to offer extremely low to no-cost back-hauling traffic for a wide coverage area. This allows you to utilize one bank of dial-up ports (which gives you the advantage of less POPs to manage, and more profitable customer-to-modem ratios as you scale) to serve dozens of small cities that are normally long distance from your current POPs. This option wasn't available until recently, and it's really worth investigating.

- Increase your coverage area by selling an interest in your company to an aggressive local telco with statewide or greater coverage, but one who doesn't understand the ISP game yet, and the two of you leverage each other's network talents.

- Increase your coverage area by buying strategic, competing ISPs, and link all of them together to form a wider coverage area.

Strategies for Reducing the Churn under Your Control

By far, the biggest way you can make an immediate impact on lowering your churn is with new subscribers who have just signed up and are therefore considered paying subscribers, but they are not loyal yet. Again, the critical difference here is that these are clients whom you've completely converted from nonpaying prospects to paying subscribers. How long you get to service them depends on what you do after the sale. Take a look at nine quick strategies that you can use to reduce churn that is under your control:

1. Offer service-level guarantees that speak to the primary fears and pains that many of your members may be feeling. This includes policies such as the following:

    No busies or it's free. This means that you didn't deserve to get paid that day if the customer experienced a true busy signal.

    High-speed bandwidth guarantee. Whenever your bandwidth exceeds 50 or 70 percent of your total, you promise to upgrade or add additional bandwidth. This guarantees your clients that if their access is slow, it's not because you oversold your bandwidth, but because there is Net congestion somewhere else.

    100 percent uptime or you don't pay. Your subscribers have a right to 100 percent uptime, even if you can't deliver it. Therefore, when you fail, that day should be credited by extending their service for a full day for their inconvenience.

    Your privacy is protected. This means you will not sell or rent their e-mail addresses or disclose their confidential customer information to anyone. This is best said on your privacy policy that is posted on your Web site.

100 percent satisfaction guaranteed or your money back. If your subscribers are not satisfied, they are going to ask for their money back anyway. Why not tell them that you are committed to removing the risk of doing business with you by putting their satisfaction above your need to get paid?

2. Get your billing straight, even if it means investing in a serious ISP invoicing system or tailoring one yourself. You will not survive long without it, nor will you be able to track trends, spot problems, be informed when a customer needs support, or be able to stop some of your subscribers who will attempt to take advantage of your inability to track them. Your subscribers deserve to be billed right, 100 percent of the time without excuses. Hire better accounting talent if you need to, but make sure you don't waste your customers' time by billing them wrong. This is a confidence destroyer if poorly executed.

3. Accept full responsibility for your subscriber's experience with your ISP. Your customer really does not care if your upstream is having problems or if your technical support people did not show up for work on time a particular night. All they care about is their experience and needs as they relate to how they use your service. No, it's not fair, but neither is life, and in the moments of truth, your subscribers will never forget how you handled their issues.

4. Educate your front line and expect them to pass internal competency tests that prove that they know what they are talking about. There is nothing worse than your subscribers speaking with technical or customer service representatives who can't answer simple questions about their account.

5. Accept every form of payment, making it easier for subscribers to stick with you. It has been proven that credit card subscribers don't cancel as easily as someone who has to write a check every month for service.

6. Update your phone system so that it works like you would like to receive service if you were the customer. Does it trap your customers in voice mail jail? How many minutes is the average caller on hold? How many calls did it drop this month? How many callers hung up before talking to a rep? You need to know what your customers' experience is like. You don't want them to feel like you use your phone system to separate you from them.

7. Set up a system where you carefully watch the login reports of your dial-up authentication servers. When you spot customers who are having trouble dialing in, after so many failed attempts, establish a routine with your technicians to e-mail or telephone your subscriber and offer assistance.

8. Does your connection software need improvement? Can your clients log in day after day, night after night, without any problems without having to relearn things? Getting connected must be a hassle-free experience and if your software or documentation does not enable that, it's time to update it.

9. Do you offer enhanced services, such as on-site setup or troubleshooting for a fee? This won't work for many of the national ISP players, but it can work for the regional and local ISPs. This is not only a great way to get to know your subscribers, but to earn billable hours while helping them get connected to the Internet.

Anything that builds confidence, is a churn buster, and anything that destroys such subscriber confidence will only increase your churn. Confidence is all about trust and how much your members have in you and your team. This is earned or lost over time.

TIP Think in terms of your confidence piggy bank. Every time you deliver great service or inspire confidence with your subscribers, you build up your goodwill piggy bank. When you destroy confidence by messing up, this piggy bank gets emptied out pretty quickly. The major advantage to being dedicated to fill it up with consistent goodwill is that when you mess up, ISPs with a full piggy bank will be quickly forgiven, whereas an ISP with a near-empty or already negative piggy bank will find themselves with an increased churn rate.

Factors Influencing Why Your Subscribers Consider Switching Providers

A significant percentage of your subscribers are going to switch providers over the next year. You need to know why they will be switching so that you can prevent it by updating your marketing to speak to the valid concerns your subscriber base has. J.D. Power and Associates did an online study of ISPs that analyzed the responses from 3,489 ISP households nationwide. The study, shown in Figure 7.2, found that the primary factors that consumers say may cause them to switch providers are connection speed (81 percent), price (68 percent), ease of use (57 percent), and e-mail service (51 percent).

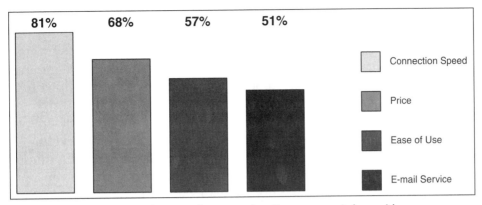

Figure 7.2   Factors that influence why your subscribers may switch providers.

Source: J.D. Power and Associates 1999 National ISP Residential Customer Satisfaction Study ™.

TIP If you've got the courage, try this: Get a list of your current paying subscribers and call or survey enough of them to give you statistically correct answers (at least 30 to 100 survey respondents) as to what factors would cause them to switch providers and what they feel are the most important features or benefits your service delivers. You not only will get *eye-opening* feedback, you may save quite a few relationships because most ISPs don't have enough time to care to find out why their subscribers are leaving.

The mere fact that connection speed ranked as one of the top reasons why existing subscribers would consider switching from their current ISP to a new ISP is actually an opportunity, considering that higher-speed Internet access services are higher-margin services and the value of a subscriber is also significantly higher as the price per month of the service goes up. With many ISPs finding the low end of the Internet access market being wiped out by the ad-supported free ISP model, there is still an incredible opportunity to provide high-speed DSL, ISDN, T1, or other connections on a part-time or dedicated basis.

If you noticed in the survey results that subscribers did not mention that they would switch because of bad or poor technical support, or busy signals, or any other common ISP problem, it's because the bar has been raised. Subscribers rightfully expect 100 percent uptime; courteous and expert technical support who do not put them on hold for long periods of time, pass the buck, or talk down to them; and no busy signals. Your subscribers certainly don't care about your cash flow problems or any equipment, people, or software problems you may be having today.

Another strategy to find out why your current subscribers would leave you is to realize that you may be able to attract and grow your ISP by focusing on delivering the exact same needs which are causing subscribers to leave your own or other ISPs. The following are two examples of such opportunities:

If speed is so important, position your marketing to talk about why your ISP is faster, what you have done behind the scenes to deliver lightning-fast service, and why your customers enjoy a different level of download speed because of your network design.

Price appears to be important to many subscribers, but don't lower your prices! Instead, increase your subscriber education through marketing so that your subscribers can better appreciate and understand the unique value that you deliver, so that they get the point that you deliver more value than it's costing them. Everyone wants to get more value than they are paying for, and with marketing, you can influence perception.

Maximizing Customer Stickiness

Customer stickiness is one of those fun buzzwords that refers to how loyal your customers are and how long they might *stick* with your ISP before departing. Obviously, the *stickier* your ISP is, the more profit and value you will receive from each subscriber who sticks with you.

One of the quickest and lowest-cost ways to get your subscribers to stick with you is to realize that people do business with people. That means you should not hide behind the veil of your almighty Web site, which does not have your name or the name of anyone at your ISP listed, nor any e-mail addresses beyond the generic info@your-company-name.com or sales@ or support@. If you want your subscribers to *stick* with you, you need to let them know a bit about yourself or at least your CEO or executive officers who are ultimately responsible for each subscriber's happiness. This includes posting a picture of you or your staff on your Web site, including a direct phone number or private e-mail address so that anyone can speak with a manager or someone who can solve problems that the front line is not handling to their satisfaction.

By giving your subscribers someone they can relate to, their confidence will rise, which will lead to more referrals. They know there is always someone they can call or e-mail if they are not satisfied and your churn will lower. One suggestion for those who fear putting their pictures or names on the Internet (which is a bit silly, because you stand behind your ISP, right?) is to create a brand name for themselves and market the brand name as the person that your subscriber base will relate to.

Here are six more suggestions to improve subscriber stickiness:

1. All new subscribers should get a personal letter from you, your name signed in blue ink, along with an e-mail from you explaining how to

get the most out of the services your ISP offers. This is also a great time to give them coupons for free Internet access trials for their friends or tell them about any referral programs which pay them cash or free service for referrals.

2. Create and send your base a monthly or quarterly newsletter that shares with them some of the many new services you offer, a peek behind the scenes, some Internet tips from your experts, and other bits of useful information that does not have a primary sales intent, but rather a *give* intent.

3. Get to know, by name, your top 20 clients (according to highest revenue), so that you can lower the risk of your most profitable clients churning.

4. Follow up with a thank you e-mail or snail mail to subscribers after they have bought or upgraded any services at any time. The *attitude of gratitude* is always appreciated and even though it may be quickly tossed out, the positive feelings toward your ISP are cumulative.

5. Do things that are above and beyond the call of duty consistently. Many items may cost very little but add great perceived value, such as extended technical support hours, free needs analysis for businesses, fast callbacks, weekend callbacks if you don't normally do them, and random gifts of information that will help subscribers get the most out of their Internet experience.

6. Invest in your subscribers by working out a deal with your local computer training provider in which it gives you exclusive coupons for $95 (or an agreed-upon amount) toward Internet basics training classes that you can give to each of your subscribers (at no cost to you) and, in turn, the training center gets to meet your subscriber base. Many aggressive computer training centers work on this model of giving away a free class to take advantage of how they market by fulfilling the needs of your subscribers. You also get a back-end benefit because well-trained subscribers require less technical support.

TIP Give your computer dealers, resellers, affiliates, associates, and any other partner who helps distribute your software dial-up kits or services assistance and extended training so that they can optimize the return on their time, labor, and resources when promoting your services. It will also endear them to you and make them stickier. Make sure you also consistently pay them on time without delay or excuses if you want their undivided attention.

CHAPTER

8

The Customer Service Role in Your ISP Marketing Strategy

*"The game of an ISP business is much like the game of racquetball.
Those who fail to master the basics of serving well, usually fail."*

UNKNOWN

Chapter 7, Strategies to Reduce Churn, covered how churn affects your bottom line. You also learned that speed is more important than service when it comes to why your existing subscriber base may switch to another provider. Or is it? A commonly quoted business statistic is that as high as 66 percent of the customers you lose come from a bad exchange with one of your employees. By the end of this chapter, you will have looked at the systems, procedures, and policies that will help you deliver topnotch customer service. There is a reason that the acronym *ISP* has the word *service* in it. However, few ISPs deliver excellent service for a myriad of reasons, none of which are really valid and none of which your customers care about.

Great customer service must start at the top of your ISP organization, not only in words, but in actions as well. That doesn't mean that if you are in a line position, you can't be where great service originates. Rather, any human being who practices the *do unto others as you would have them do unto you* can figure out what exceptional, great, okay, or lame customer service looks like, and do something to improve it.

This chapter is not only about your *customer service* people but also about how every role within your ISP must have a *service* element within it for

159

your team to be successful. Customer service must be delivered internally as well as externally. A point of clarification: Your internal people do not buy and sell from each other so calling each other internal customers is wrong, but providing service and being service-oriented whether it's for a customer or coworker is vital to the overall success of your ISP.

You must also focus on the people who focus on your subscribers. If you treat them right by caring, motivating, and making winners out of them, they'll treat your customers right, who will in turn become lifetime subscribers.

Clarify your customer service objectives by giving your team specific goals and strategies. MindSpring Enterprises, a national ISP with more than a million subscribers at the time of this writing, has what is known as the *14 Deadline Sins of MindSpring* that describe the principles of the company's customer service. You could consider creating your own kind of ISP principles plan with your own unique name. Establishing memorable customer service policies will help your team live up to the expectations of service you wish to deliver.

Customer service policies are systems that you put in place because you recognize the need to be more service-oriented or often because you had a company-wide failure with an important customer or a pattern of customer problems that you want to correct for the future. If you don't create systems to solve your customer satisfaction challenges, you will be forced to continue learning the same lessons over and over again until you create a system to prevent the problems.

Rules for Effective ISP Customer Service Policies

When you create your customer service policies and systems, consider these four rules:

1. Your end outcome for the policy must be specific, measurable, and related to the problem you are looking to correct or prevent in the future.

2. The policy must be buzzword-free so that everyone within your organization can understand it without having to be *in the know* to decipher your particular terms or language.

3. The performance of the policy must be measured daily, weekly, biweekly, or, at a minimum, monthly in order to be effective. By mea-

suring the performance of the policy, you're able to give real-time feedback to your team so it can take steps to improve in the middle of the process, not just at the end.

4. The policy must be communicated by leadership on a very frequent basis. People just forget, and it's your job if you're in leadership or management to continually remind the troops as to what your minimum service expectations are along with the tools and examples for how they can deliver excellent service.

TIP Once per month or quarter, stop your people and ask them individually or as a team if there are any current customer service policies which make things difficult or prevent them from delivering great service. Your objective is to continually update your policies to produce consistently satisfied customers.

Internal Issues That Lead to Bad Customer Service

Bad customer service can result from the following internal issues:

Joking about how dumb the customer is. You would never joke about how dumb your boss is as he or she approves your paycheck every pay period. You are lucky that you have a job and it's your subscriber's monthly subscription fee that is making your job, your next promotion, and your personal market capitalization possible. Suggest creating a strict internal policy of never slamming or joking about customers, even behind their backs; it's unprofessional and dishonorable. The pure fact that you have clients who are not Internet-savvy ensures that you will have a job or opportunity in the future.

Not following up or not following up fast enough. Your customers do not care about your needs, your network, or any of the excuses as to why you can't return their calls or e-mails within 24 business hours or less. Create an internal policy that states the maximum length of time within which 100 percent of any incoming service issue needs to be handled. If anything goes beyond that, your upper management needs to know about it. This is called an *escalation* procedure.

Relying on your subscribers to tell you when your network has a problem. You must hire a third-party service to monitor and measure your uptime, so that you are able to proactively troubleshoot and handle problems before your customers ever know there was a problem.

Poor coordination between your sales and marketing people versus your technical support and engineering people. This causes undue headaches not only internally but with your customers since they may be exposed to some of your ISP's personal chaos and many of them just won't put up with it.

Not moving fast enough internally to respond to issues. Your subscribers need to be able to get immediate assistance from a live human being who will help them in minutes every single time, if you want to keep them for a long time.

Not delivering on commitments or overpromising and underdelivering. If you say that you're going to have a problem fixed by a certain time and date, it needs to be fixed. If it looks like you won't have the problem resolved as you said you would, you have a responsibility to re-inform your clients when it will be done.

Participating in office politics, gossip, or rumors. This does not allow you to give your full attention to your customers when you waste time focusing on activities normally reserved for the soon-to-be-fired.

Telling your customers internal information that they should not be told or don't need to know. For example, blaming another department for the problems that your customer had or is having instead of taking responsibility for fixing the problem on the spot.

Management holding too much back from front line. Your front line should be empowered by management to handle a high percentage of typical customer problems instead of a labor-expensive follow-up call because management approval was needed.

As it relates to your ISP marketing strategy, your customer service strategy is the glue that holds together your subscribers' level of confidence. ISP business plans that are missing a customer service strategy should scare you. A well-executed customer service strategy is very often the deciding factor since your customers decide which ISP they like better when it comes time to evaluate their needs.

Mastering the ISP Service Moments of Truth

A *moment of truth* as it relates to your customer service strategy is any time your service people interact with a client when solving a problem. The customer's satisfaction is on the line. How you handle the challenge will determine whether you pass or fail at the moment of truth. Every day, dozens, hundreds, and even thousands of moments of truth will happen at your ISP, and your team needs to recognize the difference between normal customer conversations versus moments of truth. The moments of truth determine how long you will be able to retain your subscribers.

Some major examples of possible ISP moments of truth include the following:

- Your subscriber finally got through to you after not being able to call you at a time when your technical support or customer service hours matched his or her work schedule. This person has not been able to log in for 10 days and wants to know why his or her ISP is messed up because nothing changes on the client's end, or so he or she believes.

- Your dial-up switches in a particular POP blew up; no one has been able to log in for two hours; all of your phone lines are lit up with angry customers; and there is no known estimated time of arrival (ETA) for when the problem will be solved.

- You moved some of your customers from one Web server to another Web server and somehow your technical support team forgot to let them know about the move, which messed up their cgi-bin and rendered their Web sites useless.

- Your upstream has become unstable and for the last month has been delivering random outages, which affects your subscribers. You tell your subscribers the truth about what is happening, but they are tired of hearing you blame your vendors and just want it resolved quickly.

- Your mail server just died and your business clients are in a panic because their Internet business is effectively halted.

The important point here is not what happens but what you do about it that counts. Apologize and take total responsibility for the satisfaction of your subscribers. Offer to make it right and share with them what you or your ISP is going to do to reduce or solve the problems in the future.

TIP When the inevitable happens, and some critical part of your network goes down or becomes unavailable for a brief period of time, make sure your entire staff knows that everyone is required to stick around, no matter what time of day it is, in order to answer the phones while your technical or engineering staff solves the problem. Your nontechnical staff needs to realize that delivering great service is a team effort and the technicians should not be the only ones who must stay late when problems happen.

How to Go Above and Beyond the Call of Your ISP Duty

Every time someone on your staff goes beyond the call of duty, you are building up *goodwill* with your subscriber base. It's a lot like having money in the bank so that when bad things happen, your customers have had many excellent interactions with you and will be more likely to forgive an occasional mistake.

Because *value perceived is value achieved,* you can purposefully set up a situation in which you establish the level of expectation that your customers will receive for the value they are going to pay you. Then you strategically set up systems to make sure you exceed the expectations you set up in the first place. It is always easier to exceed your own preset levels of expectation than it is to exceed the customer's (sometimes unrealistic) level of expectation. An example might be if you offer to be available for customer support from 8 A.M. to 6 P.M., and then you have staff stay until 8 P.M. every night to answer questions that come after 6 P.M. In this case, extra value will only be delivered in the customers' minds if you educate them as to what your true hours are, so that they know you provide extended support on your dime and prove that you have your subscribers' best interests at heart by your actions.

Here are some examples of how you can go above and beyond the call of duty at your ISP:

- Cross over the preset boundaries for how long you give them technical support when their problems are clearly PC-related and not related to your ISP.

- You're watching the login server and you notice that some of your clients are not getting as fast a connection as possible, so you contact your subscribers to see if they have the latest software drivers loaded for the fastest download or connect speed possible.

- A customer is having problems paying, so you set up a payment schedule to help him or her spread the past due payments over a short period of time. This way, you can continue to provide your services while the customer brings the account current, and you don't have to terminate the account for nonpayment.

- An important subscriber or client is just not getting it and you know that this person is within driving distance, so you stop by on your way home to drop off new disks or help the customer with the problem.

- You provide a comprehensive library of resources that is only available to paying members and which saves them incredible amounts of time or research. Items include basic Internet troubleshooting tools, CGI and Perl scripts, and Web or e-mail tools.

- You provide one-page faxes that you can send to customers who have common problems for which you have a preset solution. This not only saves human technical support labor expenses, but also helps your clients become more self-sufficient.

- Your customer works unusual hours and never seems able to call for help because he or she is always working when you offer your support hours, so you set up a time after hours or on the weekend for someone to be available to support the person.

- Send a special e-mail to clients a week after they had a problem to make sure the problem got resolved. No one does this consistently, but if you do, you will quickly find yourself with thousands of loyal customers who won't leave you as quickly as others might.

- After collecting the most commonly asked technical support questions, hold a monthly, free ISP user group session with a couple of your ISP technical support people speaking or providing answers to questions from the attendees.

- You know your customer is in a particular line of business and you find articles in magazines, newspapers, or online that relate to something that might benefit that person, so you forward it with a note that simply says that you were thinking about him or her.

- You develop a system for tracking every problem your customer ever experiences with your ISP so that when new technical support reps work with your customer, they have their complete past history available in front of them. The benefit customers receive is not having to repeat themselves or their past problems every time they call for help.

- You set up a network status mailing list that your subscribers can join. Whenever you have a network problem, you send a special message to your subscribers who care about network uptime issues through this special e-mail announcement list. The value delivered is information.

- Refer to your subscriber by name during telephone calls. People like to know you care enough to remember their name throughout the call, instead of just being thought of as another member among thousands. One additional step you can take is to make a note in their file as to how they phonetically pronounce their name, so that future service people on your staff use the right pronunciation of the customer's name.

In all of these cases, you must educate your customers as to when you are giving them more than your normal policy allows for any given situation, so that they know not to expect it in the future, even though you'll do your best to support them.

Delivering great service happens one subscriber at a time. Focus your service energies on delivering a perfect customer experience every time you interact with your members and increase your level of personalization, so that each subscriber knows that he or she is special or important to your ISP.

TIP Eliminate the negative words in your discussions with your customers, such as *can't, don't, no, won't,* and *not possible.* Customers don't want to hear them anyway. Instead, replace the negative words with what you can and will do. Positive words include *yes, you got it, you bet, absolutely, no problem,* and *I'll get it done.*

Attracting, Retaining, and Training the Best ISP Customer Service Staff

> *"No employee seeks to be mediocre; all seek to be magnificent."*
> **Ken Blanchard**

Attracting and retaining high-quality customer service staff is not only necessary but also vital to gaining or maintaining your competitive advantage in the ISP marketplace. A great staff does not happen overnight. It takes a concentrated, continuous effort in the many areas outlined in this chapter. As you're reading the following strategies, circle the ones that you need to improve at your ISP, and after you get done improving each one, cross it off.

There are two basic issues that impact your ability to attract and retain the best service people: pay and praise. One of the most unprofitable things you can do is to underpay or not pay enough to attract and retain top-notch customer service talent. There is a direct correlation between the employees who genuinely take great care of each of your clients and higher pay. The old saying *you get what you pay for* applies here. Private and public praise also has an economic impact and is not only suggested, but necessary in order to supply the basic human desire for appreciation and the need to be recognized.

What Makes up a Great Customer Service Personality?

A person with a great customer service personality will have the following qualities:

Emotional maturity. The ability to maintain perspective even when things get crazy.

Genuine care and concern for others. Customers can see right through service that is not genuine (even over the telephone).

Positive mental attitude. Without it, the ability to seek win-win solutions during problem resolution may be impaired.

Ability to have empathy. The ability to respect and understand the customer's perspective, even if the customer service representative doesn't agree with it.

What Makes a Poor Customer Service Personality?

A person with a poor customer service personality will have the following qualities:

Self-centered. This is the root of a customer service representative's inability to care about the customers' needs or perspectives.

Cares more about the next job assignment rather than focusing on performing the current role. When employees think about their future in a different role, they typically have a hard time doing excellent work in their current job.

Narrow field of vision. They are only able to see their own job, and not how their job relates to other departments within the ISP organization.

Strategies to Attract Top Service People

If you want to attract A-level talent, your ISP must be run by A-level people, and your image or brand must reflect that as well. In the beginning days of your ISP, you will attract people who are looking to help build an excellent company. Somewhere along the road of growth, you will attract people who want to work for an excellent company. There is a huge difference between hiring people who want to help build an excellent company versus hiring those who wish to work for an excellent company. Your ability to tell the difference will determine how long your ISP remains an excellent company.

Another popular strategy is to always recruit. That includes being on the lookout for those who take personal pride and responsibility for going above the call of duty. When you need an important position filled, it's hard to find a great service representative right away. That's why you should always look. Find ways to bring in better and better talent whenever you're able to attract it and continue to raise the bar internally, which will push out your lowest or most-uncommitted talent.

Strategies to Retain Top Service People

Recognition of contribution is as good as money for most people, and even your best people will leave if they don't feel like you appreciate, want, respect, or are happy with their contribution. Most top performers will not settle for being ignored or wait for an annual review for feedback on their performance. This means that if you want to keep them, you're going to have to respond to their needs.

Here is a list of questions to ask yourself in order to retain your best people:

- When was the last time you asked your employees what was truly important to them? They need to know that you care enough to ask every once in a while.

- Do you provide incentives, bonuses, or any form of internal reward that is directly tied to performance? Top performers want a way they can make more money or receive more value if they crank up their contribution.

- Have you found out lately what is going on in the personal lives of your top people? Sometimes it's more profitable to not only talk about business, but also talk about issues that are currently impacting the lives of each member on your team.

TALENT ATTRACTION RESOURCE

A good place to get connected with ISPs who are looking to hire or people looking for a new ISP job is the ISP-Jobs discussion list, which is a free resource maintained at www.isp-jobs.com.

- Do you currently have an award or recognition program either on a monthly, quarterly, or yearly basis for your people? Private praise is always appreciated, but public praise and recognition is gold.

- Do you currently offer stock options for your best people? A stock option is an agreement between you and your employees that grants them a nonvoting ownership interest in your ISP; it vests over a period of time, typically three to five years. High-tech companies that rise to the top of their industry almost always do it by granting stock options to their employees.

- How does your pay compare to industry standards for similar jobs at your competitors? This is something you need to know before you get a surprise notice that you've just lost one of your best people because you weren't informed how far off your compensation was from market conditions.

- Do your people really love what they are doing? Help maximize the right person for each position, so that your people get a chance to grow and reach their full potential before quitting to go find it elsewhere. Is one of your salespeople really a technician or vice versa?

How to Train Your ISP Service People for Optimum Results

Most ISPs just throw their new people into the ring, sometimes assigning someone to look after them in the beginning. Often there is no formal program from there, no guide as to how or what great service looks like, what your minimum expectations are of them, and specifically how to deliver it. In addition to your new people, your existing team needs continual training so that team members can advance themselves and learn techniques that will improve their ability to deliver great service.

Typical service training for your ISP team can include the following:

- A clearly defined list of your customer service standards along with explanations why each one is important to the kind of service you expect from team members

- Specific job skill training or refresher courses in order to maintain a high level of skill in their job duties

- Cross-functional work group training so that they can see how their jobs impact other departments or teams within the organization

- Training in common customer problems or questions along with pre-set solutions or responses for as many issues as you can include

- Role-playing so that they can see how they are supposed to act or handle different situations before making mistakes in the real world

- Telephone listening, speaking, troubleshooting, and communication skills training

- A specific list of what bad ISP customer service versus good ISP service looks like

The ISP Service Points System

In keeping with the management by measurement philosophy, you could create a point system that rewards your employees with bonuses, incentives, and other perks as they reach different points along their way to delivering better service.

Items that you could track that would be used in a numeric point system include the following:

- Test score results from various true or false, multiple-choice, or essay questions

- Completion of different training programs

- Praise or testimonial letters received

- A reduction in the number of complaints that your ISP receives or an increase in the percent of uptime you're able to deliver through your network

- Any critical success statistic that your employees could improve or impact with their thoughtful and consistent actions

Implementing and Managing an ISP Call Center

An *ISP call center* is the group of people and support services your ISP provides for your subscribers. For many ISPs, it's one or two people who cover all of your sales and customer support functions, and for other ISPs, it's an elaborately orchestrated team of dozens to hundreds or even thousands of support, sales, and customer service professionals who support tens of thousands to millions of dial-up subscribers.

Your ISP call center, or *helpdesk* as it's often called, is a pivotal component to the level and quality of service your subscribers and clients receive from you. There are two distinct functions for your call center. They include technical support and sales. Each should have a separate focus, purpose, and leadership in order to properly deliver quality service.

A popular formula for helping you figure out how to properly staff your call center, as taken from the *Microsoft Sourcebook for the Help Desk* (Microsoft Press, 1995), is as follows:

$$\frac{\text{Calls} \times \text{Average Time}}{\text{Available Time} \times \text{Utilization Rate} \times (1 - \text{Staffabs Rate})}$$

Calls = Number of calls per day
Average Time = Average time per call (minutes as percent of hour)
Available Time = Hours per day at work times 60 minutes per hour
Utilization Rate = Percent of time on phone with customers
Staffabs Rate = Percent of time on leave or when your staff is absent

Most ISPs who are running call centers are using a 65 to 75 percent utilization rate. For example: 70 percent utilization rate would mean taking 300 calls in a day times an average of 9 minutes per call if your people worked an 8-hour day and were never absent; you would need 6.25 people to properly staff your ISP call center [300 calls × 7 minutes per call = 2,100 minutes divided by (8 hours a day times 60 = 480 minutes) × 70 percent utilization = 336 available minutes].

There are many functions within your ISP organization that you can outsource, and there are many that you should not. For example, you should not outsource your marketing——specifically as it relates to your marketing vision and overall goals of the organization, your executive talent, or your internal accounting. However, you could consider outsourcing some or all of your dial-up ports, various services you provide such as e-mail or Web-related services, or possibly even your helpdesk.

To Outsource or Not to Outsource Your ISP Helpdesk

A superior helpdesk pays off in greater customer retention and increased revenue and profits. To be effective, your helpdesk must keep pace with your ISP's corporate goals and technology advancements to ensure that you are able to effectively support whatever new technology or software your organization adopts. This makes it essential that your ISP reviews, measures, and enhances your helpdesk operations on a regular basis to ensure continued optimal performance and return on investment (ROI).

If you are an ISP that wishes to focus on being purely a sales and marketing organization, it could make sense to outsource your helpdesk to a specialist who focuses its core business on mastering helpdesk technology, methodology, professional staffing, and the related processes, while you return to your core competencies. There are disadvantages also, and you should evaluate which strategy will produce the highest returns for your ISP, your short- and long-term goals, and your immediate needs.

Outsourcing your helpdesk does not have to be an all-or-nothing type of arrangement but rather can be something that augments your existing support after-hours. This allows you to reduce internal labor expenses and only pay for additional support when you need it or for after-hours support when it may be cheaper to buy the shared time of someone who is staffing a helpdesk center around the clock.

Advantages of Outsourcing Your Helpdesk

There are several advantages to outsourcing your helpdesk:

Allows you to return to your core business. By removing the burden of supporting and staffing your helpdesk, outsourcing frees up your existing employees' time, reduces the need for more management staff, and allows you to focus your time on driving sales. Unless the company you hired goes out of business, it never calls in sick.

May reduce your operating costs. If you don't have to maintain your helpdesk, you remove the expenses associated with hiring and maintaining a staff, such as the elimination of hiring, recruiting, and training fees; insurance benefits; vacation pay; having to purchase new office equipment; and renting office space.

Increases your flexibility. By outsourcing your helpdesk, you are able to buy highly trained helpdesk assistance anytime you need it to handle your helpdesk duties, day or night, including your overflow needs and full 24 by 7 support.

Superior reporting. A well-managed outsourced helpdesk service will give you daily reports on call center volume. With those utilization numbers, you're able to more accurately make decisions that affect your ultimate profitability and productivity.

Leverages helpdesk and call center expertise without the high up-front capital costs. You make money by offering Internet access to a pool of dial-up ports that you manage, which in effect allows you to make money off a shared resource. Outsourcing your helpdesk is very similar in that your outsource company has a pool of technical and customer support personnel to whom it sells a shared access.

Disadvantages of Outsourcing Your Helpdesk

Outsourcing your helpdesk can have several disadvantages, including the following:

Lost customer contact. If you're not interacting with your customers on a daily basis, how are you going to get feedback on how to improve? What about the lost opportunities to up-sell and cross-sell additional goods and services?

The success of your ISP is outsourced. Your reputation is on the line. Can you really trust it to someone else? Will someone else care as much as you do about the level of service you are looking to provide?

You lose creative and innovative control. Sometimes success is created when you're able to make hundreds of small changes in the way you do business. When your helpdesk is outsourced, you can't make minor adjustments along the way since your needs must align with the needs of your outsource vendor.

Questions to Ask When Considering Outsourcing Your ISP Helpdesk

If you are considering outsourcing your ISP helpdesk, the following are some questions that you need to ask:

- Can the hired company provide private-labeled services so that your subscribers never know that you outsourced your helpdesk operations?

- How well does the firm track its telephone statistics and does it provide daily or real-time statistics reporting? You need this information for your own management.

- What is the length of its average support call? How many problems is the company able to handle on the first call?

- What is its average phone queue size, meaning what is the average hold times that your subscribers could experience?

- What are its minimum requirements that each technician must meet in order to work for the firm?

- What are its minimum standards for the level of service it wants to provide or guarantee?

- What is its trouble or problem escalation procedure when things go wrong?

- How long has the company been around? This is a major decision and vendor stability is very important.

- Is the company flexible enough to create a custom solution that fits perfectly with your current ISP structure?

- What makes its ISP outsourcing solution unique?

- Is it the right fit for your ISP's current size and your intended growth over the next 12 to 36 months?

- What is the company's basic pricing structure? How does its pricing structure relate to your needs? Is it per subscriber, per minute, per incident?

TIP Why not ask the company to which you may outsource your helpdesk for its technical support number and run some tests on its technicians to see how well they perform? How deep do they go? how well do they handle the entire call? were they professional? and could you live with this kind of support for your subscriber base? Make sure you also speak to the company's existing clients to see how many of the company's claims are true and whether their clients are satisfied.

How Outsourced Services Are Priced

Each helpdesk provider prices its services differently. You must find one that matches your needs perfectly. Most are priced per minute, per incident, or per subscriber, and quite a few have hidden or additional fees, such as long-distance charges, private-labeling premiums, extra charges for e-mail support, and after-hours support costs.

Additional ISP Call Center Services

Additional options include the following:

In-sourced helpdesk support or consulting. If you'd like to retain your own in-house helpdesk, but want some of the expertise and management services that many of the helpdesk outsourcing providers make available, why not hire them to manage your in-house helpdesk operations? Many of them provide consulting and some even take full on-site responsibility for your helpdesk while preserving your business processes, culture, and brand or image of your company. This can give you the helpdesk productivity and performance advantage that is sure to be a competitive advantage.

Enhanced ISP call center services. Many helpdesk providers are really telemarketing firms who have recently converted, upgraded their technical support skills, and repositioned themselves as helpdesk providers. That means many of them are ready and equipped to handle all of your business calls, scheduling, order-processing, dispatching, and call-screening services, which might also include direct sales, market research, lead qualification, and almost any traditional call center service your ISP might need.

The *Call Me Back Voice Button* concept. A new technology is becoming more popular, and that is providing your Web-surfing clients or prospects with a *Click to Call* button. The client can click, which will initiate a teleconference between the client and your ISP customer service center using a separate telephone line. Eventually, this same technology will coordinate with caller-ID and your subscriber database to pop up their records for your call center technician to see their past history or get ready to annotate.

Customer Relationship Management

Customer relationship management (CRM) is a term that defines every process that you do in order to understand and adapt to the complex and changing relationships with your subscriber base. Everyday, the amount of information available about your subscribers increases as your clients interact with your ISP and the services you offer them. This interaction creates new opportunities to use that information to deliver more of what your customers want and enjoy and get a higher return from each client.

Specifically, CRM refers to the collection of tools that you use in order to maintain long, positive, and profitable customer relationships, including marketing campaign management, sales force automation, sales analysis, sales forecast, mobile access for your sales reps, service tools, call center monitoring, routing and management, communication, back-office integration, intranet design and implementation, customer inquiries management, customer personalization, and anything that involves one-to-one marketing at its best.

TIP The Peppers and Rogers Group (Don Peppers, Martha Rogers, and Bob Dorf) literally wrote the book on CRM: *The One to One Fieldbook: The Complete Toolkit for Implementing a 1 to 1 Marketing Program* (Bantam Books, 1999). It's worth picking up if you have not read it yet.

Large ISPs, in which more complete systems are needed end to end, will be impacted by CRM issues as opposed to small ISPs who can get the job done without any red tape. It's relatively easy to coordinate the efforts of a couple dozen people on your ISP team; but when that number gets into the hundreds or thousands, a whole new set of processes is needed to navigate through customer service-related issues.

Improving your CRM systems begins with getting feedback from your subscribers, so let's take a look at how to get more feedback than you ever wanted, so that you can improve.

Feedback Forms

You need feedback from your subscribers because you do not have the right to assume that you know how satisfied or dissatisfied they are until you ask them for their input. Asking for customer input not only helps you to identify the real issues that affect your clients, but you also could discover issues that you thought were solved but actually were not. Feedback from a subscriber gives you the heads up.

Where to Distribute Your Feedback Forms

There are a number of places to distribute your feedback forms:

Your Web site, on the main page and placed throughout your entire Web site. This will be your lowest-cost feedback form but it will produce the highest results. Make the form simple and include the following fields: FROM: (e-mail address), NAME (optional), a drop-down list with which to select the area of your service the customer wishes to give you feedback on, and then a huge COMMENTS field, which gives the customer at least 22 lines to submit the message. For the comments field, add HTML code so that it does not scroll horizontally and subscribers can view the comments they send you without having to scroll horizontally.

With your dial-up kits when sent to new subscribers. Make it a one-page flyer with questions about their views of how it felt getting started with your ISP process and any suggestions for improvements. On the back of the flyer, or with a separate envelope, provide a Business Reply Mail (BRM) prepaid response item. Your response rate will be significantly less if you expect the customer to pay for postage.

After each Web site design, programming, or service job. This is the same kind of form as you sent to your dial-up subscribers. It can be customized to allow for feedback about the kinds of Web, e-mail, or Internet services you deliver. Include a prepaid return envelope.

In your ISP monthly e-mail or paper newsletter. This is a good place to ask for more specific feedback each month about different areas of your ISP business such as dial-up, Web hosting, and dedicated access, and gives you an opportunity to educate everyone as to the other services they may not have known you provided.

Never underestimate the power of asking customers for their opinions. Many ISPs report seeing a significant increase in customer referrals, confidence, and new business requests purely because they've shown that they care about improving and they want and value their customers' feedback.

Strategies to Increase the Volume of Feedback

What follows are strategies you can use to increase the volume of feedback you receive:

- Set up a contest where every month or quarter, you give away a free month or year of dial-up Internet access to everyone who fills out the feedback form.

- Hold a sweepstakes that is only valid if customers return the form within 30 days of signing up with your ISP.

- If customers are giving you feedback from your Web site or via e-mail, make sure you reward them with an autoresponder that thanks them personally for their input, and tells them how you're going to use the information they provided to improve your services. Then, after you have solved or addressed their feedback, let the customers know what you've done about it so that they know that sending in feedback is worth their time. In the future, they will reward you with even more valuable information that you can use to increase your sales and service to them.

- Reward your subscribers with a free book, report, or e-book that allows them to maximize their Internet experience with the use of your services.

- Make it easy for them to give feedback. You may also consider creating a feedback@your-company-name.com e-mail address.

Taking an Effective Customer Service Survey

Surveys are different from feedback forms in that surveys generally ask for more input in multiple sections. Surveys are for more than a generic comment about improving one area of your ISP.

Reasons for an ISP customer service survey often include the following:

- To simply find out what your subscribers think about your ISP, products, and services

- To identify the biggest gripes, complaints, or reasons your clients may consider switching to a different ISP

- To find out what services your subscribers would like you to offer next or in addition to your current offerings

- To help you establish marketing and sales budgets or forecasts based on perceived demand

- To help you establish customer-friendly policies (sometimes when you are stumped about how to implement a new policy you know you need to implement, it's nice to survey your clients to get real-time feedback as to their opinions on the topic)

TIP In addition to external surveys of your subscriber base, you should also survey your internal people to find out from time to time what needs to be improved or what is messed up and needs immediate attention. Make sure you allow for feedback anonymously in addition to feedback that is signed by name, so that you can capture all thoughts designed to help you improve your ISP.

In order to be effective, your survey must do the following:

- Have a start date and end date, so that you can tally the results at some predetermined point in time

- Be measurable so that you can score yourself based on the feedback

- Be secure and confidential, so that negative feedback makes it into the final tally in addition to positive feedback

- Be easy to understand and quick to fill out

- Have unbiased questions from which you can get the truth

- Be relevant to areas that you are committed to improving; otherwise, any feedback you receive won't be acted on, and therefore may be a waste of your time

Helping Your Technicians to Understand Marketing

If everyone is in sales, why is it that the people that your subscribers trust the most seldom know how to maximize their influence for a positive gain for your bottom line or to help and improve your sales and revenue goals? There seems to be a dichotomy between many techie types versus sales and marketing types that says that if you are an ISP technician, you could never stoop to become involved in sales-related issues, because sales and marketing people are evil. That is just nonsense.

There is a rare breed of ISP technician out there who is also sales-savvy. This unique individual is sometimes called a sales engineer and is often involved in selling dedicated Internet access accounts. Unfortunately, it is relatively difficult to find or attract these rare birds, so here are six steps for making your regular nonsales techie types understand marketing enough to possibly stop fighting with you or your sales team long enough to get something positive done as a team:

1. Awareness and education alone will not help your techies understand why you need things done certain ways in order to meet customer expectations or be marketing and sales smart.

2. Involve your technicians in the marketing campaigns you're launching. They will be involved as your network scales anyway, and they have a right or a need to know anyway.

3. Involve your technicians in sales incentives so that they can benefit from the rewards of helping your sales team grow your ISP revenues.

4. When hiring, let your potential technical support or engineer candidate know that your ISP's success is based on everyone being in sales. While this does not include cold calling or relying on sales performance for how technicians draw their paychecks, it needs to be made clear upfront how important you value their contribution in helping your sales team drive sales.

5. Share with and expect your technical support people to know every price of every major product or service your ISP delivers. This isn't that difficult and it will help in situations in which technicians will be able to recommend other services to the clients they regularly deal with on technical support issues.

6. Forget about trying to get them to understand and just keep on hiring and firing until you find the right mix of technical troubleshooting savvy and marketing and sales knowledge. Immature technicians

who don't care about the sales needs of your ISP organization should be let go immediately or replaced with someone who will care beyond the minimum.

Running Internal versus External Promotions to Drive Sales

Internal promotions can be a highly effective way of achieving your sales results. This key point is often ignored. An internal promotion is one where your employees are given a program, contest, incentive, or bonus for going above the call of duty to increase sales, margins, speed, level of service, or any objective of the organization. To be effective, it must be something that can be measured, such as sales, average ticket size, gross margin, average on-hold wait time, or percentage of problems solved in the first call.

It should come as no surprise that sales teams get the bulk of any internal incentive programs. This is an even greater reason to move some of your external marketing dollars over to your internal promotion budget.

The Incentive Federation conducted a study that was based on the written responses from 6,500 sales, marketing, and human resource executives in a cross section of U.S. businesses. It found the following results when it comes to choosing which incentives would be the most powerful to achieve the corporate goals.

Selected Types of Motivators Used by Respondents

AWARD	PERCENT USING
Cash awards	63
Gift certificates	54
Merchandise	51
Discounts or rebates	43
Individual travel	38
Time off from job	34
Group travel	29
Debit cards	4

Source: Incentive Federation

From the study, it appears that cash is king as the best way to reward your people when doing internal promotions. It may be easier to give gift certificates, as they are easier to write off as business expenses rather than pure cash, but sometimes cash can come in the form of a bonus or extra commission on the employee's next paycheck. Cash can be very instantly gratifying, but has less brag power than other incentives when it comes to sharing the news with coworkers.

The following are suggestions for typical ISP internal promotions that you might run:

- Every new employee gets $20 in cash for the first five praise or testimonial letters that he or she receives from a customer on the customer's company letterhead.

- The top person in your sales office who signs up the most new dial-up accounts gets a gift certificate for two at a local steak or seafood restaurant.

- For some reason, everyone on your team loves volleyball as a sport, so you offer a brand new volleyball and self-standing net kit (valued at about $250) for the next person or team who brings in a higher percent increase in performance this month over the same time a year ago.

- The salesperson with the highest average ticket size will get an opportunity to use your company's buying power to save 40 percent on his or her next vacation expenses.

- Anytime your technical support team pulls off a new record for longest number of days in uptime, each member gets a chance to rotate taking a day off with pay as the reward.

- Have everyone in your sales team vote for which technician provided the most positive support in helping them drive their sales, and reward that person with a gift certificate for four cases of a preferred beverage.

- There is no reason why your people can't give incentives to each other—they do not always need to come from management.

TIP After you start using anything other than cash for your incentives, make sure that the gift certificate or merchandise that you offer is wanted or needed by your team. You want the reward to be relevant and closer to home for them instead of what you would have liked to win yourself.

Strategies for Running a Successful Internal Incentive Program

Typically an ISP will spend between 5 to 10 percent of the incremental sales that an incentive program will generate in order to fund and administer the program. The following are the steps for creating a program that has a win-win profile for your people, management, and owners.

Your Internal ISP Incentive Program Goals

What is the end outcome you're looking to generate out of this program? Are you looking to bring on more new customers during this period versus last year same time or are you looking to increase the average ticket size of each sales rep's orders? Your first step is to quantify your goals into measurable, attainable, realistic goals.

You must also consider your market conditions. It may be unrealistic to ask your sales team to bring on a 5 percent growth in local market share this month if you know there are five new ISP competitors moving into the area during the same period.

Next, focus on the challenges you are facing internally, such as prospects not converting into paying subscribers, or your sales team is not up-selling enough dedicated accounts compared to the industry average or what you believe should be possible based on experience. Ask yourself why your team is not achieving the intended goals. The answer to that question could help you choose which incentive program and which items will be involved with which team members.

Incentive programs are usually based on sales performance this year versus last: the percent increase above your plan or forecasts, number of units sold (such as number of dial-up, ISDN, DSL, T1, or any dedicated Internet access account sold); sales of high-profit or high-margin items (such as Web site design or any labor billable sale), or simply an improvement in the number of qualified leads that your team generates.

Develop a Budget for Your Incentive Program

Your budget must be based on the incremental profit projected to come from this program. Typically 10 to 30 percent is spent on running the program and 70 to 90 percent of the remaining balance is spent on rewards or prizes.

Here's an example: You currently sell 20 dedicated DSL connections a month and you want to raise it to 30 new dedicated DSL accounts per month. For this example, use $700 per month as the amount that you get for each dedicated DSL account sold. If you are able to sell 30 dedicated accounts per month instead of 20, the incremental revenue is (Old Way:

$700 \times 20 = \$14,000$ monthly or $\$168,000$ annually)—(Projected Future: $700 \times 30 = \$21,000$ monthly or $\$252,000$ annually), which gives you a difference of $84,000 annually or $7,000 more monthly in gross revenues. Assuming that you have a 30 percent margin, it means that each month you bring in $7,000 more in revenue and create $2,100 more in gross profit monthly or $25,200 annually. You now know that you can spend up to $25,200 on your incentive program without going broke, but realistically you will set a budget of ($25,200 \times 10$ percent$) = \$2,520$ for your total incentive budget for this internal promotion.

> **TIP** While it might be tempting to calculate the preceding formula in addition to the new market value each of those subscribers brings your ISP, resist the temptation and only create internal incentive budgets based on the positive cash flow that you can count on.

Create the Rules of the Internal Incentive Game

An ounce of prevention is worth a pound of cure when it comes to creating the rules of your incentive program. Spell out the rules very clearly and anticipate issues, such as a tie, and get feedback from your team before you release it to make sure the rules you create are easily understood and not confused.

Your rules must allow for a simple, fair, quantifiable program during a finite period of time. You also could consider adding some spice to it, such as a Supersalesperson Bonus award for anyone who sells the most during the last two weeks of the contest, or whoever gets beyond $5,000 in collections in a given week earns 2 percent more bonus on top of the current commission structure during the program.

Choose the Awards and Prizes

This is the most important part of the program, since the correct prizes will properly motivate your people whereas the wrong prizes may stagnate your program or doom it from the start.

Your sales team is sophisticated. Therefore, don't insult team members' intelligence by offering a generic or no-name-brand product; you'll lose the effectiveness that a name-brand product might be able to create in terms of bragging rights. Your incentives should be something your sales team would be proud to tell their friends they won or earned.

Promoting and Tracking the Program Internally

The next step is to let everyone know about the program. This is typically done in a one- to two-hour meeting. In addition to passing out a printed copy of the incentive program, send everyone an e-mail reconfirming the rules of the program and details. Your goal is to cheerlead this new program while educating everyone about the benefits of what they will receive if they meet the realistic goals that are set.

Post the program in your sales office to remind everyone daily so that everyone involved can focus on improving his or her chances of winning. You also could have a party to celebrate the start of the program, so that everyone knows how big of a deal this is. Throughout the program, send motivational e-mails to your team members to help them achieve their best.

You may also want to get the awards on display so that everyone can see what will be won or what is available for the winners so they can visualize receiving it and enhance their short-term performance.

Award Fulfillment

Remember that public praise and recognition has a value—sometimes more than cash—to most people, which means you must make sure everyone in your office knows who won which incentives. The ISP CEO should be present to congratulate your highest performers and give out the awards.

While it does not seem very difficult to deliver the awards or prizes, make sure that delivery of the prizes has the exact same high priority that delivering paychecks on payday has, so that future programs are not in jeopardy because your people don't have high confidence in what you say you are going to do versus what you actually do.

Evaluating the Program's Effectiveness

Did you achieve the increases you expected? How many team members participated or took the program seriously? Why did some of your team members succeed while others failed during the same time period? What could have been the results if you did not do the incentive program?

In addition to your own analysis of the incentive's effectiveness from a business perspective, make sure you get your team's input and feedback on what the members thought of the campaign, so that you can get the best overall program perspective and figure out which incentive program should be next.

The Most Important Secret to Keeping New Subscribers

If there ever was a greatest moment of truth, it's when your new subscribers experience their first month with your ISP. This period of time is the single most important time between you and your new subscribers, which is followed by how you handle problems down the road in your efforts to retain new and existing subscribers.

Your objective is to convert 150 percent of your new prospects who are in either your free trial period or have signed up to give your ISP a try. If you are able to pull the near impossible, and get 100 percent to sign up and become a paying subscriber, where does the other 50 percent come in? You want 100 percent of the new subscribers who join you to refer their friends and family to you, so that you immediately are able to sign them up as well. So, in effect, this is a two-part challenge:

1. To find a way to achieve a 100 percent retention of your new subscribers

2. To find a way to get a significant number of your new subscribers to tell their friends about your ISP and get them signed up as well before the month is over

If you've done your homework and know your current conversion ratio of how many new subscribers drop off during their first month of usage, you may become shocked to find out you've got money slipping out the back door; it's time to fill the hole with a solution. With all the effort it takes you to acquire a new subscriber, in addition to the typical $10 to $120 you could pay to acquire the customer, it makes sense that you might want to beef up your processes and procedures to retain as many new subscribers as possible.

The secret to keeping new subscribers is to create systems at your ISP that facilitate a perfect experience for your new customers, which makes them feel welcome, happy, and smart that they chose a good ISP that is going to take care of them. This includes a follow-up call or a series of calls to make sure they are able to not only get connected, but all of their initial questions get answered and their expectations are met.

The ISP Angel Concept

Give your follow-up strategy for new customers a brand name, such as [insert your ISP's name] Guardian Angels, or [insert your ISP's name] Angels, or any other brand name which suggests a nontypical experience might be had with an interaction with one of these special team members.

The *ISP angel* is the person or team assigned to actively monitor new customers who are signing up to make joining your ISP as painless as possible. These people have been empowered by your management to handle almost any challenge that your new subscribers could encounter and they step in to make sure billing is also handled correctly and perfectly. Typically your angels would be your senior-level staff or employees who have at least 6 to 12 months of experience assisting normal client questions or problems.

How to Acquire New Subscribers via Strategic Acquisition of Other ISPs

Growth through targeted acquisitions is one of the fastest ways to increase your subscriber base and leverage your talent and market position. This high-growth strategy is usually reserved for the advanced ISP growth guerilla that has the vision to see beyond its normal everyday growth strategies and those of its competitors. It requires a different skill set than normal sales and marketing growth tactics but, with proper planning, this strategy can be applied by an ISP of any size.

Most ISPs only acquire subscriber bases or other ISP assets, but never the full ISP business. This is done to avoid unnecessary liability, as it is much easier, cleaner, and faster to buy the assets of an organization than to acquire the unknown and often hidden liabilities that creep up long after the original owner has cashed out. Unknown liabilities can include an excess of outstanding customer refunds, bad debts, accounts receivable which do not fully collect, and past accounts-payable debts that are unsatisfied or were accidentally not recorded on the books.

Growth through acquisitions comes in three main flavors:

1. **Customer base acquisitions only.** This is by far the most popular form of ISP growth strategy. Deals can be started and finished in a few weeks to a month.

2. **Customer base, plus network and talent.** This is done when an ISP investor or interested party cannot or does not wish to grow without additional network infrastructure or the talent to run such an operation. Some deep-pocket businesses have found that sometimes it costs less to buy an organization in order to acquire the talent and expertise within the ISP than it costs to organize and build it separately.

3. **Acquisition of the whole ISP operation.** When publicly traded ISPs have a pooling of their interests, many times the entire ISP organization is acquired or merged including all assets and liabilities.

Growth via acquisition is not for everyone, and in fact, there are many types of ISP operations and owners who should not attempt an acquisition. Here are some reasons why you *should not* try to acquire an ISP:

Lack of business maturity. Seasoned veterans have the advantage here.

Inability to master the basics of running an ISP organization. Before you leave your comfortable ISP nest to conquer the world by attempting to acquire some of your competitors, you must prove to yourself that you can run a basic ISP business. Such experience will be invaluable in helping you navigate what a good or bad subscriber base acquisition might look like.

Inability to manage positive cash flow, manage your finances, or read basic financial statements. You cannot make good acquisition decisions until you can master your ISP's finances first.

The acquisitions would take you too far out of your comfort zone. When the cost of having to relearn how to play the ISP game would be a competitive disadvantage for you after the acquisition, then you know the timing is not right for your ISP to be making acquisitions.

Lack of cash or access to capital. Without cash, your only alternative is to give up a percentage of your equity to acquire other ISPs or their subscriber bases. This may not always be to your advantage.

For those who are ready for the challenge, following are some of the pluses of growth via acquisition(s):

- Faster growth allows you to catapult yourself to the top of your niche faster.

- You are removing a competitor from the marketplace.

- You are creating a stronger, dominant force in your market to take on a larger opponent; each ISP may have failed to compete with it separately before the acquisition but they can succeed together.

- Economies of scale may reduce your operating costs.

- It improves your market value and perceived strength in the market place, which can increase investor and subscriber confidence or perceived value.

- Pooling of interests may significantly reduce your marketing costs to fight each other if you are considering acquiring a competitor while returning a higher number of new subscribers.

- It is one way to acquire technologies or systems you may not have had or developed yourself.

Disadvantages of acquiring other ISPs or their subscriber bases can include the following:

- Culture clash may spark employee revolts, loss of key talent, loss of productivity, or employee sabotage.

- Upsetting the customer base always causes higher attrition rates.

- Subscriber base may not be loyal and many subscribers could disconnect after a month or two, causing you to record a much higher churn ratio than your normal subscriber churn.

- You or your network may not be ready to handle the untold or unforeseen network scalability needs, causing bad service to be delivered at a critical moment for your new subscribers.

- Unreported liabilities or customer refund requests that become your responsibility out of goodwill or a poor contract may cause unplanned financial losses.

The Typical ISP Acquisition Cycle

Just like every sale has a *sales cycle,* when you are acquiring an ISP or an ISP subscriber base, there is an *acquisition cycle* that takes place. This cycle can take anywhere from a week to several months and depends on multiple factors, including how close you and the seller are to each other in terms of being ready to deal.

Figure 9.1 shows the steps involved in making an ISP acquisition. It starts out with your ISP acquisition staff doing the fieldwork to identify the best opportunities so that a decision to engage a possible seller can be determined. Once you have a willing seller and you believe there is a high chance of acquisition success, you're able to proceed to the next step, which is performing an in-depth valuation of the business and offering a letter of intent.

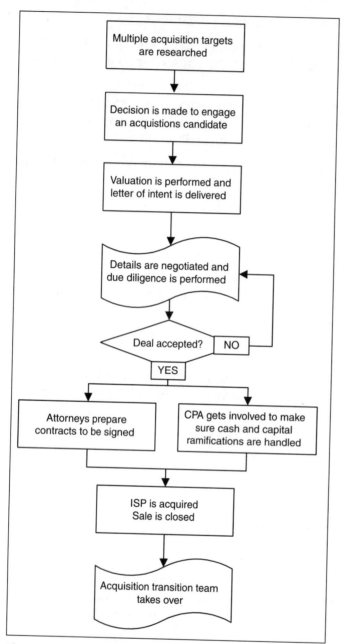

Figure 9.1   A typical ISP acquisition cycle.

This is the time the *information collection phase* begins. Your acquisition team will spend an enormous amount of time getting to know the details of this acquisition opportunity, meeting the people, getting cross reports on various aspects of the ISP to see if they add up with each other, and being diligent.

As you negotiate, if the global aspects of the deal are close, it's time to bring in your attorneys to draft an initial asset purchase agreement. This document will then be negotiated further as you continue to uncover more details about the ISP. Once you have an agreement, or when you are very close, you'll need to get your CPA or chief financial officer involved to help navigate how the deal will occur from a cash and tax consequence perspective.

The final step is for your legal counsel to draft the final agreement to be signed at closing when you will deliver the first check and close the deal. It's at this point that you also receive the supporting customer information and further details that you were not privy to until the closing of the deal. If everything checks out, you'll move onto turning this acquisition over to your ISP acquisition transition team, which will lay out the course for the fastest and highest conversion rate possible.

It should be noted that this is a highly simplified view of a typical ISP acquisition cycle. There could be other variables, such as escrow accounts established by third-party intermediaries or additional members of your staff working with your acquisition candidate to determine suitability or compatibility of the acquisition candidate with your existing operation.

Creating Your Own ISP Acquisitions Department

An *ISP acquisition department* is a team of people that is responsible for scouting, developing, and qualifying ISP acquisition possibilities for your ISP to consider buying. Typically, the person who heads this function has the same qualifications as your vice president of business development and either has full responsibility to carry out the deals or qualifies the best opportunities for the president or CEO.

You do not need an entire team of people to create an acquisitions department. One person can fulfill the role. The goal is to create the perception that your ISP is in the business of acquiring other ISPs, or at least their subscriber bases. By establishing a formal acquisitions team, you establish the upper hand early on in the negotiation process. With the perceived upper hand, the acquisition candidates know they must meet your requirements in order to be considered for purchase. Using this method, you are not going to be at the mercy of an ISP that is ready to sell, but only on its terms.

If you're an aggressive ISP looking to grow fast through acquisitions and you've secured enough capital for a serious round of acquisitions, you may wish to have an acquisition administrator on staff who carries out some or all of the following duties:

- Joins all of the ISP e-mail discussion lists looking to identify ISPs on the edge, ISPs getting ready to sell, or even ISPs who are doing a fire sale (a bad position for them to be in, but a great buying opportunity)

- Attends all of the major ISP conventions and trade shows, including ISPCON, the ISP Forum, ISP Summit, and local or regional ISP trade events

- Joins and attends all local, state, or regional ISP trade association events to scout for acquisition opportunities

- Continually identifies ideal ISP acquisition candidates and sends personal letters to them to open a dialog with your ISP (this will help you to gauge their level of interest)

- Acts as the initial liaison between your ISP and potential candidates to answer common questions to free up your ISP's CEO from dealing with candidates that don't meet your ideal acquisition criteria

Your ISP Acquisition Checklist for Identifying Great Opportunities

There is no perfect checklist for identifying ideal acquisition candidates. Each acquiring ISP and each selling ISP has a very unique set of needs. What follows is a general checklist of basic commonsense items to request when identifying an ISP acquisition possibility.

- Size of ISP in terms of how many paying subscribers it has on a monthly basis broken down by price point and service type

- Geographic layout of where the subscribers are concentrated compared to where your POPs are deployed

- Method of payment by the paying subscribers, broken down by payment type (i.e., cash, check, credit card, checking outdraft, other)

- How much does the ISP owner want per subscriber? What type of deal is he or she looking for?

- Reason for selling. Why is this ISP trying to sell its business or client base?

- Complete list of the owners and shareholders in the firm

- List of any legal proceedings against the company now or at any time in the past

- Which core business the ISP focused on, including samples of the past year of marketing materials

- Financial statements that include audited income statements (profit and loss) and balance sheets for the past three years, including the company's accountant's compilation letter

- Current year-to-date (YTD) income statement

- Three years of tax returns, along with any management explanation as to why they don't match the previously mentioned financial statements

- Records of accounts receivable including bad debts and a complete aging schedule

- Records of accounts payable (whether you are acquiring these or not)

- Long-term notes, lines of credit, or mortgages owed (if you are acquiring any of this, you have a right to copies of these notes)

- Copies of the company's facilities and equipment leases along with vendor contact information

- Copies of leases, contracts, and all written agreements between the ISP and its customers

- Existing contracts with employees, including agreements that might cover nondisclosure, noncompete, surrender of invention rights, compensation, commission, bonus, options agreements, and any related agreements that cover benefits to which your employees are entitled

- Copies of patents, trademarks, or copyrights the ISP possesses

- Complete list of domain names the ISP owns that would be included in any possible deal, along with the last 12 months of page views (a *page view* is equal to one person viewing one page) and unique session performance statistics

- A credit check through your favorite credit bureau, such as Trans Union or Dun & Bradstreet. The $50 to $250 you'll pay for such a report could help you improve your negotiating position. You will know whether the ISP you are attempting to acquire is in financial arrears or is really in a fire sale status and must sell soon, even though it hasn't given you this information.

TIP If you're going to assume anything before investigating possible acquisition opportunities, you can assume that what you would want if your ISP was being acquired is seldom what someone else would want when looking to sell his or her ISP. The bottom line is that you want to ask questions to uncover the unique needs and wants of the owners of the ISP you are considering.

Creative Techniques to Acquire More Bang for Your Acquisition Buck

No one said that every ISP acquisition has to be done traditionally—by paying cash for subscribers. Just like creating innovative marketing, you can design creative acquisition deals that transcend the norms and create win-win profitable deals if you're willing to think outside of the box.

The criteria for determining whether you acquired more bang for your buck is unique to each ISP and depends on how you determine value. For some, acquiring more subscribers at a cheaper rate than past deals might be the measuring stick, while others who are able to acquire a subscriber base with payments over time might benefit more by considering their cash flow situation.

Defining the Ideal ISP Acquisition for Your Business

If your acquisition possibilities are in tune with your business goals and needs, you will receive a higher return and more leverage through this mode of growth. Because time is of the essence, it is important to establish criteria that will help you categorize and locate meaningful acquisition opportunities.

Here is a partial list of ideal ISP acquisition strategies:

- ISPs that have realistic valuations and expectations of how much the ISP or their subscriber bases and assets are worth

  Reason: All of the best fundamentals are worthless if you and the current owner of the ISP are in dispute over valuation of the assets. It is best to work only with ISP owners who are based in reality or at least the same reality that you subscribe to when it comes time to set a buying or selling price.

- ISPs that are continuing on with another area of their business and only wish to sell their dial-up access clients

  Reason: These ISPs are concerned with their name and reputation and are not usually in a "Let's dump it all and get out" mode. These ISPs are more stable and will be more helpful in a positive transition than ISPs that will never see or hear from their clients again because they are leaving the industry.

- ISPs who have a solid price point or higher and have maintained it for more than one year

   Reason: If the subscriber base you are acquiring is used to paying the same or more than you charge, then it is likely it will continue paying, resulting in lower churn.

- ISPs with more than 5,000 subscribers

   Reason: Whether you are acquiring 500 or 5,000, the amount of time it takes to structure the deal is similar. All things equal, you get more bang for your time buck by raising the minimum number of subscribers you are looking to acquire.

- ISPs that are in the same geographic space that you currently serve and will not require installation of new POPs in order to serve the newly acquired customers

   Reason: Less new coverage area during an acquisition equals higher return and leverage from existing POPs, unless you are looking to grow into new regions.

- ISPs with large Web-hosting subscriber bases

   Reason: This will vary from ISP to ISP, but for some ISPs, Web hosting and related services create a serious second profit center that can be enhanced with strategic acquisitions.

- ISPs with 50 to 100 percent growth rates and less than 20 percent annual churn

   Reason: These important numbers determine future recurring revenue, growth, and attrition. If you are looking for fast growth after the sale, seek out ISPs that have growth or momentum indicators and are cranking out strong numbers and minimizing churn.

- ISPs with solid advertising revenue streams

   Reason: This could be because you don't have a good advertising stream yourself and would like to improve yours. If you derive a solid percentage of your ISP revenue from advertising and wish to augment it, find ISPs with solid revenue streams from advertising.

Create an acquisition model that works for your ISP and stick to it, even when tempting opportunities come across your desk. The more in tune your acquisition model is with your overall corporate objectives and available capital or resources, the greater your leverage and ability to identify the best opportunities.

Searching for the ISP Fire Sale

Fire sales are some of the best buying opportunities. Fire sales occur whenever an ISP is forced to sell its business because of a lack of capital, financial troubles, lack of interest, divorce, or legal proceedings against it which appear insurmountable, just to name a few reasons.

There are risks to acquiring an ISP subscriber base with pennies on the dollar. The largest risks include mismanagement of its subscriber base, poor service, poor record keeping, disorganized databases, high churn, and low or stagnant growth. The old cliché "buy low, sell high" applies here, but be careful not to waste your valuable time pursuing cheap deals while ignoring more profitable opportunities.

David Shires, who has participated in dozens of ISP acquisitions and is one of the people in charge of acquisitions for Voyager.net, has this to say: "A bad deal at a good price is still a bad deal."

Using Historical Data to Protect Your Interests

In addition to your right to ask for current information and data, you have the right to ask for all historical data dating back to the first day of the ISP's operation. This could include sales, margins, profits, growth rates, churn rates, modem ratios, and more, sorted by month. By collecting historical data, you can ask more intelligent questions about inconsistencies during the life of the ISP.

Shires says that by the time a company is ready to sign on the dotted line for an ISP acquisition, he already has over 20 inches of historical paperwork documenting the ISP's history. This depth of research into operating history and condition weeds out the bad deals, ensures lower churn during the conversion, and increases the likelihood of a positive return on the investment (positive ROI).

Geographic Acquisition Leverage

When reviewing a possible acquisition, keep in mind that a higher percentage of subscribers in your targeted geographical coverage area will result in higher returns by leveraging your existing infrastructure.

If you have a national footprint because of an alliance with a dial-up POP wholesaler, make sure that your acquisition targets map well with your existing POP reach. Make a list and get to know all of the other ISPs using the same wholesale provider in order to identify which ones may be interested in getting out of the business. If your wholesale dial-up POP provider won't give you a list of its customers, start your own public e-mail discussion list for ISPs who use the same wholesale provider and invite your competitors to join in.

Creative Structuring of the ISP Acquisition Payout

There are literally dozens of strategies with which to structure your ISP acquisitions. There is no law stating that you must acquire them all the same way. For maximum benefit, structure each acquisition in a way that results in maximum return while you manage downside risk potential.

Here are four quick strategies on how to pay out for your acquisition(s):

- 75 percent down at close, 25 percent down in 30 days
- 50 percent down at close, 25 percent in 30 days, 25 percent in 60 days
- 90 percent down at close, 10 percent in 30 or 60 days
- Multiple payouts, depending on which ISP assets are purchased. For example: 75 percent down at close and 25 percent in 45 days for the customer base; 100 percent down at the time of close for any hardware or network assets purchased; and 50 percent down on any domain names being purchased separately; and 50 percent upon successful transfer of ownership of said property to your name or business.

There is no limit to the possibilities of how you can structure your offer. A sale can only happen when a willing buyer meets with a willing seller and the two parties agree on the price and terms.

TIP The whole point of structuring your payout during an acquisition is to keep the ISP you are acquiring properly motivated to help you complete the deal with your largest upside potential while managing the risk of the downside.

Acquisition Using Equity as Your Capital

Publicly traded ISPs acquire using equity as their capital when it makes sense or when the deal is large enough. Privately traded ISPs can also make acquisitions with equity ownership in their ISPs or through a combination of equity and cash.

You may not find high success with this method. The majority of ISPs looking to sell search for a cash exit without seller-based financing. But it does not hurt to make it an option during your negotiation if the deal is large enough and the resulting combined ISP can leverage goals more successfully than each ISP separately.

If you decide to offer cash plus equity, you could lower your negative cash flow and acquire a greater strategic advantage in your marketplace because of your ability to hold onto more of your cash assets and reduce overall liabilities.

For example: Your ISP is valued at $20 million, and you want to acquire an ISP with 10,000 subscribers at a cost of $400 per subscriber that converts. Assuming 80 percent convert, instead of paying the ISP $3.2 million ($400 × 8,000), you offer $200,000 in cash up front so that the owner has some money to spend immediately (handles some of the psychological or emotional seller needs). Then you give the ISP you are acquiring a $3 million interest in your ISP or a 15 percent nonvoting rights interest. To make this successful or even possible, you will have to convince the selling ISP how much your stock is worth today and how much it will be worth in the future. You want the seller to see how a $3 million interest or a lousy 15 percent of your business can quickly multiply if and when your ISP is sold or goes public in the future.

Using equity for ISP acquisitions is not best for the following situations:

- Small deals, that is, anything under 10,000 subscribers

- When the value of your money and your time or labor resources would be better spent elsewhere

- When you have access to low-interest capital from a lending institution or another source that makes it easier to pay cash outright, allowing you to retain all of your existing equity

- When the legal costs to structure the deal outweigh the value of the overall deal

- When the short-term gain of avoiding negative cash flow outweighs the long-term gain of your market capitalization over the next 24 to 60 months

Components of the ISP Asset Purchase Agreement

An *asset purchase agreement* is the contract that your attorney will draft for you. It is the legal, binding agreement between you and the ISP who is selling to you. This chapter covers the very basics of such an agreement. However, you should always consult your lawyer to assist you with any purchase transaction.

Asset purchase agreement styles differ from lawyer to lawyer. It's best when making an acquisition that you and your legal team are the ones writing the asset purchase agreement. What follows is a sample to give you a feel for what you should include.

Introduction Statement. This includes your legal corporate name, address, and who is representing your firm, and the same legal corporate name, address, and name of the person who is representing the ISP you are buying.

Preliminary Recitals and Statement of Intent. The seller agrees to sell, and you, as the purchaser, agree to buy its assets as set forth in your agreement. The purpose of this section is to outline the intent of this entire agreement. This is only a global review of the deal and is subject to the details that follow.

Asset Purchase. Within this section you will list a separate section for each of the kinds of assets you are purchasing, such as customer bases, accounts receivable, employee contracts, equipment, or network contracts. You'll want to go into great detail describing the assets, so there is no future confusion as to what is being purchased and what is not.

Purchase Price and Consideration. The total purchase price of the entire agreement along with step-by-step provisions for how it shall be paid are disclosed in this section. If you've got an escrow account involved, this is where you disclose the details. Optionally, how the account receivables will be paid is also discussed in this section.

Transition of Customers Understanding. The more information you have upfront, the less confusion during the actual transition period. You'll want to be very detailed and thorough when you describe to the seller how you want the transition period handled. The purpose of this section is to avoid future misunderstandings as well as unnecessary litigation if things go wrong during the transition.

If you are setting up an offset for subscribers who do not convert, this is the section that typically carries that understanding, along with in-depth definitions of how you will determine whether it's a successful transition or not. You'll also want to require the seller and its agents or employees to assist in the conversion process as much as possible.

Assumption of Liabilities, Contractual Obligations, and Assignment of Contractual Rights. *Assumption of liability* can be defined as any situation in which you are buying a debt, which is something that you will owe someone else after the deal. This could include prepaid subscribers, customer refunds, telecommunications circuit charges, equipment leases, and so forth.

Representations and Warranties. This is where the seller makes representations and warrants that it has the right to do this deal. The language asserts that it is a company in good standing; that the customer agreement is exactly as it said it was in the preliminary due diligence; that there have not been any material adverse effects since it has disclosed the information prior to signing; that there is an absence of litigation against the seller; that all titles and liens against any asset being acquired are owned or cleared at this time; and that all government permits are handled.

Conversely, you as the buyer also represent in this section that you have the power to make this acquisition happen and that you have your corporate act together.

Indemnification. You release the seller of liability and it releases you, in case anything happens that may lead to litigation. Normally you can try to start by making this lopsided so that the seller releases you fully and you only release it partially, but in almost all agreements, you end up indemnifying each other equally so that you can get on with the deal at hand.

This section also determines who pays for what, if legal battles occur between the two parties involved after the deal is closed.

Closing. This section notes the closing date, time, and place for you and the seller to sign the agreement. It also can include a list of various kinds of information that should be delivered by both parties to each other. For example, you as the buyer will probably be delivering a down payment check, and the seller will probably be delivering all books, records, supporting documentation relating to the customer list, equipment list, employee list, bill of sale, noncompete agreements, and all other documents required by you, the buyer.

Miscellaneous. This section declares the governing state for this agreement (usually the state of the buyer). This section also states that this is the entire agreement between both parties and overrides any verbal discussion prior to closing; that any subsection of this agreement will be binding even if any other subsection is in default or is breached; and that each side has certain rights to request relevant information that is required and must be furnished with proper request.

Signatures. The legal representatives of each organization, with their titles and the date, sign this section. This is often done in front of a notary public whose witness gives the document an extra degree of professionalism and binding certainty.

Exhibits.

- The customer list (detailed in printed form) and an electronic spreadsheet or database of the same information
- Accounts receivable list
- Customer contracts
- Equipment asset list
- Any assumed equipment leases or network/telecommunication circuit agreements
- Noncompete agreement

    You may wish to attach an exhibit for any item that needs more in-depth description or clarification.

Optional Items. Other items you may wish to include in your asset agreement follow:

- Referral fees that the seller can receive in addition to the deal for any future client or new subscriber that it refers to your ISP
- How customer payments to the ISP will be handled postsale
- Contingencies as to what will happen if parts of the agreement fail. This is your backup plan.

When Acquisitions Go Wrong

Acquisitions go wrong for a lot of reasons, many of which can be prevented. The best defense against bad deals is a strong offense during the due diligence phase of your investigation into the selling ISP's operations. The more information and cross-examining you're able to do with your acquisition candidates, the higher your chances are of not having an acquisition go wrong.

Here is a list of possible items that can go wrong during an ISP acquisition, along with some suggested remedies that may help you prevent the worst case scenario:

- Actual subscriber base is not the same size as the ISP warranted it would be.

Remedy: Legal recourse so that you pay only for subscribers that convert. Subscribers that don't convert are not paid for.

- Higher than industry standard churn rate. This means that after you did the acquisition, less than 80 percent of the subscribers you just bought switched over to your service.

   Remedy: Who messed up in this case? Did your acquisition team mess up the acquisition transition process or did the actions of the seller impact its own subscriber base negatively which caused a low conversion? Solution: Add a section to your acquisition contract that specifically states how the transition period will take place.

- A high percentage of the subscribers you just acquired have informed you that they have more months prepaid than the ISP you bought them from indicated.

   Remedy: Get a schedule added to your contract that lists customers from the database, along with their renewal dates. Make sure your acquisition contract has economic remedies for you if the selling ISP misrepresents any information in the deal.

- During the transition period, the seller's network fails and puts you in jeopardy—your new customers might bail before you get a chance to bring them safely onto your network.

   Remedy: Have a *fallback* plan in place in case this happens. Assume it's a real possibility since the ISP you are acquiring could have been on the brink of falling apart at the seams from lack of proper capitalization. Your fallback plan can include having your senior system administrators step in and help restore the seller's network to see if you can minimize the damage.

- Employees of the seller who may be about to lose their jobs sabotage the deal, for any reason.

   Remedy: Get the seller's employees involved or suggest strongly to your acquisition candidate that you wish to meet and talk with the team leaders who will be in charge of the acquisition transition period. Information is power here. You should also know the reporting structure of the ISP you are acquiring so that you can escalate issues before they become big economic problems for you. If the ISP you are acquiring will no longer be running a business at all, either make offers to their best employees to work at your ISP as part of your acquisition or, as part of the deal, help them find new jobs elsewhere.

- Your own employees sabotage the deal, for any reason.

  Remedy: Fire them. You have a planned process; you are going to work that process perfectly, improve on mistakes, and stop mistake patterns immediately. You are going to measure your transition process daily and weekly to make sure it is going as planned. Anyone who works for you should be loyal to that plan.

- Many of the new subscribers who are converting to your network are not getting the same connection speeds they were at the ISP you acquired or they are having compatibility problems they didn't have before.

  Remedy: Acquire the entire dial-up network of the ISP you are buying so that the subscribers will not experience any difference in dial-up quality or conditions. For those for which this is not an option, alert your transition team to look for compatibility problems. Keep those subscribers on the seller's network until your top engineers can figure out the lowest-cost way to bring them onto your network without delivering new problems.

- A competitor is tipped off that you're doing an acquisition and swoops in to take advantage of your new subscribers who may be fed up with the ISP you are acquiring and on the verge of switching.

  Remedy: Keep all acquisition talks private and highly confidential until after you have signed on the dotted line. The less time you give your competitors to react, the faster you'll be able to work your transition team into getting the conversion going. If it's too late and your competitors are marketing hard to your new subscribers-to-be, make sure you aggressively communicate the new benefits subscribers will receive from you and make sure your service team is operating at above-average standards.

- You're not staffed well or your network's capacity is not enough for the new load on it; the surge of new subscribers who are converting to your ISP is starting to leave because it appears you do not have your act together.

Remedy: Only do acquisitions when you and your team are not in crisis management. The old saying *An ounce of prevention is worth several pounds of cure* applies here. For the network-planning purposes, a T1 of bandwidth can handle 200 concurrent connections on average, which is about 2,000 subscribers per T1 or (1.544 Mbps) when utilizing a ratio of 10 users for every one Internet access port. Your existing server load will also need to be balanced or capacity increased, as this is part of the equation.

The following problems apply to ISP acquisitions in which you are acquiring the complete ISP, instead of the subscriber base only. Acquiring a complete ISP can include the subscriber base, employees, accounts receivable, accounts payable, other assets and liabilities, and existing client and vendor relationships.

- The ISP you just acquired has many hidden skeletons in the closet which means that after a month into the acquisition, you find that there are untold liabilities where creditors and customers are looking to you to make right the wrongs that your seller made when it was in control. Because of poor records, you're unable to sort things out very well.

    Remedy: Only acquire the assets of the seller, instead of its corporate shell. By doing this, you shield yourself from being liable for the history of the ISP you just acquired.

- You cancel some of the sellers circuits that you no longer need since you're able to transition the subscribers onto your network, but you are hit with a costly early circuit termination charge.

    Remedy: Get a copy of all contracts for all circuits that are in place ahead of time so that early circuit termination charges are dealt with before you sign the deal. Circuit charges are a liability in all cases unless you're a telecommunications company that can retariff them in which case you're able to deliver economic value to the ISP who would be stuck with these expenses on its way out of the business.

- A culture clash with the staff of the seller and your staff causes problems, lack of follow-through, sabotage, lack of attentiveness to customer service issues, and other network or subscriber satisfaction issues.

    Remedy: Get what information you can about the staff before the acquisition. Immediately after the deal, analyze and reorient your new staff members into your culture or give them a chance to exit by helping them find new jobs elsewhere.

- The new or used equipment you just acquired as part of the deal has liens on it that you did not know about and the bank or leasing party is trying to repossess it.

  > *Remedy:* Lease transfer documents should be included in the agreement or as part of the schedules to be completed concurrently with the signing of the overall contract. You, the buyer, need to know whether there is any money owed on the equipment before the acquisition, not after.

- You're having a hard time collecting several thousand dollars of the accounts receivable (AR) that you acquired.

  > *Remedy:* First, never buy AR at face value. Always buy it based on a discounted value—a guesstimate that only 50 to 75 percent of it will actually pay up. During your diligence, find out how clean the AR really is by studying the aging and any history you're able to secure from the acquisition candidate. Preacquisition, study any account that is more than 90 to 120 or more days past due. The farther the debt owed is past due, the less likely you will ever get paid.

ISP Acquisition Safety Net Tips

The larger the deal, the higher the level of written contract protection you will need to ensure that the covenants, representations, and warranties of your agreement are obeyed. It should go without saying that 100 percent of all ISP acquisitions should be done with the assistance of your legal counsel. Here are three quick tips on how to increase the safety of your acquisitions:

1. Never assume that just because you have a signed acquisition contract that you can't keep negotiating if the other side failed to deliver on any of its contractual obligations. When either party fails any of its obligations, the party must prove in a court of law, if it ever goes that far, that it mitigated its damages, which means that the offending party did something to reduce the problem it just created. The more possible scenarios you can list in your contract and what will happen if those events occur will make problem resolution postdeal much faster and easier.

2. To put 100 percent down at signing is silly. Instead, give the seller a significant amount of the value as a down payment at closing. Then, either escrow or hold back 10 to 50 percent of the remaining balance

for a period of 30 to 120 days so that adjustments can be made on which clients convert and what problems are encountered.

3. Put an equal amount of effort into contingency planning as you do into normal due diligence during an acquisition in case things go wrong.

Managing the Acquisition Transition Period

The *transition period* starts the minute you sign a contract to acquire someone's subscriber base and ends when all of the new subscribers are under your billing and network umbrella. It's during this critical period that you need to maximize and leverage your efforts and all your experience to get the highest conversion rate.

Larger ISPs have acquisition transition teams, but smaller ISPs will have to get more creative to pull off the increased labor demands during the transition period. Typically, this period lasts from three weeks to between four and six months and depends on the complexity of the sale.

Your critical success indicators during this period include the following:

Conversion rate. How many subscribers convert to your network as a number or percentage of the total number of subscribers acquired?

Conversion speed (time cycle). This relates to how fast you can get them from the other ISP's network over to your network. The quicker you can get the bulk of the users onto your network, the more time you'll be able to identify the problem subscribers who are not able to convert as easily and need extra attention.

New member confidence. How can you begin to educate and inspire confidence and excitement in your new subscribers so they feel good about the fact that you are their new ISP host?

Network uptime of seller. You want to layer your technical support and engineering skills over the seller's team so that you are able to generate good team karma while keeping your new subscriber's experience hassle-free.

Many of the same lessons learned in Chapter 7, "Strategies to Reduce Churn," also apply here with respect to your ability to keep your churn low and your conversion high. The transition period is one of the most exciting times during the acquisition cycle as it can give your ISP a competitive advantage if you're able to maximize your success in conversion rate.

ISP Case Studies

"Success leaves clues."

ANTHONY ROBBINS

If it is true that "success leaves clues," then this chapter is packed with clues from successful ISPs in multiple different market niches. Each of the following ISPs share their strategies, expertise, and experience. As with all things that change rapidly, please note that many of the ISPs listed in this chapter will have grown significantly or will have been acquired by the time you are reading this chapter. Nonetheless, these stories bear telling.

National ISP Case Study: EarthLink

Number of subscribers:	3 million or more
Year business founded:	1994
URL:	www.EarthLink.net/
Number of employees:	4,000
Number of POPs:	890–1,500+
Business niche or USP:	Business and consumers
Organization structure:	Public: NASDAQ: ELNK

Financing:	IPO
City and state of headquarters:	Atlanta, Georgia, USA
Name of interviewee:	Mike McQuary, President
E-mail for public inquiries:	Not applicable
Sales phone number:	(800) 395-8425

History, Vision, and Quick ISP Facts

EarthLink and MindSpring merged in the fall of 1999, creating a superISP. MindSpring is a leading national Internet service provider; it offers local Internet service in more than 890 locations throughout the United States. The MindSpring Biz division is a leading provider of Web hosting services and domain registrations and offers other value-added services such as Web page design. EarthLink is the world's largest independent Internet service provider and through its unified EarthLink Sprint Internet access service, the company makes the Internet relevant to and productive for hundreds of thousands of individuals and businesses every day. It provides a full range of innovative access and hosting solutions to thousands of communities internationally from more than 1,500 points of presence. EarthLink and Sprint Corporation (NYSE: FON) have formed a broad business relationship to create an Internet service with the potential to reach millions of new customers. Sprint is a global communications company and one of the world's largest carriers of Internet traffic.

ISP Strategies for Success

You must have a business model that can be profitable. AOL and EarthLink/MindSpring have actually demonstrated that their business models work—no one else has done that yet. Investors will not continue to fund bad Internet businesses, so you need to find ways to fund your ISP from your revenues. Write a three-year business plan that shows how you are profitable in the third year and then stick to the plan.

The value of an ISP is not based on number of subscribers—its value is based upon a multiple of future cash flows. When growing your ISP through acquisition, depending on your cost structure, you should never pay more than the expected lifetime cash flows of the customers you are looking to acquire.

There is no single best way to acquire new subscribers, as you need to have a differentiated service and create awareness around your brand. Price cutting just artificially shifts around price-sensitive customers who have no loyalty.

The number one way to reduce churn is to offer great service or offer proprietary applications that others can't match. The least-effective way to build an ISP is to bring in lots of subscribers by spending lots and lots of money, all the while hoping to get bought by a bigger ISP or rescued by advertising dollars from your portal.

Your marketing budget should be between 10 and 25 percent of your gross sales, depending on your cost structure and should be flexible enough to grow at market rate without sacrificing your path to profitability.

In order to retain top talent, you need to have a compensation system that rewards employees when the company does well, and that means stock options.

Future for EarthLink.net and the ISP Industry

A new ISP would be looking at some ugly business prospects right now. With the current rebates for PCs which include a three-year commitment for the supplied ISP service (from a few big ISPs), it would be tough for a new player to make any impact unless it was going to enter that fray and be willing to endure huge financial losses. The ISP business has always been tough, and it's getting tougher.

EarthLink's prediction is that the ISP business will come to look like the long-distance phone industry: there will be three to five major players who make up 90 percent of the industry and then a bunch of smaller players who will fight for the scraps.

Cable and DSL will be the contenders for the future of broadband.

A word about the free ad-supported ISP model: Like their free predecessors, they will all be out of business within 18 months. Ad revenues will not support quality Internet service. Remember, too, that this is different from the European ISP model in which the phone calls themselves are metered and provide revenue for the ISPs.

Regional ISP Case Study: Atlantic.Net Internet Services

Number of subscribers:	24,000+
Year business founded:	1995
URL:	www.atlantic.net/
Number of employees:	60+
Number of POPs:	50

Business niche or USP:	Consumer first, businesses second, wholesale dial-up provider third
Organization structure:	Privately held, profitable
Churn rate:	2–3 percent per month
Financing:	Private investment by current owners
City and state of headquarters:	Gainesville, Florida, USA
Name of interviewee:	Brian Bess, Marketing Director
E-mail for public inquiries:	sales@atlantic.net
Sales phone number:	(800) 422-2936

History, Vision, and Quick ISP Facts

Atlantic.net is the fifteenth fastest-growing private company in Florida. It experienced a 328 percent increase in revenues from 1996 to 1998. Starting out as a computer retail store, Atlantic.net focused first on the consumer clients with increased attention to business needs, such as Web hosting and e-commerce solutions. Business clients are more loyal and spend more than their consumer counterpart. Atlantic.net also leverages its facilities-based network to provide wholesale dial-up access for its competitors. Serving over 50 cities now in the southeastern region of the United States, Atlantic.net is a certified CLEC, and leverages this status to build what it calls *SuperPOPs*, where it consolidates its dial-up centers for increased economic leverage and profit. It has made nine strategic acquisitions to grow its subscriber base and is also very focused on organic growth.

ISP Strategies for Success

Putting the customer number one and delivering good service are Atlantic.net's most important distinctions. It is able to pull this off, in part, by having tough goals for its ISP call center where it works hard to answer every call under one minute and has a low abandonment rate (people who hang up before they reach a human). Respecting its clients and notifying them when things go wrong is also very important for good ISP-subscriber relations.

Atlantic.net believes its current subscriber base is valued around five times or more of its annual revenues and currently has a price point of $19.95 for its dial-up Internet access rate.

On acquiring other ISPs, the company had this advice to offer:

- Check the records thoroughly of the acquisition candidates you are evaluating. Computerized records are absolutely essential when an ISP goes over 1,000 subscribers.
- During the conversion, communicate with the acquired company's customers a lot by sending numerous e-mails, telling them what is happening, how it will affect them, and calling them personally if need be in order to get the highest conversion rate possible.
- Atlantic.net's conversion rate has averaged 80 percent for its last nine acquisitions.

Future for Atlantic.net and the ISP Industry

As one of the last privately held big ISPs in Florida and the surrounding area, Atlantic.net's future looks very bright. It has been approached by many suitors and has decided that it is having too much fun to sell out at this time. If there could be one thing that would significantly improve conditions for Atlantic.net and the ISP industry, it has stated that the break up of the incumbent telecommunications monopolies would be a major factor.

International ISP Case Study: I-Link

Number of subscribers:	250+
Year business founded:	1995
URL:	www.ilink.fr
Number of employees:	4
Number of POPs:	1
Business niche or USP:	Business and Administrations—primarily serving business
Organization structure:	Privately held, slightly profitable
Churn rate:	Not applicable
Financing:	Private investment by original owner
City and state of headquarters:	Albi, Midi-Pyrenees, France
Name of interviewee:	Denny Adelman, Owner-Director

E-mail for public inquiries: info@ilink.fr

Sales phone number: +33-5 63 54 81 77

History, Vision, and Quick ISP Facts

I-Link (*Internet en Pays de Cocagne*, which means Internet in a Land of Plenty) is located in southwest semirural France. It was founded and is run by American entrepreneur Denny Adelman who left the American rat race eight years ago to live in la belle France. He created a basic French corporation that is called a SARL. A SARL, while similar to a U.S. subchapter S corporation, does not have the advantages of its American counterpart.

The free ISP model has been a great success in Europe, and in France has been responsible for 75 percent of total new connections in the last nine months. This has obviously hurt the not-free access market.

But some of these new "internauts" have already found the service level lacking, and I-Link has been able to convince users to join its service in those cases where the free model "costs too much." It helps that three times in the last two years I-Link has been cited as best access provider in Midi-Pyrenees (the region where it's located) by the French Internet press.

Its average dial-up service goes for 100 francs per month unlimited including Value Added Tax (VAT), which equates to about $14 US. This is at the high end of not-for-free dial-up fees in France. The majority of I-Link's dial-up access sales are sold in three-month or one-year prepaid accounts.

However, over 50 percent of I-Link's sales comes from other Internet activities, mainly Web site and intranet design, hosting, and training.

Because 56 percent of the French economy is controlled by the public sector, the major potential clients in any region of France are always the various administrations. I-Link, therefore, counts many of the administration members as clients.

What many Americans pay for a T1 (1.544Mbps) of bandwidth would only get you about 64K in France. I-Link has a 128K connection that costs it approximately $2,000 US per month.

This is a small ISP business and plans to stay that way. In a land that is suspicious of its entrepreneurs (even though it is the French that coined that word!), Adelman would rather continue to be creative, dynamic, and a pioneer than become a municipal employee, which was what was suggested to him when he first moved to France.

ISP Strategies for Success

In France, it doesn't appear possible to be an access provider only. One must look for value-added services for businesses in order to survive.

Future for I-Link and the ISP Industry

I-Link will not be doing much more to attract more consumer subscribers, but it will continue to explore new ways to deliver valued-added services for businesses.

France Telecom (the French telephone monopoly until January 1998) stills controls a large percentage of the market. It, like other incumbent telecommunication companies across Europe, is fighting tooth and nail to keep what it has, and national deregulation commissions are notoriously lax in enforcing new antimonopoly laws. This, coupled with the fact that a small elite controls a big percentage of the businesses and civil servant positions in the country, does not make it easy for small businesses and start-ups in the Internet or telephony sector.

One bright hope: Europe got the mobile phone thing right the first time around, settling on the GSM (Global System for Mobile communication) standard, whereas the U.S. counterparts are still fighting to agree on a standard. Mobile wireless Internet communications will create many new industries and opportunities for entrepreneurs in Europe in the future.

Regional ISP Case Study: iServe Internet, Doing Business as Qserve Internet

Number of subscribers:	1,650+
Year business founded:	1997
URL:	www.qserve.net/
Number of employees:	9
Number of POPs:	665
Business niche or USP:	Residential dial-up
Organization structure:	Privately held, profitable
Churn rate:	2.5 percent per month
Financing:	Privately financed (credit cards, shoe-string)

City and state of headquarters: Carmel, Indiana, USA

Name of interviewee: Jamie Brown, CEO

E-mail for public inquiries: jkb@qserve.net

Sales phone number: (888) 704-7261

History, Vision, and Quick ISP Facts

The college buddy ISP: Right out of Purdue University, Jamie Brown got started in computer repair/sales and getting people on the Net through a relationship with another ISP. Things went sour, so Brown, some college buddies, and one of the ISP employees thought to themselves, "Gee, we could do things better," so they started their own ISP on a shoestring of $7,000 and a lot of long hours of hard work.

They pride themselves on having a real person answer the phone and the fact that their subscribers' inquires get answered promptly. Their subscribers know that they care and Jamie's team will often work on their customers' computers for free to get their problems fixed if their technical support is unable to help them over the phone. Offering the lowest rate in their local market ($12.95 on a one-year prepay or $14.95 per month) has also been successful for them.

ISP Strategies for Success

Being a computer repair store with a retail location makes a real difference to this company's dial-up access subscribers. Word of the great lengths it takes to fix customer problems is spread quickly by word of mouth from its satisfied and happy members. If the boat gets a little rocky (meaning things go wrong), the Qserve team knows that because they care and give their subscribers extra perks, they are cut some slack when problems happen.

Brown recommends that you do not cut corners when setting up your business. He believes you should take time to research a name, trademark it, and enforce the marks. This will save you a lot of time and energy, especially if someone challenges you later.

He also recommends that you should not allow your customers to take advantage of you, by ensuring that billing terms and procedures favor your positive cash flow needs. You can do this by implementing procedures that make getting paid simpler and create an ease for dealing with your ISP. The subscribers who pay by check are the ones who are late and who you have to chase after for payment. ISPs offer a service that must be paid for in advance. No payment, shut the account off. If this was any other industry, such as the cellular industry, and you don't pay your bills, the service is shut off—oftentimes when you need it the most. The ISP industry should be the same in that regard.

Future for Qserve.net and the ISP Industry

Qserve is going to continue expanding its coverage areas in all locales, especially to suburbs and rural areas. These areas will be less influenced by cable and DSL. Qserve feels that until the costs of bandwidth come down significantly, DSL will be hard to offer at the level of service its customers are enjoying. [In Indiana, Ameritech won't sell dry pairs (2 copper wires with no dial tone on them) yet anyhow.] There will always be a market for ISPs that offer the level of service Qserve works very hard to offer, along with computer repair services that such companies as Gateway do not offer.

Those at Qserve see the next five to 10 years as a growth period since they believe that there is only a small fraction of the potential subscriber pool online now. These next years will allow service-oriented ISPs to grow into viable, standalone entities that are not threatened by rollups and buyouts.

Qserve is in it to grow and is not ready to hand over control of its subscriber base for a short-term reward, when it knows that with some courage, the future will be much brighter and rewards much greater if it keeps working at it.

The ISP industry is still *very* young, and the Qserve team thinks that many ISPs are making a big mistake to get out of the business prematurely. There are only so many portals that people will tolerate or embrace and it seems that portals are popping up like dandelions in the backyard every day. Content is very important; without access it really doesn't matter. Qserve believes its model will survive well into the next phase of its business growth.

Regional ISP Case Study: Snake River Valley Net, Inc.

Number of subscribers:	7,000+
Year business founded:	1994
URL:	www.srv.net/
Number of employees:	10+
Number of POPs:	4

Business niche or USP:

Consumer first, T1s, farmers, rural market

Organization structure:

Privately held, break-even profitability

Churn rate:

2–5 percent per month

Financing:

Private investment by original owners; acquired by consulting company to provide Internet services for them in addition to other clients

City and state of headquarters:

Idaho Falls, ID USA

Name of interviewee:

Hollis Henry, Director of Marketing and Sales

E-mail for public inquiries:

sales@srv.net

Sales phone number:

(208) 524-6237

History, Vision, and Quick ISP Facts

SRV.net was started as a nonprofit organization and was actually a home-based business. It was then purchased by Scientech.com and became a subsidiary designed to serve its corporate needs as well as the needs of the local Idaho Falls region. Currently it serves a geographic region that includes 75,000 households and has no plans for offering nationwide access. It has four T1s of bandwidth for redundancy and runs a 12:1 ratio of clients to modems. A general manager and board of directors oversee SRV.net's operation. To date, 100 percent of its growth has been organic.

ISP Strategies for Success

One way SRV.net has found to reduce the high cost of equipment is to lease many of the network hardware and software that it takes to run its ISP rather than buying it and amortizing the capital expenditures.

SRV.net believes that many ISPs have failed because of being undercapitalized. It believes it has a market advantage by being owned by a larger corporate parent that is not subject to the hair-raising demands of the sometimes low-margin dial-up services market. Also, by having the backing of a stronger parent company, it is able to offer a better level of service in the rural markets it serves, whereas some of its competitors barely even have a full T1 circuit, or redundancy for that matter.

SRV.net cautions other ISPs that their local telecommunications provider may not be able to respond as fast they need. It also advises others to always coordinate their capacity needs with their marketing, so that they stay ahead of the curve.

Excellent customer service can and must be delivered, and SRV.net does random customer polls to find out how others feel about its service. The majority of subscribers who leave SRV.net get a questionnaire or quick poll to find out why he or she left. SRV.net wants to know and track the top five reasons why subscribers are leaving it, so that it can keep its churn rate low.

In order to retain top talent, SRV.net believes that people need to feel valued, know that management appreciates them, and work in an atmosphere in which employees feel a sense of ownership in their positions. The company has just implemented bonuses and incentives that are designed to reward employees who do a great job of reducing churn or other critical success indicators that it has deemed important for its business.

In order to improve *customer stickiness*, SRV.net delivers free seminars for its clients and its marketplace. It has found this an effective strategy to return clients who may have left, keep current clients longer, attract new clients, and provide added value at the same time.

Radio advertising and word of mouth are very effective for SRV.net to drive new membership interest and help maintain market awareness about the ISP. Print ads have not been as effective.

Future for SRV.net and the ISP Industry

Serving the needs of business and consolidation among the ISPs is what SRV.net believes will be the future for the ISP industry. With U.S. West and other local incumbent telecommunications providers being slow to bring new technology to remote regions and the lack of cable modems, rural ISPs will have an advantage all of their own in meeting the increasing local demand that the big ISPs can't fulfill.

National ISP Case Study: VillageNet Inc.

Number of subscribers:	70,000
Year business founded:	1994
URL:	www.villagenet.com/
Number of employees:	Not available
Number of POPs:	Not available
Business niche or USP:	Family-oriented Internet service

Organization structure:	Publicly held: OTC-BB: VILN, profitable
Churn rate:	1–1.5 percent per month
Financing:	Separate division of parent company from start; reverse merger with VillageWorld.com to become publicly traded
City and state of headquarters:	Bohemia, NY USA
Name of interviewee:	Jeffrey Meltzer, Senior Network Administrator
E-mail for public inquiries:	sales@villagenet.com
Sales phone number:	(516) 218-9090

History, Vision, and Quick ISP Facts

VillageNet is a community-oriented Internet service provider specializing in educational and family-based Internet services with a local emphasis on business advertising and shopping, chat rooms, and parent/student/teacher interaction. The company also offers systems-integration services, specializing in network design, implementation and maintenance, and providing Internet/intranet messaging and security products. VillageNet is a value-added government and commercial reseller for Cisco Systems and FORE Systems and is authorized to sell and install their products to public entities in New York (e.g., school districts) without public bidding through those companies' New York State contracts.

VillageNet seeks to acquire compatible Internet companies that currently outsource the backbone and support services offered by the company. It has grown organically to date, but will be adding a nonorganic growth strategy through strategic acquisitions to fuel its future success.

It has partnered with Rhythms NetConnections for deploying nationwide DSL and believes that DSL is the future access transport of choice for multimegabit access.

ISP Strategies for Success

To provide great service means to be reliable. Reliability must be number one, and this is one of the primary reasons VillageNet has been able to keep customer churn below industry averages. It is able to provide less than 1 percent per month of downtime by only deploying quality equipment, such as Cisco, Lucent, and Sun products, as well as having trained experts on staff who can support the best hardware and software.

Dr. Frankenstein monster theory: To grow to beyond your capacity is stupid. Don't bite off more than you can chew. Slow, controlled growth is not only the right way, but should be the only way an ISP can deliver great service while scaling its business to the top.

It also believes that its low employee turnover is because it puts its people first and has excellent upper-level management.

Future for VillageNet and the ISP Industry

VillageNet believes in nationwide growth, and unlike other ISPs that are looking to get bought out, it is looking to grow the business and maximize shareholder value. Like the advent of the television and automobile, the Internet is the next big thing and ISPs will be in one of the greatest businesses to profit from this growth explosion. The fantastic growth of the industry will change the way the world works and communicates. Voice Over IP (VOIP) will become the next big communications medium.

Afterword

The future of the ISP industry is one filled with change, evolution, excitement, and challenges as regulatory hurdles are overcome to deliver consumers and businesses the best possible Internet access service. Unlike the telecommunications industry, which has had almost a full century to develop and mature, the ISP industry is expected to evolve and change just as it has since the early 1990s.

One thing is certain: The demand for Internet access will continue to climb for the next decade as more consumers and businesses get online. In addition, the demand for Internet-aware devices and appliances (the microwave, refrigerator, home heating and cooling systems, entertainment center, and so forth) will increase, which will require access to the global network we now call the Internet.

Will the free ISP (advertiser-supported) model crush the fee-based ISP industry? The answer is no, but it will have a serious impact on the future of the ISP industry in that it will eventually wipe out the entire bottom layer of the low-price or almost-free ISP pricing model. It is unlikely to replace the fee-based ISP model until the free ISP model is able to deliver expert technical support upon demand and high bandwidth availability—two items that appear impossible to deliver at this time. It will force the average-size ISP to focus on delivering higher-bandwidth broadband solutions, such as DSL, T1, DS3/T3, and ATM, because there will always be businesses that don't have time for monkeying around with free ISPs that may have a hard time returning simple support calls.

ISPs of the future will also have an incredible opportunity to fulfill the enormous needs of small to medium-size businesses that need services such as high-speed dedicated access, virtual private networks (VPNs), e-commerce hosting solutions, remote access, and eventually voice- and fax-over-IP services.

ISPs that serve big businesses will have the ability to supply or become part of the emerging Application Service Provider (ASP) market. More businesses will begin to outsource many of their information technology (IT) department functions, including software, hardware, and networking applications, and ISPs will be in a perfect position to be able to step in and solve their problems. Expect that your service revenue from labor services will increase and, for the first time, even exceed your Internet access fees.

One major roadblock for many ISPs is that they don't have the telecommunications industry expertise to navigate and deliver end-to-end solutions for their business clients. Therefore, ISPs will begin to pair up with competitive local exchange carriers (CLECs); incumbent local exchange carriers (ILECs); and communications, computer equipment, and software value-added resellers (VARs) in an effort to leverage their existing infrastructure for a greater return.

The international ISP scene will be one of opportunity, as less than a third of the world is connected. Here, the international ISPs have the advantage of watching the buying trends of their U.S. counterparts. You can expect many ISPs from the United States to become more involved in international ISP marketplaces utilizing existing international local ISP experts.

Vinton Cerf is famous for championing "The Internet is for everyone." This is not a fad, but a trend you can bank on, especially in the emerging ISP wireless market. Businesses and individuals want Internet access everywhere they go in order to get stock market quotes and execute trades, get news, weather, sports, and other related information in addition to voice/fax and other data communication, regardless as to where they are on Earth.

In conclusion, you can expect that the ISP market will be in high demand for the next decade. Valuations for subscribers will continue to climb. Consolidation will continue to remove major players from the market. The number of ISPs will continue to increase as new niche players set up shop to dominate specific segments of the ISP market. The common voice network will shift from the incumbent telephone companies to the data IP network as Voice Over IP (VOIP) solutions become a reality for ISP deployment. DSL will replace T1 and fractional T1 circuits as the high-speed bandwidth of choice. More ISPs will leverage their reach into their subscriber base by adding major advertising revenue streams. And finally, there is no better time to be a part of the ISP industry if you've got the cash, persistence, drive, and determination to succeed.

ISP Business Plan Sample

By Jason Zigmont, jason@howtosell.net, www.howtosell.net

Note: QEI.net is a fictitious company. All the information in this ISP Business Plan Sample has been provided as a model. Any and all data including pricing, market conditions, and competition are for modeling only. It is strongly recommended that those readers using the ISP Business Plan Sample as a model for their own plan access current statistics.

Business Plan

Date _____

Contact:
James Doe
President
100 Main Street
Berlin, CT 06037
Phone (860) 555-0000
Fax (860) 555-0101
E-mail *jdoe@QEI.net*
www.QEI.net/

The content of this report is confidential and is the sole property of QEI.net. Its use is strictly limited to those readers authorized by the company. Any reproduction or divulgence of the content of this report without the written consent of the company is strictly prohibited.

TABLE OF CONTENTS

Executive Summary

Business Concept and Mission Statement

QEI.net was founded in 1998 by James Doe to provide Internet service to niche markets that have been neglected by other ISPs. The company's stated philosophy is to provide unmatched service on a personal level to end users while maintaining profitability. By designing a scalable internal structure, QEI.net will be "Putting the service back in Internet Service Provider."

Internet Service Providers have been around since the late 1980s and have developed and matured into a heavy-growth market. The company will provide dial-up access to the Internet with quality personal service which is lacking in the current Internet market.

QEI.net will specifically market to Connecticut's extensive middle- to upper-income population and small office/home office (SOHO) market. This niche is willing to pay a premium price for the premium service QEI.net is offering. From a competitive standpoint, this is currently an untapped market. Importantly, this niche is not as strongly affected by price or offers for free Internet access.

Operating Plan Summary

QEI.net will provide the highest level of service and customer satisfaction through rigid adherence to established procedures and an ongoing process of evaluation and improvement. All of QEI.net's staff will be trained to answer both customer service issues and technical questions—something very few providers offer.

The company will provide reliable dial-up Internet access through its relationship with XYZ provider. The company decided to partner with XYZ rather than do the connectivity in-house because outsourcing dial-up is more cost-efficient and provides a more robust and reliable solution.

Marketing Plan Summary

QEI.net's product will be marketed to middle- and upper-income residential users and small office/home office users. The company's sales will be sufficient to break even and gain a market share of 5,000 users in the first planning year. This plan includes intensive customer interaction to foster additional word-of-mouth sales, the largest source of sales for ISPs, and to consequently bring down the cost to acquire customers.

Financial Plan Summary

Mr. Doe will provide the initial $150,000 of working capital that the company needs through its crucial first year. The company feels that with adequate controls, QEI.net's sales figures and cash budget can be maintained, resulting in annual sales of $772,533.25 and a cash balance of $107,875.09 at the end of planning year one.

Business Description

Business Name and Location

Business Name:	Quick Easy Internet (QEI.net)
Legal Name:	Quick Easy Internet
Location:	100 Main Street Berlin, CT 06037
Telephone:	(860) 555-0000
Fax:	(860) 555-0101
Contact Person:	Mr. James Doe

Business History

QEI.net is a start-up Internet Service Provider. Located in Berlin, Connecticut, the company was founded on October 1, 1999, by James Doe, its president, and is legally incorporated in Delaware.

Business Concepts and Mission Statement

QEI.net was founded to provide Internet service to niche markets that have been neglected by other ISPs. The company's stated philosophy is to profitably provide an unmatched level of service on a personal level to end users. By designing a scalable internal structure, QEI.net will "Put the *service* back in Internet Service Provider."

QEI.net will specifically market to Connecticut's extensive middle- to upper-income population, and Connecticut's small office/home office (SOHO) market. This niche is willing to pay a premium for the premium service QEI.net is offering. From a competitive standpoint, this is currently an untapped market.

QEI.net expects this commitment to personal service to increase word-of-mouth sales, and to therefore lower customer acquisition costs and raise profits. QEI.net will then up-sell its existing loyal user base to raise the average ticket size per user.

Market and Target Customer Group

QEI.net is an Internet Service Provider, SIC code 7375, and provides Internet connectivity to business and residential users. There are currently 5,078 national and local ISPs in North America according to *Boardwatch*, Directory of Providers, October 1999. QEI.net's competitors include national providers such as AOL, MindSpring, and Prodigy, but more directly local providers such as RCN, SNET Internet, DSL.net, and Netplex.

ISPs traditionally market to individuals who have a high level of disposable income and a need for Internet access. Overall, approximately 42 percent of adults say there is a personal computer in the home. According to a poll in *USA Today*, October 1998, of the 42 percent of adults with computers, 74 percent have a modem and 65 percent have Internet access.

QEI.net will initially launch its services for planning year one in Connecticut and expand to New York, Massachusetts, and Rhode Island in planning years two and three. Connecticut was chosen because of its lack of strong competition and above-average level of disposable income. Connecticut's current population is 3,274,000, with 1,230,479 occupied households. Connecticut's per capita income of $32,177 is the highest in the United States according the 1992 U.S. Census.

Description of Operations

A combination of somewhat unique but highly successful marketing and operating strategies will be crucial to QEI.net's success. The most important is the commitment to providing quality, responsive service to the end user. QEI.net has arranged agreements with the Internet industry's leading providers to supply reliable, high-speed access to QEI.net users.

QEI.net offers an unprecedented 100 percent service level agreement (SLA) to business and residential users backed up by a 30-day money-back guarantee.

QEI.net's sales strategy continues the company's personal service strategy. QEI.net will have more personal contact than normal with end users, including configuration of the users' computers in their homes or businesses. The company will also use a network of authorized resellers to extend reach and impact.

Management Profile and Needs Assessment

QEI.net's management team consists of the CEO, James Doe; Vice President of Sales and Marketing Jane Smith; and CTO Don Stevens. James Doe earned an MBA from Harvard and brings five years of business experience in the Internet market to the company. Before entering the Internet market, he was a published writer on business issues, specializing in emerging technical companies, including ISPs. Mr. Doe owns 50 percent of QEI.net.

Jane Smith has a BS in marketing from Loyola College and has been in the high-tech industry for the past seven years. During this time, she has held the positions of vice president of marketing, director of product development, and sales manager at multiple companies.

Don Stevens has a BS in computer science from MIT and has been in the Internet market for the past four years. At MIT, Mr. Stevens worked on some of the prototypes for current Internet architectures.

The company's commitment to service is going to require the hiring of an experienced operations manager. This manager will be crucial to expanding QEI.net and will lead to the need for regional managers as QEI.net expands into additional states.

Financial Profile

Mr. Doe has provided all of the current seed money for QEI.net. QEI.net currently has $150,000 in cash reserves, but expects to expend much of that in the first six months of marketing and sales. QEI.net is not an established business and therefore does not have any cash reserves beyond Mr. Doe's investment.

Industry Analysis

Industry Description

The Internet was originally designed by the U.S. Advanced Research Projects Agency (ARPA) for military and educational use in the 1960s and 1970s. In the early 1980s, the face of the Internet changed with the addition of the World Wide Web (WWW), which brought commercialism to the Internet. The WWW and the commercial side of the Internet created a market for retail Internet Service Providers.

ISPs are classified under SIC code 7375, Information Providers. ISPs provide end-user access to the networks of computers that make up what is commonly known as the Internet. These computers are interconnected to help disseminate information and enable commerce and business transactions.

The ISP market has changed greatly since its inception and continues to change daily. Decisions by the Federal Communications Commission (FCC) and local Public Utilities Commissions (PUCs) threaten to change the face of the Internet completely. New technologies are being developed, and support for digital subscriber lines (DSL), cable modems, and wireless access is growing.

Some technologies are not feasible for ISPs to implement. Currently, cable access is only available from cable companies because they are not required to provide open access to their facilities. Groups such as the OpenNet Coalition and ISP/C are lobbying for cable access and may change the availability to ISPs.

Keeping up with the changes in the ISP market is one of the hardest challenges of being an ISP. These changes mandate that ISPs have to constantly upgrade equipment and take a loss on the capital equipment they own. Not only are there technical issues, but with each new technology, ISP marketing and business practices change.

Currently, the market consists of two main segments: business and residential users. Residential users use low-speed 56Kbps analog dial-up and 128K ISDN service. Businesses connect both by dial-up and digital fractional and full T-1s at up to 1.544Mbps speed, and even by DS-3 and OC-3 connections at 45Mbps and 155Mbps speeds, respectively.

Industry Competition

The market for ISPs has evolved from a market in which a company that was originally a bulletin board system (BBS) was the only provider in the area to a variety of ISPs providing dial-up access in a given area. This variety ranges from the mom-and-pop shops, which are usually technocentric people, to the regional and national providers, which tend to be more businesslike and less technically adept.

Many of the existing local providers started as hobby ventures that eventually turned into businesses. Local providers tend to be run by technical people who started the ISP to provide access to their friends or who originally ran free BBSs. As a result, local providers generally tend to provide good connections but lack the business and marketing skills. Usually, local providers are smaller and have a smaller coverage area, which leads to trouble growing into a sustainable business.

Beyond technical strength, local providers tend to be able to offer better personal service because they have a lower total user base. There is a trend with new local providers to become *virtual ISPs* or *VISPs*. These providers tend to be run by business-oriented people. QEI.net could be classified as a VISP since it outsources the most essential technical duties.

Local providers in Connecticut include Kilroy's Internet at ~1,000 subscribers; Cyberzone at ~3,500 subscribers; Connix, which recently sold to Business Online, at ~7,500 subscribers; and Netplex at ~10,000 subscribers. (All subscriber numbers are approximate based on research done by Mr. Doe.)

Regional and national providers, in comparison with local providers, tend to be more business oriented and have only the base-level technical knowledge required at an ISP. In general, regional and national providers are larger and have a greater coverage area than local providers. Regional and national providers have been very successful at mass marketing and adding users, but due to their size have lost the personal touch and personal service that users want.

Some regional/national providers who service Connecticut include Southern New England Telephone (SNET) Internet at ~150,000 subscribers; RCN/Erols at ~500,000 subscribers; Prodigy at ~550,000 subscribers; Earth-Link at ~3,000,000 subscribers; NetZero at 1,700,000 subscribers; and America Online (AOL) at 16,000,000 subscribers.

The ISP end-user pricing model has been somewhat determined by the market and has evolved into the "$19.95 Unlimited Access Model." This model is a misnomer. Users do not truly have unlimited access. QEI.net is positioning itself as a high-quality, high-service provider and will charge 20 percent more than industry average in return for a higher quality of service. (It will charge $23.95 per month for residential dial-up access.)

Recently, an ad-supported free model has become a strong competitor in the low-end dial-up market. QEI.net's higher quality will allow QEI.net to stay out of the price wars and will allow the company to stand out from the crowd.

QEI.net is going to position itself as a local provider with exceptional personal service while positioning itself to become a regional/national provider. Therefore, the company's direct competitors will be the local providers and national providers, such as EarthLink, which at this point provides the best national service in the United States.

As it grows, QEI.net will continue its commitment to provide quality, personalized service in two ways:

- By training its support people to handle both customer service and technical support issues to help users solve their problems quickly

- By segmenting the company's user base so that users deal with the same group of customer service or technical support personnel each time they call

Industry Growth and Sales Projections

As Internet acceptance and reliance on the Internet has grown, the market of people who want to be on the Internet has grown exponentially and will continue to grow exponentially. The rapid growth and development of the Internet industry has resulted in a large number of services being offered by 5,078 national and local providers in North America per the October 1999 *Boardwatch* Directory of Service Providers.

While the ISP market has undergone some consolidation in the past two years, the actual number of ISPs has grown. Consolidation in the ISP market is due to multiple factors. Many of the local ISPs are having trouble independently financing and running their businesses and therefore are looking toward regional and national providers to purchase them and rid them of their business problems. Regional and national providers are looking to grow as fast as possible to gain market share and are looking to acquire local providers. But users do not like being bought and sold. Every time a local provider is sold, it provides an opportunity for other providers to gain the users who do not like being sold. This belief is proven in the fact that in most acquisitions, ISPs loose between 20 and 30 percent of their subscriber base during the transition.

International Data Corporation (IDC) estimates that by the end of 2002 the number of Internet users will be over 135 million in the United States, a 29 percent compound annual growth rate since 1997. In addition to this growth rate, there will be an average 3 percent overall *churn* each month. This churn number is the number of users who switch ISPs every month. New ISPs, such as QEI.net, benefit from the growth of Internet users as well as the users who leave other providers each month.

The bulk of revenue for an ISP currently comes from Internet access, but there is a trend toward gaining additional revenue from value-added services. Forrester Research (Forrester) projects that revenue from Internet access services in the United States will grow from $4.7 billion in 1997 to $15.3 billion in 2001. A 1997 Jupiter Communications Research report projected that independent ISPs would serve approximately 79 percent of the households with Internet access in the United States.

An October 1998 *USA Today* poll found that about 42 percent of adults say there is a personal computer in the home. Of the 42 percent of adults with computers, 74 percent have a modem and 65 percent have Internet access. The poll also stated that in households with an income of over $75,000/year, which encompasses a majority of Connecticut households, the number of homes with a PC is over 75 percent.

Market Analysis

Market Area and Market Sales Potential

QEI.net's target market will initially consist of the state of Connecticut. Connecticut is the third-smallest state in the United States and has a population of 3,274,000. Connecticut's per capita income of $32,177 per person ranks number one in the United States, according to the 1992 U.S. Census. This high per capita income provides for a high average level of disposable income and an average household income of around $65,000/year.

An average household income of $65,000 puts the percentage of households with computers at 57 percent. There are 1,230,479 occupied households in Connecticut. An average of 57 percent of households in Connecticut with computers yields a target market of 701,373 households. On average, 74 percent of those households with computers have modems, or 519,016, and 65 percent, or 455,892, have Internet access.

Connecticut's relatively small size, a mere 4,862 square miles, allows contact to be made with all 156 towns. Connecticut's close proximity to New York City has created a large population of commuters who live in southern Connecticut's Fairfield County and work in NYC. On average, residents of Fairfield County have an income of over $125,000.

Hartford, Connecticut, is the insurance capital of the world. This provides for a large amount of employees who make greater than $40,000 yearly and provides a ready market for premium services.

Groton, Connecticut, and the surrounding areas are heavily dependent on defense contracts. With the reduction in defense spending in the United States, this could have a negative impact on QEI.net's sales in that specific area.

Locating QEI.net's headquarters in Berlin, Connecticut, allows for low-cost office space and a centralized location. Berlin is the geographical center of the state and within short driving distance of Massachusetts, Rhode Island, and New York, all logical locations for expansion of the company's services.

Target Market Description

The company's target market consists of residential customers, and small office/home office (SOHO) customers who are looking for quality service and are willing to pay for it. QEI.net expects 90 percent of its business to come from residential customers and 10 percent from SOHO customers. This market has currently been buying from value-priced providers but at the expense of service downtime, busy signals, and bad service.

A survey of business users showed that price is the fifth most important concern when choosing an ISP. Connection availability, network performance, network capacity, and mean time to repair were ranked before price in ZDNet's 1998 ISP ratings. Surveys of residential customers have given the same or similar results.

Some small to medium-size ISPs have adopted the service model with a price higher than $19.95 unlimited access. Those ISPs that do tend to have fewer customers, but have a higher profit margin and a higher profit overall when compared to their $19.95 competitors.

In order to reach customers looking for a premium service, the company will focus on the areas in Connecticut with higher average incomes. QEI.net will work with companies to provide premier Internet access to their employees, offer special arrangements to civic organizations, and partner with resellers while the company's own sales force reaches SOHOs. QEI.net has already secured multiple essential relationships to kick start the company's sales.

QEI.net's reseller plan includes provisions to train and update resellers monthly on changes in QEI.net's services. QEI.net also plans to hold cooperative seminars at the resellers' and partners' locations, resulting in publicity for QEI.net and its partners.

The company will offer unsurpassed individual service, including set up of end users' machines in their homes through its network of support installers. This is an important tool in keeping the personal touch and helping users who are new to the Internet get online and orientated with the Internet.

Market Competition

In Connecticut the provider with the largest amount of known users is a division of the local Incumbent Local Exchange Carrier (ILEC), Southern New England Telephone (SNET). SNET Internet currently has approximately 150,000 users and offers access throughout, and only in, the state of Connecticut. SNET Internet, primarily a telephone company, has a reputation for bad service but gains privileges that other ISPs cannot have. While some of these privileges may not be legal or allowed by the PUC or FCC, they still exist. Such privileges include better install times, better line quality, and advertising and billing on the user's telephone bill.

America Online is the national provider with the largest impact in Connecticut, although the number of users that AOL has within Connecticut is unknown. AOL focuses on getting new users online. AOL used its size through mass distribution of start-up software and remains a tough competitor. AOL is a slow service with subpar customer service but is a good ISP for beginners because its software is very easy to use.

RCN, which acquired Connecticut ISPs Erols, JavaNet, and NAI, has been increasing marketing in Connecticut and currently has approximately 75,000 customers. RCN is looking to become a customer's complete service provider by offering telephone, cable, and Internet service. RCN's service receives mixed reviews, but is currently the best in Connecticut.

There are many local providers that service Connecticut, but not one of them claims a significant market share. Netplex and Connix both have very good personal service, but lack the marketing and capital to grow into a large ISP. Still, their relatively small sizes make them competitors because they provide quality service.

QEI.net will position itself to compete with the regional and national providers by providing local provider service on a wide-scale level. By marketing against the national providers and providing a high level of service, including a service level agreement, the company expects to be able to sign up those users who have had bad service with the national providers. QEI.net will also use its value-added services, currently consisting of value-added e-mail, to entice customers. For $5.00 per month and a registration fee with Internic, customers can have their e-mail addresses as @theirdomain.com.

Sales Forecast

The company conservatively estimates that by the end of planning year one, it will have 4,000 56K dial-up customers, 500 128K ISDN customers, and 500 virtual domain hosting customers. This will result in revenues of $772,543.25 in planning year one. This will also result in monthly recurring revenue of $145,800 at the end of planning year one. A full sales forecast is available in the appendix in Table A.1.

Marketing Plan

Marketing Plan Summary

The QEI.net marketing plan outlines the strategy that will be used to market the company's services and set marketing controls. QEI.net's product will be marketed to middle- and upper-income residential users and small office/home office users. The company's marketing should be sufficient to break even and to gain a market share of 5,000 users in the first year.

Situational Review

The market.   Approximately 42 percent of households in the United States have one or more computers in the home. In Connecticut, approximately 57 percent of the households have one or more computers. Approximately 74 percent of these computer users have modems and 65 percent have Internet access. This makes for a total of approximately 519,016 potential Internet users in Connecticut.

The majority of users with Internet access are middle- and upper-income consumers. Their motivations for purchase are as follows:

- To enhance communication capabilities by using e-mail, IRC, and other forms of electronic communications
- To research and buy products online

- For recreation
- For educational uses
- For business uses

User sign-up.   The main method of user sign-up of end users will be through direct contact with end users. End users will be able to sign up via telephone, online via a Web page, via fax, or through QEI.net's sign-up server. The company will also use resellers and referral programs through computer stores, video stores, affinity groups, and employee benefit programs.

The competition.   The intention to mass market QEI.net's services will put the company in direct competition with national providers with established brands. Management conservatively estimates that the company's high level of service and guarantees will allow the company to gain market share of ~1 percent for a total of 5,000 users during its first year. Customer surveys and interviews substantiate these estimates.

Strategic Opportunities and Threats

The company's business model offers the following strategic advantages and opportunities:

- Consumers have shown in multiple surveys that they are willing to pay a premium price for quality service.
- QEI.net has a significant advantage over its competitors. The company's product guarantees end users quality of service (QoS) via a service level agreement (SLA) of 100 percent uptime and no busy signals. A SLA provides a means for users to receive a prorated amount of money for service problems or interruptions. SLAs have been offered to large business users but never to SOHO users and residential users.
- SLAs and guaranteed QoS are required in many up and coming Internet services such as voice-over-IP and Internet Teleconferencing.
- A high level of service is proven to increase word-of-mouth sales and referrals. Most ISPs state that the majority of their sales come from word of mouth. Once the company acquires 5,000 users in its first year, customer acquisition costs will decrease. Quality service will also help to lower the company's churn rate.
- QEI.net currently has a high level of marketing expertise that will speed time to market for the company's products.

- QEI.net currently has signed deals with computer stores, affinity groups, and a large insurance company to promote its services.

- Additional value-added services, such as e-mail at virtual domains.

The company's business model faces the following strategic threats:

- QEI.net has no established reputation or brand in the Connecticut market.

- QEI.net's competitors already have an established brand and foothold in the market.

- Competitors could realign their offerings to offer a higher level of service and offer SLAs to end users.

- QEI.net's price is higher than its competitors.

Marketing Goals

- Given QEI.net's stated dial-up price of $23.95 per month per user, the company's goal is $100,000 gross profit in planning year one.

- Capture 1 percent of the target market, or 5,000 users, during planning year one.

- Generate sales revenue of $750,000 in year one, and a monthly recurring revenue stream of $145,000 per month by end of year one.

- Conduct a wide-scale advertising program to build brand awareness, product awareness, and gain additional users.

- Expand the number of resellers, affinity groups, and companies who offer the company's services by 10 percent monthly.

- Increase average ticket size to $30 per month per user by up-selling additional services, higher-speed connections, and training.

Marketing Strategy

The important features of the marketing strategy of QEI.net are as follows:

Target market.   Upscale households with middle- to upper-incomes and small offices/home offices. Particularly homes and offices with computers and modems.

Positioning.   The QEI.net service has a strong advantage over competitors. The company's product guarantees end users quality of service (QoS) via a service level agreement (SLA) of 100 percent uptime and no busy signals. SLAs and guaranteed QoS are required in many up and coming Internet services such as voice-over-IP and Internet Teleconferencing.

Product. Initial entry into the consumer market will be with dial-up access, 56K analog and 128K ISDN, and Web hosting. In addition to dial-up and Web hosting, QEI.net, through its partnership with Critical Path, will be able to offer value-added e-mail services. As the need for higher-speed services increases, QEI.net will offer partial and full T-1s and, where available, XDSL services.

Service. All of QEI.net's products are backed by a no busy signal guarantee, a 100 percent uptime service level agreement, and money-back guarantee. Beyond technical service superiority, QEI.net will offer unsurpassed customer service and technical support. The company will offer guaranteed hold times of less than three minutes for customer service or technical support. Initially, QEI.net will offer 9 A.M. to 9 P.M. staffed support, with after-hours support via a pager system. As QEI.net grows, and demand increases, the company will go to a staffed 24 by 7 support center.

Price. Standard pricing will be as follows:

- Analog (56K) dial-up $23.95/month
- ISDN (128K) dial-up $50.00/month
- Dedicated dial-up (24 by 7 connection) $100.00/month
- Virtual domain name hosting $50.00/month
- Additional e-mail box $5.00/month

All accounts include five e-mail boxes with POP3, SMTP, and Web Mail access, and 10 megs of hard drive space for user Web pages. User Web pages have a 0.5GB transfer limit per month. Virtual domain hosting accounts have a 2GB limit and are aimed toward businesses. Users may have their e-mail @ their vanity domain for an additional $5 per month. Dial-up accounts are unmetered connections with a daily limit of six hours/day or 180 hours per month. All accounts have a $25 setup fee.

User sign-up. The main method of sign-up of end users will be through direct contact with end users. End users will be able to sign up via telephone, online via a Web page, via fax, or through our sign-up server. The company will also use resellers and referral programs through computer stores, video stores, affinity groups, and employee benefit programs.

Sales force.   QEI.net will maintain an inside sales force of two people after initial ramp up to target the small office/home office market. The staff will be well trained and experienced and will have the technical knowledge to sell the products and provide tier-one support. QEI.net will also have a staff of well-trained customer service reps/technical support reps who will handle inbound sales for residential users. In addition to QEI.net's own sales force, through our partner and reseller relationships, we could gain as many as 10 more in the first year.

Promotion.   QEI.net's entry into the market will be accompanied by an intense six-month campaign consisting of aggressively seeking partners to promote the company's services; weekly training sessions and informative seminars taught by QEI.net staff; direct mailings; and internal sales contests and telemarketing.

Advertising.   Advertising will be strong but localized and will leverage cooperative and barter situations whenever possible. QEI.net's partner program includes co-op marketing dollars in return for 15 percent coverage of the partner's ads. The company has also established a relationship with the local country radio station to barter ads for Internet services, and a similar relationship with a statewide newspaper. The company will also purchase radio ads at local radio stations and display ads in local newspapers during its first six months and cut back to line ads in all newspaper Internet directories with the occasional special advertising blitz.

Marketing Budget

The yearly marketing budget is as follows.

PLANNING MONTH	TOTAL
Flyers and chatchkies	$8,000
Seminars and trade shows	$12,000
Print advertising (display)	$28,000
Print Internet directory line ads	$12,000
Radio advertisement	$30,500
TV advertisement	$36,000
CD-ROMs	$15,000
Direct mail	$15,500
Reseller program and co-op marketing	$12,000
Total Marketing Budget	$170,000

This represents a total $170,000 spent on marketing, or 22 percent of sales. The entire monthly marketing budget is represented in the appendix in Table A.2.

Marketing Controls

The sales and profit performance of QEI.net will be monitored and evaluated on a monthly basis. The primary tool for this is the monthly budget concentrating on the number of new users. Projected monthly values serve as targets against which actual monthly data are compared and evaluated. The monthly comparisons are made by calculating a variance for each budget item. The variances of revenue are calculated at the actual value minus the budgeted value. The variance calculations for expense or outflow items are reversed. Thus, a positive-valued variance indicates a favorable occurrence and a negative-valued variance an unfavorable outcome.

Operating Plan

Operating Plan Summary

This operating plan describes the business concept and operating strategy that will be the primary reasons for QEI.net's success. The high level of service and high level of customer satisfaction will be achieved through rigid adherence to established procedures and an ongoing process of evaluation and improvement.

Situational Review

The company will initially have two bases of operations: one in Berlin, Connecticut, for personnel, and one in Hartford, Connecticut, for equipment and connectivity. The personnel office is 1,000 square feet and is located at 100 Main Street, Berlin, CT. This location was chosen due to favorable rental rates and terms and geographical location in the center of Connecticut, close to all major Connecticut interstate highways. All operational equipment is located at 1 Constitution Plaza in Hartford, CT, at XYZ provider's collocation facility. This location was chosen because it is a carrier-class facility with ample connectivity and telco facilities as well as our relationship with XYZ provider.

Operations

QEI.net's operations are broken into two parts: customer service and technical support and providing Internet connectivity. All of QEI.net's customer service and technical support staff are trained to handle both technical support and customer service. By having staff cross-trained, the company can reassign personnel to technical support or customer service dependent on call overflow. When users call in to sign up, they speak with a customer service representative (CSR) who takes all of their billing information and inputs it into the billing and account creation system. The CSR then gives the customer three options (all options are included in the set-up fee):

- The CSR can give them the set-up information over the telephone or via fax for instant access. (For advanced users.)

- Customers can use the CD-ROM that will be sent out priority mail to get set up. (For novice users. All users are sent a CD-ROM of useful software that will set up their machines.)

- Customers can set up a time for a technical representative to come to their homes or businesses within three days and set up their computers. (For beginning users.) Site visits will be limited to one hour, and the user's computer must be fully set up and located in a room that has a working telephone connection before the technician arrives. Any time past one hour will be billed at a rate of $50 per hour.

QEI.net includes on-site setup for end users within the setup fee. QEI.net will have a network of employees and partners who will go to the users' homes or businesses, set up their machines, orient them with the company. The company does this to extend its commitment to quality service and reduce technical support calls. In breaking it down to three choices, the company has found that experienced users will call technical support less often, and the start-up CD-ROM coupled with on-site setup helps to limit technical support calls until there is a problem truly out of the customer's hands.

The company has the added advantage of being located in an area with an ample workforce and a local college, CCSU, located only 10 minutes away. All support personnel will be trained and hired by Mr. Stevens and the operations manager.

Initially both technical and customer support will be available only from 9 A.M. to 9 P.M., with a pager system for after hours with on-call support personnel. As the user base grows and demand increases, the company will move to a staffed 24 by 7 support center.

QEI.net's CTO will handle all high-end Internet connectivity issues. Internet connectivity will be provided by multiple means. QEI.net has signed an agreement with XYZ provider to provide wholesale dial-up ports. In researching dial-up solutions, Mr. Stevens found that the capital cost and maintenance cost are much higher to do in-house dial-up services than to outsource. The company evaluated multiple providers and tested connect speeds, fast busies, throughput, and price and chose XYZ provider. XYZ provider uses Lucent Portmaster 4 equipment and has multiple redundant connections to UUNet, Cable and Wireless, Sprint, and its own peering agreements.

The company has gone into an agreement with XYZ provider to provide wholesale dial-up ports, QEI.net's own telephone numbers, proxy radius, and reverse address translation of dialupport.qei.net. This agreement allows QEI.net to position itself as owner of its own equipment and controller of its own modem-to-user ratios.

All Internet providers oversell their modems by a certain ratio, which allows providers to make a profit. As a provider grows, it can have a higher user-to-modem ratio, and if the provider is willing to accept busy signals during peak times, it can raise the ratio. For example, AOL, during its peak time, had a ratio of 35:1. Currently, AOL runs a 25:1 ratio. Average ISPs run a 10:1 ratio, with some of the better providers running a 6.5:1 ratio. QEI.net has decided to purchase enough wholesale ports for an operational user-to-modem ratio of 6:1. This, coupled with the 10 percent overage agreement with XYZ provider, will allow the company to provide a no busy signals guarantee.

QEI.net has not signed an exclusive contract and has contingency plans in case XYZ provider runs out of capacity, goes out of business, or otherwise cannot provide service.

The company also has a 100 percent uptime guarantee SLA with XYZ provider for all services purchased from XYZ provider. The company also has an internal policy stating that when user-to-modem ratios reach 5:1, it will order additional modem ports to allow for the 30- to -45-day time period it may take XYZ provider to provision additional phone lines from the local telephone company or competitive local exchange carrier (CLEC).

QEI.net will also purchase rack space and connectivity for its servers, routers, and connections from XYZ provider. Initially, QEI.net will run four Linux boxes, which will run radius authentication, Web services, domain name services, and the company's billing and sign-up services. These boxes will be directly connected via 100 base T Ethernet to XYZ provider. By having multiple boxes and multiple direct connections to XYZ provider, QEI.net can maintain its 100 percent uptime guarantee. As QEI.net grows, it will place routers within its rack space at XYZ provider to provide fractional T-1, full T-1, and even DSL services. All systems are Y2K-compliant and will be backed up daily. Weekly backups will be taken to off-site storage at QEI.net's Berlin, Connecticut, facility.

In order to provide fault-tolerant, reliable, feature-rich e-mail to end users, QEI.net investigated multiple solutions including in-house and outsourcing. The company found that it could not maintain reliability and scalability in-house and therefore chose Critical Path to provide outsourced e-mail. In choosing Critical Path, QEI.net received a SLA from Critical Path and the ability to offer additional features, including Web mail. Web mail will provide an additional revenue source as the company grows. This is a value-added service that costs the company nothing to provide.

Quality Control and Customer Service

Customer service and technical support calls will be tracked within the billing system to provide a way for management to analyze problems and employee effectiveness. Customers will be polled quarterly for their input and ways to make QEI.net better.

The company will monitor all services, including outsourced solutions, 24 by 7 and have the technician on duty paged for remedy. Customers will be notified in advance anytime QEI.net or one of its providers needs to do maintenance that may influence service. This will provide a way to lower the mean time for repair and minimize outages.

QEI.net will also provide for both internal and external examination and utilization graphs of all Internet connectivity and modem usage. Customers will receive a report of uptime and availability on a monthly basis and may then request any moneys they may be due through their SLA. QEI.net will also use the reports of monthly uptime and availability to assess problem areas and what remedies can be taken.

Organization Plan

Organizational Plan Summary

This plan describes the organization structure and key personnel that will be required to support QEI.net's initial launch and sustain QEI.net through the first planning year. Key personnel will be crucial for the expansion of QEI.net into other states in planning years two and three. QEI.net is incorporated in the state of Delaware.

Situational Review

QEI.net's initial organizational structure reflects the limited needs of its single-location operation. An organization chart depicting this basic functional structure is shown in Figure A.1 of the appendix to this plan. James

Doe oversees all company operations as CEO. Jane Smith, VP of sales and marketing, organizes all of the company's sales and marketing. Don Stevens, CTO, handles all high-end technical issues and trains and hires technical staff. The operations manager, whose position is currently open, manages the day-to-day operations and is responsible for customer service and technical support operations.

Management Philosophy

QEI.net's management philosophy stems from Mr. Doe's personal commitment to helping both employees and customers alike. This philosophy is stated best in a quote by noted sales trainer and speaker Zig Ziglar. He states, "You can have everything in life you want if you just help enough other people get what they want."

This philosophy of helping others carries through all areas of the company. In helping end users and the company's employees, QEI.net will be able to retain both end users and quality employees. Retaining quality employees will be one of the hardest challenges for management. The employment market for skilled people with Internet experience is fierce and highly competitive.

Mr. Doe further believes the following:

QEI.net exists to service our customers. QEI.net is here to provide a service to our customers. The company is committed to providing the ultimate in service and reliability to our users. The company wants its users to believe always that they are getting their money's worth, and that they tell others that they believe so.

Employees are the company's most important assets. Hiring and training employees at all levels is essential to providing the company's high level of service and reliability. Without our employees, the company could not keep customers happy and would not have a viable business model.

Good service will be rewarded while bad service will be punished. Service is king at QEI.net. Those employees who constantly provide good service to our end users will be rewarded. Those who do not provide good service are not an asset to the company and will be reprimanded appropriately. The company will also hold weekly meetings that include a 15-minute session on helpful tips to help service customers better. The company will also ask employees to share success stories, tips, and news items which will be good for cross-training as well as morale.

Key-Personnel Assessments

As indicated on the organization structure chart (Figure A.1 in the appendix to this plan), QEI.net's management team consists of the chief executive officer, vice president of sales and marketing, chief technology officer, and an operations manager. A summary of the background and qualifications of each position-holder is given in the following sections.

Chief Executive Officer

James Doe has a BS in management from the University of Georgia and an MBA from Harvard. His five years of business experience in the Internet market include positions as director. More recently, he served as general manager of a successful e-commerce company with a recent successful initial public offering. Before entering the Internet market, he wrote on business issues of growing technical companies, including ISPs.

Vice President of Sales and Marketing

Jane Smith has a BA in marketing from Loyola College and has been in the high-tech industry for the past seven years. During this time, she has held positions as vice president of marketing, director of product development, and sales manager at multiple companies. Ms. Smith has been responsible for the entire marketing of a successful Internet start-up company and has helped organize marketing for an industry trade association and its associated trade show.

Chief Technology Officer

Don Stevens has a BS in computer science from MIT and has been in the Internet market for the past four years. Before working at QEI.net, Mr. Stevens was the systems administrator for one of the largest providers in Connecticut, which later was sold to a national provider. While at that ISP, Mr. Stevens successfully maintained a 99.9 percent uptime, unheard of at that time. At MIT, Mr. Stevens worked on some of the prototypes for current Internet architectures.

Key-Personnel Needs

The key-personnel need currently includes an operations manager. This position is depicted in the organization structure chart in Figure A.1 in the plan's appendix.

Operations Manager

This position-holder will be heavily involved with the day-to-day operations of the company. This individual will manage the day-to-day operations and is responsible for customer service and technical support operations. The individual must possess good managerial skills, an attention to detail, and good customer interaction skills. The individual will be responsible for setting and maintaining schedules, hiring, training, and firing staff, and helping staff with customer problems and problem resolutions. This person must have a bachelor's degree in business or a related area or appropriate experience. This person must also demonstrate good management and interpersonal skills.

Compensation and Incentives

QEI.net's corporate charter authorizes 200,000 shares of common stock. These shares have an assigned par value of $0.50. Only 140,000 shares are outstanding. The distribution of shares is as follows:

James Doe has ownership of 100,000 shares, or 50 percent of the total amount of authorized shares. The total value of these shares represents compensation for Mr. Doe's time, effort, and expertise provided to the business and capital contributed to the company. Mr. Doe also receives a $30,000 per year salary.

Jane Smith, in return for her extensive work in development of the company's sales and marketing program, owns 20,000 shares, or 10 percent of the total amount of authorized shares. Jane Smith also receives a $40,000 per year salary and has performance-based bonuses tied to sales of up to $20,000.

Don Stevens, in return for his extensive work in technical development and research of systems for the company, owns 20,000 shares, or 10 percent of the total amount of authorized shares. Don also receives a $40,000 per year salary and has performance-based bonuses tied to system uptime of up to $20,000.

The operations manager will have stock options and a salary to be determined. Salary and options will be determinate on the experience and skills the operations manager brings to the company.

At the date of this writing, the company has no management contracts or employment agreements outstanding. Mr. Doe fully realizes that in order to attract a qualified person for the planned operations manager position, such considerations may be necessary.

At the date of this writing, QEI.net has no outside members of the board of directors. Mr. Doe has discussed seats on the board with a local venture capitalist and a local financial consultant. Both individuals would bring much expertise and possibly opportunities for financing needed for expansion into additional states and growth of QEI.net. An annual stipend of $5,000 per individual has been discussed as possible compensation for their services.

Financial Plan

Financial Plan Summary

This financial plan outlines the financial strategy that will be used to manage effectively the company's initial growth in sales, cash flows, and earnings over the next year. As discussed in the cash planning sections of this plan, the initial financing provided by Mr. Doe will provide the company with enough support for working capital needs to take the company through its crucial first year. The company feels that with adequate controls, QEI.net's sales figures and cash budget can be maintained and annual sales of $772,533.25 will be achieved with a planning year-ending cash balance of $106,300.15.

Situational Review

Annual financial statements are not available for QEI.net, a start-up with no history. All numbers are based on industry standards and Mr. Doe's experience in the Internet market.

QEI.net's growth from $0 in sales to annual sales of $772,533.25 with a recurring monthly revenue stream of $145,800 will not be an easy task. Budgetary numbers beyond the half-year point rely on sales being on track. Any variance will throw off other parts of the budget. The company feels optimistic that it can make its sales numbers and will end up with a monthly recurring revenue stream of $145,800, allowing the company to expand in its second year.

Financial Goals

The management team of QEI.net has instituted control measures designed to accommodate and anticipate the exponential growth in sales and keep costs down. The company's goals are as follows:

- Achieve monthly recurring sales revenue of $145,800 in the first year
- Maintain a cash-positive budget without soliciting additional funds
- Keep cost of goods down while providing high levels of service

Cash Flow Planning

QEI.net's short-term cash plan was prepared using the cash budget contained in the appendix in Table A.3. The cash flow budget shows the importance of recurring revenue and its effect on the cash in hand. The cash budget also reflects the cash nature of accounts and lack of credit given to end users.

QEI.net will be able to function without outside capital due to the $150,000 Mr. Doe invested initially in QEI.net to get the company through its crucial first year. If sales figures are low, either the budget will have to be adjusted or addition funds secured during the planning months five through seven.

Table A.1 Sales Forecast

PLANNING MONTH	1	2	3	4	5	6
# of Dial-up Accounts Added	50	75	125	160	215	300
Total # of Dial-up Accounts	50	125	250	410	625	925
Dial-up Revenue Total	$1,197.50	$2,993.75	$5,987.50	$9,819.50	$14,968.75	$22,153.75
# of ISDN Accounts Added	5	10	15	20	25	35
Total # of ISDN Accounts	5	15	30	50	75	110
ISDN Revenue Total	$250.00	$750.00	$1,500.00	$2,500.00	$3,750.00	$5,500.00
# of Web Accounts Added	5	10	15	20	25	35
Total # of Web Accounts	5	15	30	50	75	110
Web Revenue Total	$250.00	$750.00	$1,500.00	$2,500.00	$3,750.00	$5,500.00
# of set-up fees	60	95	155	200	265	370
Set-up fee revenue total	$1,500.00	$2,375.00	$3,875.00	$5,000.00	$6,625.00	$9,250.00
Total Monthly Recurring Revenue	$1,697.50	$4,493.75	$8,987.50	$14,819.50	$22,468.75	$33,153.755
Total Monthly Revenue	$3,197.50	$6,868.75	$12,862.50	$19,819.50	$29,093.75	$42,403.75

Financial Controls

Operating costs, sales, and marketing budgets will be monitored on a monthly basis to ensure that the adopted quality control measures remain effective. Should any part of the budget be skewed, management will adjust for the change.

Appendix

7	8	9	10	11	12	TOTAL
375	450	525	550	575	600	4000
1300	1750	2275	2825	3400	4000	4000
$31,135.00	$41,912.50	$54,486.25	$67,658.75	$81,430.00	$95,800.00	$429,543.25
45	55	65	65	75	85	500
155	210	275	340	415	500	500
$7,750.00	$10,500.00	$13,750.00	$17,000.00	$20,750.00	$25,000.00	$109,000.00
45	55	65	65	75	85	500
155	210	275	340	415	500	500
$7,750.00	$10,500.00	$13,750.00	$17,000.00	$20,750.00	$25,000.00	$109,000.00
465	560	655	680	725	770	5000
$11,625.00	$14,000.00	$16,375.00	$17,000.00	$18,125.00	$19,250.00	$125,000.00
$46,635.00	$62,912.50	$81,986.25	$101,658.75	$122,930.00	$145,800.00	$647,543.25
$58,260.00	$76,912.50	$98,361.25	$118,658.75	$141,055.00	$165,050.00	$772,543.25

Table A.2 Marketing Budget

PLANNING MONTH	1	2	3	4	5	6	7	8	9	10	11	12	TOTAL
Flyers and Tchotchkes	1000	500	500	500	500	500	500	500	500	1000	1000	1000	8000
Seminars and Trade Shows	1000	1000	1000	1000	1000	1000	1000	1000	1000	1000	1000	1000	12000
Print Advertising (Display)	3000	2500	2500	2500	2500	2500	2500	2500	1500	2000	2000	2000	28000
Print Internet Directory Line Ads	1000	1000	1000	1000	1000	1000	1000	1000	1000	1000	1000	1000	12000
Radio Advertisement	3000	3000	2500	2500	2500	2500	2500	2500	1500	2000	2000	4000	30500
TV Advertisement									3500	9000	11500	12000	36000
CD Roms	1000	1000	1000	1000	1000	1000	1000	1000	1000	1500	1500	2000	15000
Direct Mail	1500	1500	1500	1000	1000	1000	1000	1000	1500	1500	1500	1500	15500
Reseller Program and Co-op Marketing	1000	1000	1000	1000	1000	1000	1000	1000	1000	1000	1000	1000	12000
Total Marketing Budget	12500	11500	10000	10000	10000	10000	10000	10000	12500	20000	22500	25000	

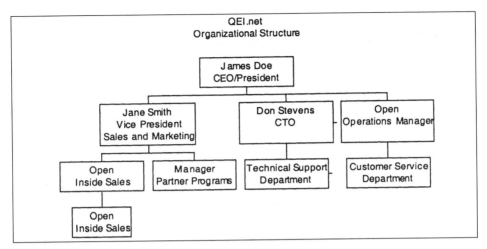

Figure A.1   Organizational structure.

Table A.3 Cash Budget for Pro Forma Planning Year 1

PLANNING MONTH	1	2	3	4	5	6
Total Cash Inflows:	$3,197.50	$6,858.75	$12,862.50	$19,819.50	$29,093.75	$42,403.75
Cash Outflows:						
Cost of Goods Sold	$611.30	$1,477.75	$2,954.85	$4,883.95	$7,387.45	$9,947.95
Wages and Salaries	12,250.01	12,250.01	12,250.01	12,250.01	12,250.01	$17,500.00
Payroll Taxes	$1,470.00	$1,470.00	$1,470.00	$1,470.00	$1,470.00	$2,100.00
Fringe Benefits	$1,715.00	$1,715.00	$1,715.00	$1,715.00	$1,715.00	$2,450.00
Rent & Leases	$2,500.00	$2,500.00	$2,500.00	$2,500.00	$2,500.00	$2,500.00
Utilities	$750.00	$750.00	$750.00	$750.00	$750.00	$750.00
Capital Expenditures	$10,000.00					
Internet Connectivity	$1,000.00	$1,000.00	$1,000.00	$1,000.00	$1,000.00	$1,000.00
Travel and Entertainment	$1,250.00	$1,250.00	$1,250.00	$1,250.00	$1,250.00	$1,250.00
Marketing	$20,000.00	$17,500.00	$15,000.00	$10,000.00	$10,000.00	$10,000.00
Postage and Supplies	$250.00	$250.00	$350.00	$450.00	$500.00	$500.00
Accounting and Legal	$500.00	$500.00	$500.00	$500.00	$500.00	$500.00
Miscellaneous	$500.00	$500.00	$500.00	$500.00	$500.00	$500.00
Total Cash Outflows	$52,796.31	$41,162.76	$40,239.86	$37,268.96	$39,822.46	$48,997.95
Net Cash Flow	−$49,598.81	−$34,304.01	−$27,377.36	−$17,449.46	−$10,728.71	−$6,594.20
Plus: Beg. Cash Balance	$150,000.00	$100,401.19	$66,097.17	$38,719.81	$21,270.35	$10,541.64
Ending Cash Balance	$100,401.19	$66,097.17	$38,719.81	$21,270.35	$10,541.64	$3,947.44

7	8	9	10	11	12	TOTAL
$58,260.00	$76,912.50	$98,361.25	$118,658.75	$141,055.00	$165,050.00	$772,533.25
$13,950.55	$18,783.95	$22,129.45	$27,053.80	$32,667.10	$38,630.00	$180,478.10
$20,500.00	$23,500.00	$28,500.00	$33,500.00	$33,500.00	$33,500.00	$251,750.05
$2,460.00	$2,820.00	$3,420.00	$4,020.00	$4,020.00	$4,020.00	$30,210.01
$2,870.00	$3,290.00	$3,990.00	$4,690.00	$4,690.00	$4,690.00	$35,245.01
$2,500.00	$2,500.00	$3,500.00	$3,500.00	$3,500.00	$3,500.00	$34,000.00
$750.00	$750.00	$750.00	$750.00	$750.00	$750.00	$9,000.00
	$5,000.00		$5,000.00		$5,000.00	$25,000.00
$1,000.00	$1,000.00	$2,000.00	$2,000.00	$2,000.00	$3,000.00	$17,000.00
$1,250.00	$1,250.00	$1,750.00	$2,000.00	$2,250.00	$2,500.00	$18,500.00|
$10,000.00	$12,500.00	$17,500.00	$22,500.00	$25,000.00	$25,000.00	$195,000.00
$500.00	$650.00	$750.00	$850.00	$925.00	$1,000.00	$6,975.00
$500.00	$500.00	$500.00	$500.00	$500.00	$500.00	$6,000.00
$500.00	$500.00	$500.00	$500.00	$500.00	$500.00	$6,000.00
$56,780.55	$73,043.95	$85,289.45	$106,863.80	$110,302.10	$122,590.00	$692,568.16
$1,479.45	$3,868.55	$13,071.80	$11,794.95	$30,752.90	$42,460.00	
$3,947.44	$5,426.89	$9,295.44	$22,367.24	$34,162.19	$64,915.09	
$5,426.89	$9,295.44	$22,367.24	$34,162.19	$64,915.09	$107,375.09	

(continues)

Table A.3 (*Continued*) Wages and Salaries

PLANNING MONTH	1	2	3	4	5	6
Mr. John Doe	$2,000.00	$2,000.00	$2,000.00	$2,000.00	$2,000.00	$2,500.00
Ms. Jane Smith	$3,000.00	$3,000.00	$3,000.00	$3,000.00	$3,000.00	$3,33.33
Mr. Don Stevens	$3,000.00	$3,000.00	$3,000.00	$3,000.00	$3,000.00	$3,33.33
Operations Manager	$3,000.00	$3,000.00	$3,000.00	$3,000.00	$3,000.00	$3,33.33
Technnical Support/ Installer	$1,250.00	$1,250.00	$1,250.00	$1,250.00	$1,250.00	$2,500.00
Customer Service Rep						$2,500.00
Telesales						
Telesales						
Technnical Support/ Installer						
Customer Service Rep						
Technnical Support/ Installer						
Customer Service Rep						
Total Salaries	$12,250.01	$12,250.01	$12,250.01	$12,250.01	$12,250.01	$17,500.00

7	8	9	10	11	12	TOTAL
$2,500.00	$2,500.00	$2,500.00	$2,500.00	$2,500.00	$2,500.00	$27,500.00
$3,333.33	$3,333.33	$3,333.33	$3,333.33	$3,333.33	$3,333.33	$38,333.31
$3,333.33	$3,333.33	$3,333.33	$3,333.33	$3,333.33	$3,333.33	$38,333.31
$3,333.33	$3,333.33	$3,333.33	$3,333.33	$3,333.33	$3,333.33	$38,333.31
$2,500.00	$2,500.00	$2,500.00	$2,500.00	$2,500.00	$2,500.00	$23,750.00
$2,500.00	$2,500.00	$2,500.00	$2,500.00	$2,500.00	$2,500.00	$17,500.00
$3,000.00	$3,000.00	$3,000.00	$3,000.00	$3,000.00	$3,000.00	$18,000.00
	$3,000.00	$3,000.00	$3,000.00	$3,000.00	$3,000.00	$15,000.00
		$2,500.00	$2,500.00	$2,500.00	$2,500.00	$10,000.00
		$2,500.00	$2,500.00	$2,500.00	$2,500.00	$10,000.00
			$2,500.00	$2,500.00	$2,500.00	$7,500.00
			$2,500.00	$2,500.00	$2,500.00	$7,500.00
$20,500.00	$23,500.00	$28,500.00	$33,500.00	$33,500.00	$33,500.00	$251,749.93

Table A.3   (*Continued*) Cost of Goods Sold

Assumptions: 6:1 User:Modem Ratio, 2 e-mail accounts per dial-up account, 2.5 e-mail accounts per ISDN and Web Hosting, 2 megs of HD space, and .1 GB of data transferred per dial-up and 10 megs of HD space and 1 GB data transferred per web hosting.

PLANNING MONTH	1	2	3	4	5
56k Dial-up					
Number of Users	50	125	250	410	625
Number of Ports	9	21	42	69	105
Number of E-mail Accts	100	250	500	820	1250
Megs of hd space	100	250	500	820	1250
GB transferred	5	12.5	25	41	62.5
Cost per port	$45.00	$45.00	$45.00	$45.00	$45.00
Cost per e-mail acct	$0.65	$0.65	$0.65	$0.65	$0.65
Cost per meg hd space	$0.01	$0.01	$0.01	$0.01	$0.01
Cost per GB transferred	$3.00	$3.00	$3.00	$3.00	$3.00
Total port cost	$405.00	$945.00	$1,890.00	$3,105.00	$4,725.00
Total e-mail cost	$65.00	$162.50	$325.00	$533.00	$812.50
Total hd space cost	$1.00	$2.50	$5.00	$8.20	$12.50
Total GB transferred cost	$15.00	$37.50	$75.00	$123.00	$187.50
Total Cost per month	$486.00	$1,147.50	$2,295.00	$3,769.20	$5,737.50
Total Cost per dial-up	$9.72	$9.18	$9.18	$9.19	$9.18
ISDN Dial-up					
Number of Users	5	15	30	50	75
Number of Ports	2	5	10	17	25
Number of E-mail Accts	13	38	75	125	188
Megs of hd space	10	30	60	100	150
GB transferred	0.5	1.5	3	5	7.5
Cost per port	$45.00	$45.00	$45.00	$45.00	$45.00
Cost per e-mail acct	$0.65	$0.65	$0.65	$0.65	$0.65

6	7	8	9	10	11	12
925	1300	1750	2275	2825	3400	4000
155	217	292	380	471	567	667
1850	2600	3500	4550	5650	6800	8000
1850	2600	3500	4550	5650	6800	8000
92.5	130	175	227.5	282.5	340	400
$40.00	$40.00	$40.00	$35.00	$35.00	$35.00	$35.00
$0.65	$0.65	$0.65	$0.65	$0.60	$0.60	$0.60
$0.01	$0.01	$0.01	$0.01	$0.01	$0.01	$0.01
$3.00	$3.00	$3.00	$3.00	$3.00	$3.00	$3.00
$6,200.00	$8,680.00	$11,680.00	$13,300.00	$16,485.00	$19,845.00	$23,345.00
$1,202.50	$1,690.00	$2,275.00	$2,957.50	$3,390.00	$4,080.00	$4,800.00
$18.50	$26.00	$35.00	$45.50	$56.50	$68.00	$80.00
$277.50	$390.00	$525.00	$682.50	$847.50	$1,020.00	$1,200.00
$7,698.50	$10,786.00	$14,515.00	$16,985.50	$20,779.00	$25,013.00	$29,425.00
$8.32	$8.30	$8.29	$7.47	$7.36	$7.36	$7.36
110	155	210	275	340	415	500
37	52	70	92	114	139	167
275	388	525	688	850	1038	1250
220	310	420	550	680	830	1000
11	15.5	21	27.5	34	41.5	50
$40.00	$40.00	$40.00	$35.00	$35.00	$35.00	$35.00
$0.65	$0.65	$0.65	$0.65	$0.60	$0.60	$0.60

Table A.3 (*Continued*) Cost of Goods Sold

PLANNING MONTH	1	2	3	4	5
Cost per meg hd space	$0.01	$0.01	$0.01	$0.01	$0.01
ISDN Dial-up					
Cost per GB transferred	$3.00	$3.00	$3.00	$3.00	$3.00
Total port cost	$90.00	$225.00	$450.00	$765.00	$1,125.00
Total e-mail cost	$8.45	$24.70	$48.75	$81.25	$122.20
Total hd space cost	$0.10	$0.30	$0.60	$1.00	$1.50
Total GB transferred cost	$1.50	$4.50	$9.00	$15.00	$22.50
Total Cost per month	$100.05	$254.50	$508.35	$862.25	$1,271.20
Total Cost Per ISDN	$20.01	$16.97	$16.95	$17.25	$16.95
Web Hosting					
Number of Users	5	15	30	50	75
Megs of hd space	50	150	300	500	750
GB transferred	5	15	30	50	75
Number of E-mail Accts	15	45	90	150	225
Cost per meg hd space	$0.01	$0.01	$0.01	$0.01	$0.01
Cost per GB transferred	$3.00	$3.00	$3.00	$3.00	$3.00
Cost per e-mail acct	$0.65	$0.65	$0.65	$0.65	$0.65
Total hd space cost	$0.50	$1.50	$3.00	$5.00	$7.50
Total GB transferred cost	$15.00	$45.00	$90.00	$150.00	$225.00
Total e-mail cost	$9.75	$29.25	$58.50	$97.50	$146.25
Total Cost per month	$25.25	$75.75	$151.50	$252.50	$378.75
Cost per hosting account	$5.05	$5.05	$5.05	$5.05	$5.05
Total Variable COGS	$611.30	$1,477.75	$2,954.85	$4,883.95	$7,387.45

6	7	8	9	10	11	12
$0.01	$0.01	$0.01	$0.01	$0.01	$0.01	$0.01
$3.00	$3.00	$3.00	$3.00	$3.00	$3.00	$3.00
$1,480.00	$2,080.00	$2,800.00	$3,220.00	$3,990.00	$4,865.00	$5,845.00
$178.75	$252.20	$341.25	$447.20	$510.00	$622.80	$750.00
$2.20	$3.10	$4.20	$5.50	$6.80	$8.30	$10.00
$33.00	$46.50	$63.00	$82.50	$102.00	$124.50	$150.00
$1,693.95	$2,381.80	$3,208.45	$3,755.20	$4,608.80	$5,620.60	$6,755.00
$15.40	$15.37	$15.28	$13.66	$13.56	$13.54	$13.51
110	155	210	275	340	415	500
1100	1550	2100	2750	3400	4150	5000
110	155	210	275	340	415	500
330	465	630	825	1020	1245	1500
$0.01	$0.01	$0.01	$0.01	$0.01	$0.01	$0.01
$3.00	$3.00	$3.00	$3.00	$3.00	$3.00	$3.00
$0.65	$0.65	$0.65	$0.65	$0.60	$0.60	$0.60
$11.00	$15.50	$21.00	$27.50	$34.00	$41.50	$50.00
$330.00	$465.00	$630.00	$825.00	$1,020.00	$1,245.00	$1,500.00
$214.50	$302.25	$409.50	$536.25	$612.00	$747.00	$900.00
$555.50	$782.75	$1,060.50	$1,388.75	$1,666.00	$2,033.50	$2,450.00
$5.05	$5.05	$5.05	$5.05	$4.90	$4.90	$4.90
$9,947.95	$13,950.55	$18,783.95	$22,129.45	$27,053.80	$32,667.10	$38,630.00

ISP Business Resources

Before you invest in a highly paid ISP consultant, you may wish to refer to the dozens of extremely valuable free or low-cost ISP resources in the following list. Many of these services and resources provide keen insights into every aspect of the ISP industry. This list was carefully selected; however, for every listing provided, at least a half dozen additional resources can be found. This list attempts to provide the best of the best here. Please be aware that technical and engineering ISP resources have been omitted on purpose. (ISP technical resources can be found in Huston, *ISP Survival Guide: Strategies for Running a Competitive ISP,* John Wiley & Sons, ISBN: 0-471-31499-4.) Enjoy!

ISP Media Sites: Editorial, Opinion, Debate, and Community

internet.com's **ISP-Planet.com** (http://ISP-Planet.com/). The Intelligence Center for the ISP Community offers daily editorial insight, commentary, and opinions about every aspect of the ISP industry. Many high-profile authors and ISP insiders contribute a weekly or monthly column to this resource.

internet.com's ISP-News (http://internetnews.com/isp-news/). This site delivers news coverage on the latest products, technologies, and services relevant to Internet Service Providers and their customers.

The ISP-Lists E-mail Discussion List Community (http://ISP-Lists.com/). This is an excellent gathering place for tens of thousands of people who discuss more than 40 different ISP-related topics from business, marketing, to CLECs, technology, and more!

Jason Zigmont's HowToSell.net (www.howtosell.net/). This site provides daily and weekly editorial insights into ISP sales, marketing, and management resources.

Tucows's ISP News Site (http://ispcentral.tucows.com/index/).

Mike Cassidy's ISP Portal (www.isportal.com/). This site will keep you on top of the ISP news stories, press releases, white papers, and buyer's guides.

David's Amazing ISP FAQ (www.amazing.com/internet/). This is one of the older ISP resources and includes many ISP technology-related links and resources.

Microsoft's ISP Industry Resource Guide (www.microsoft.com/isn/isp/default.asp). This site tracks ISP industry trends, product and company news, and exclusive insight into Microsoft Internet services and strategies.

So You Wanna Be An ISP? (www.vicnet.net.au/help/tips/ISP/isp.htm). An Australian perspective with excellent ISP resource links.

Inet-Access E-mail Discussion List. To join, send an e-mail to list-request@ inet-access.net with *subscribe* in the body.

ISP Financial Media or Business Sites

I$P Media Business Corporation (www.ispreport.com/). This subsidiary of Rampart Associates produces the monthly *I$P Report.*

Wall Street Research News (WSRN)'s INTERNET ISP/ACCESS INDEX: ISPS.I (www1.wsrn.com/links/l.cgi?symbol=ISPS).

ISP-Investor Discussion List (ISP-Investor.com/).

MCG Credit Corporation (www.mcgcredit.com). This corporation publishes a free-distribution newsletter that covers mergers and acquisitions, and valuation trends in the broader communications industry.

Major ISP Trade Shows and Conferences

Penton Media's ISPCON (www.ispcon.com/)
First Conferences Ltd.'s The ISP Forum (www.theispforum.com/)

Internet Service Providers Consortium's (ISP/C) ISP Forum (www.ispf .com/)

Penton Media's ISP World division of Internet World (www.internet-world.com/)

ISP Trade Magazines

Penton Media's *Boardwatch* Magazine (www.boardwatch.com/)
ZD's *Inter@ctive Week* (www.interactiveweek.com)
Penton Media's *Internet World* Magazine (www.internetworld.com/)

ISP Organizations and Associations
National (United States)

Internet Service Providers Consortium (ISP/C) (www.ispc.org/) Small to medium-size ISPs
Internet Service Provider Business Forum (www.ispbf.org/) Medium to large ISPs
CIX: The Commercial Internet eXchange Association (www.cix.org/) Medium to large ISPs
openNET Coalition (www.opennetcoalition.org/) Fighting for broadband rights
United States Internet Providers Association (www.usipa.org/)
CAUCE, The Coalition Against Unsolicited Commercial Email (www .cauce.org/)
The North American Network Operators' Group (www.nanog.org)

Regional (United States)

The California Internet Service Providers Association (www.cispa.org/)
Coalition of Utah ISPs (www.cuiisp.org/)
Colorado Internet Cooperative Association (www.coop.net/)
Florida Internet Service Provider's Association (www.fispa.org/)
Internet Providers Association of Iowa (www.ipai.org/)
Minnesota Internet Services Trade Association (www.mista.org/)
Mississippi ISP Association (www.mispa.org/)
New Mexico Internet Professionals Association (www.nmipa.org/)
Oregon ISP Association (www.orispa.org/)
Texas Internet Service Provider's Association (www.tispa.org/)

Virginia ISP Alliance (www.vispa.org/)
Washington Association of ISPs (www.waisp.org/)
Wisconsin Internet Service Providers (www.wsta-net.org/)

International ISP Trade Associations

Asia Pacific Internet Association (www.apia.org/)
Australia's Internet Industry Association (www.iia.net.au/)
South Australian Internet Association Incorporated (www.saia.asn.au/)
Tasmanian Internet Association (www.tia.asn.au/)
Western Australian Internet Association (www.waia.asn.au/)
Service Providers Industry Association—Australia (www.span.net.au/)
ISPA Austria (www.ispa.at/)
Internet Service Provider Association Belgium (www.ispa.be/)
The British Columbia Internet Association (www.bcia.bc.ca/)
Canadian Association of ISPs (www.caip.ca/)
European ISP/C Mirror site (www.euro.ispc.org/)
EuroISPA, the pan-European association of the Internet Services Providers Associations of the countries of the European Union (www.euroispa.org/)
EuroISPA (http://euro.ispa.org.uk/)
Irish Internet Association (www.iia.ie/)
Italian ISPA (www.itb.it/ispa/)
Internet Association of Japan (www.iaj.or.jp/iaj/index-e.html)
The Internet Service Providers Association of South Africa (www.ispa.org.za/)
Internet Services Providers Association of the United Kingdom (www.ispa.org.uk/)

Get Your ISP Listed for Free Exposure

internet.com's The List (http://thelist.internet.com/). The definitive buyer's guide to Internet Service Providers. The List allows you to find a provider that offers the access speed and computing services that satisfy your needs and budget.
Barkers.org's ISP National Access Guide (www.barkers.org/online/). Online connection comparing national ISPs and online services.
Providers of Commercial Internet Access (POCIA) (www.celestin.com/pocia/).

1-888-ISP-FIND (http://ispfinder.com/). The easy way to find a local service provider.

Internet Access Providers Meta-List (www.herbison.com/herbison/iap_meta_list.html). Hundreds of pointers to resources for finding Internet access providers and information on how to select a provider, with separate pages for all U.S. states, Canadian provinces, and over one hundred countries.

Yahoo! (http://dir.yahoo.com/Business and Economy/Companies/Internet Services/Access Providers/Directories/). Yahoo! publishes an excellent link to many of the ISP access lists.

Network-USA (www.netusa.net/ISP/). WWW-based Internet Service Providers catalog has an international listing of ISPs.

Boardwatch's ISP list (http://boardwatch.internet.com/isp/ispform.html).

The Directory (www.thedirectory.org/). The directory of Internet Service Providers, Web-hosting companies and bulletin board systems.

The Ultimate ISP List (www.internetlist.com/).

The ReCellar (www.recellar.com/). Web hosting.

C | Net's Ultimate Web ISP List (webisplist.internetlist.com/).

ISP Industry Research Analysts

internet.com's AllNetResearch (www.allnetresearch.com/). The superstore for Internet research.

The Burton Group (www.tbg.com/). Focuses on analysis of emerging network-computing technologies.

Cahners In-Stat Group (www.instat.com/). Helping you make better business decisions through real-time research.

internet.com's CyberAtlas (http://cyberatlas.internet.com/). Internet statistics and market research for Web marketers.

Forrester Research (www.forrester.com/). Helping business thrive on technology changes.

Gartner Group (http://gartner11.gartnerweb.com/public/static/home/home.html). Access to extensive collection of IT research and analysis.

International Data Corporation (www.idc.com/). The industry's most comprehensive resource on worldwide IT markets.

META Group (www.metagroup.com/). IT research and unlimited analyst consultation.

NUA Internet Surveys (www.nua.ie/surveys/). Often covering the online/ISP access industry.

Patricia Seybold Group (www.psgroup.com/). Strategic technology and business solutions.

StatMarket (www.statmarket.com/). Accurate Internet statistics and user trends in real time. A WebSideStory production.

Yankee Group (www.yankeegroup.com/). Strategic planning, technology forecasting, and market research.

Zona Research (www.zonaresearch.com/). Information and advice for the Internet industry.

Miscellaneous ISP Resources

Microsoft Internet Explorer ISP Kit information: www.microsoft.com/Windows/IE/ISP/default.asp

Netscape Navigator ISP Kit information: http://home.netscape.com/ partners/distribution/index.html

Information for ISPs working with **WebTV:** www.webtv.com/company/isps/

Dawn McGatney's "Every ISP In Your Town and The Universe": http:// dogwolf.seagull.net/isplist.html

ISP Newsgroups (USENET)

alt.internet.access
alt.internet.access.wanted
alt.internet.services
alt.online-service

Recommended Reading

"The human spirit needs to accomplish, to achieve, to triumph to be happy."

BEN STEIN

The following is but a short list of my reading favorites. I've actually read many, many books in the area of personal and professional development. Once you get past the contradictions that many of the top scholars and authors have, what trickles down are a few books that fall into the category of universal principles. In addition to basic sales, business, advertising, public relations, and marketing-related books, I've also listed some of the best ISP business resources I know. Enjoy!

ISP Business

ISP Liability Survival Guide: Strategies for Managing Copyright, Spam, Cache, and Privacy Regulations. By Tim Casey, John Wiley & Sons, ISBN 0-471-37748-1 (to be published in the spring of 2000)

ISP Survival Guide: Strategies for Running a Competitive ISP. By Geoff Huston, John Wiley & Sons, ISBN 0-471-31499-4

Business Building Basics and the Internet

Advertising on the Internet, Second Edition. By Robin Zeff, John Wiley & Sons, ISBN 0-471-34404-4

Awaken the Giant Within: How to Take Immediate Control of Your Mental, Emotional, Physical & Financial Destiny. By Anthony Robbins, Fireside, ISBN 0-671-79154-0

Creating the High-Performance Team. By Steve Buchholz, Thomas Roth, and Karen Hess (editor), John Wiley & Sons, ISBN 0-471-85674-6

Customers for Life: How to Turn That One-Time Buyer into a Lifetime Customer. By Carl Sewell and Paul B. Brown, Pocket Books, ISBN 0-671-02101-X

The Dilbert Principle: A Cubicle's-Eye View of Bosses, Meetings, Management Fads & Other Workplace Afflictions. By Scott Adams, Harperbusiness, ISBN 0-887-30858-9

The E-Myth Revisited: Why Most Small Businesses Don't Work and What to Do About It. By Michael E. Gerber, Harperbusiness, ISBN 0-887-30728-0

Getting Connected: The Internet at 56K and Up. By Kevin Dowd, O'Reilly, ISBN 1-565-92154-2

Guerrilla Marketing Online Weapons: 101 Low-Cost, High-Impact Weapons for Online Profits and Prosperity. By Jay Conrad Levinson and Charles Rubin, Houghton-Mifflin, ISBN 0-395-77019-X

How to Build an Internet Services Company from A to Z. By Charles H. Burke, Quality Books, Inc., ISBN: 0-935563-03-2

How to Master the Art of Selling. By Tom Hopkins, Warner Books, ISBN 0-446-38636-7

1001 Ways to Reward Employees. By Bob Nelson and Ken Blanchard, Workman Publishing, ISBN 1-563-05339-X

Principle-Centered Leadership. By Stephen R. Covey, Fireside, ISBN 0-671-79280-6

See You at the Top. By Zig Ziglar, Pelican, ISBN 0-882-89126-X

Success Through a Positive Mental Attitude. By Napoleon Hill and W. Clement Stone, Pocket Books, ISBN 0-671-74322-8

Swim With the Sharks Without Being Eaten Alive: Outsell, Outmanage, Outmotivate, and Outnegotiate Your Competition. By Harvey Mackay, Ballantine, ISBN 0-449-91148-9

The 22 Immutable Laws of Marketing: Violate Them at Your Own Risk. By Al Ries and Jack Trout, HarperBusiness, ISBN 0-887-30666-7

Web Site Stats: Tracking Hits and Analyzing Web Traffic. By Rick Stout, Osborne McGraw-Hill, ISBN 0-078-82236-X

What Makes People Click: Advertising on the Web. By Jim Sterne, Que Education and Training, ISBN 0-789-71235-0

World Wide Web Marketing, Second Edition. By Jim Sterne, John Wiley & Sons, ISBN 0-471-31561-3

ISP Glossary

This glossary provides business, technical, and user terms commonly used in the ISP industry.

ACK (acknowledgment) a message that confirms receipt of some other message. This is most commonly used by domain registrars when approving an update or transfer of a domain name.

ad impressions one impression would equal one person viewing the ad at one time.

ad inventory the total number of ad impressions your network can deliver in a given period of time.

angel investor an individual who invests money in your organization.

anonymous FTP a mode of operation for the File Transfer Protocol (FTP), which permits a remote user to obtain transfer of a particular collection of files without authentication.

announcement list e-mail list of people to whom you can send an announcement or newsletter directly or with the assistance of an e-mail list server.

ASCII (American Standard Code for Information Interchange) provides a seven-bit pattern for each of 128 common characters; often used in an eight-bit form by appending a zero bit or parity bit.

ASN (Autonomous System Number)   used in BGP4 routing; a unique identifier for your network.

ASP (Application Service Provider)   third-party entities that manage and distribute software-based services and solutions to customers across a wide area network, such as the Internet.

ATM (Asynchronous Transfer Mode)   a switching technology that organizes digital data into 53-byte cells or packets and transmits them over a medium using digital signal technology. ATM is implemented by hardware and is a key component of broadband communication.

AUP (Acceptable Use Policy)   a policy outlining what an ISP's user can or cannot do as a member of the ISP's service.

authentication   a security function with which the data received is confirmed to have been sent by a particular user.

backbone   a large transmission line or provider that carries data gathered from smaller lines that interconnect with it. Many tier-one providers are called backbones because they carry capacity around the globe on their own private network, rather than passing packets from one network to another to reach common destinations.

bandwidth   range of frequencies present in an analog signal; also used to measure the size of an ISP's total available capacity for throughput in or out of their network to the external Internet.

banner ad   usually referred to as a 468 by 60 pixel Web banner that is used for advertising purposes.

banner ad server   a server that manages Web banner or button ad campaigns, including displays, clickthrough, and other statistics useful for marketers.

BGP4 (Border Gateway Patrol)   a protocol for exchanging routing information between gateway hosts in a network of autonomous systems.

browse   to view a document often created using HTML with a Web browser.

byte   eight bits of data used as the code for one character; generally the code is ASCII.

cable modem   a modem that operates over a cable TV coaxial line.

carrier   (1) signal in a data channel; (2) commercial organization that provides communication services among geographically dispersed locations.

CGI (Common Gateway Interface)   standard way for a Web server to pass a Web user's request to an application program and to receive data back to forward to the user.

circuit in electronics, a closed path through which a signal current can pass; in telecommunications, a path from one point to another through which a signal can pass.

CLEC (Competitive Local Exchange Carrier) a telephone company that competes with Incumbent Local Exchange Carriers (ILECs) by providing its own switching and network.

closed list list server that supports input from and output to a specified list of users for which it is configured.

confidentiality exists when information is disclosed only to those intended to receive it.

congestion in a network, excessive traffic which causes delays and possibly losses of data because of packet loss or other errors.

conversion rate the number of prospects who become customers divided by the number of prospects.

CPM (cost per thousand) advertising term that refers to the price of advertising per thousand impressions.

CSU/DSU (channel service unit/data service unit) provides the telephony interface for circuit data services. A CSU connects a terminal to a digital line; a DSU performs protective and diagnostic services for a telecommunications line. Required on each end of a T-1 or T-3 connection.

CTR (clickthrough rate) equal to the number of clicks on an advertising medium divided by the total displays of the medium.

DCF (discounted cash flows) a valuation model that takes the historical cash flows of the ISP combined with projected future cash flows of the business that then calculates a time-value discount rate to the future cash flows to translate them to present value. The value of the business is the net present value of the future expected cash flows.

discussion list an e-mail-based forum, otherwise known as a list community, where members come together to discuss different topics, both personal and professional, all depending on the list's charter or purpose.

DNS (Domain Name System) Internet service that provides for lookup of the IP address associated with a particular name or a domain name lookup based on an IP address.

Domain name your unique identifier on the Internet. Example: Your-Company-Name.com. *See also* **URL.**

DS0 (Digital Signal Level 0) specification for transferring digital signals over a single channel at 64 Kbps on a T-1 facility.

DS1 (Digital Signal Level 1) specification for transferring digital signals at 1.544 Kbps on a T-1 facility (or at 2.108 Mbps on an E1 facility outside the United States).

DS3 (Digital Signal Level 3) specification for transferring digital signals at 44.736 Kbps on a T-3 facility.

DSL (Digital Subscriber Line or Loop) any digital subscriber line that often offers high-bandwidth capacity over two pairs of copper wires.

E1 a WAN transmission circuit, predominately used outside the United States, that carries data at a rate of 2.048 Mbps.

E3 a WAN transmission circuit, predominately used outside the United States, that carries data at 34.368 Mbps.

EBITDA (earnings before interest, taxes, depreciation, and amortization) a common method of business valuation in the telecom industry.

e-mail electronic mail.

Ethernet a LAN protocol that supports transfer rates up to 10 or 100 Mbps; supports several different media types.

e-zine e-mail newsletter or announcement list.

facility-based ISP an ISP that owns its own dial-up access hardware, servers, and telecommunications equipment.

FAQ (frequently asked questions) a list of the most frequently asked questions on a particular topic. Found in most formats, including HTML Web pages and traditional printed formats.

firewall network element used to protect hosts from hostile attacks.

flame an insulting message sent to another person or group of people. A *flame war* often occurs in mailing lists and USENET; a flame has very little value for the participants but allows Internet users to vent.

FTP (File Transfer Protocol) Internet application protocol for transfer of files between hosts.

full duplex property of a communication link or network whereby a node can both send and receive data simultaneously.

GIF (Graphic Image Format) standardized format for a computer image composed of individual pixels.

half duplex property of a communication link or network whereby a node can either send or receive data but not do both simultaneously.

host computer connected to a network capable of communicating data between its applications and those of other computers on the network.

hypertext elaborated text which can be specified as to font, color, size, and so forth and may contain symbolic links that can be followed automatically to other text, either within the hypertext document or to external documents and multimedia objects.

HTML (Hypertext Markup Language) the set of markup symbols or codes inserted in a file intended for display on a Web browser whereby the markup tells the Web browser how to display a Web page's words and images for the surfer. The World Wide Web Consortium (W3C) is the governing body for standards in the HTML industry.

HTTP (Hypertext Transfer Protocol)   application layer protocol used to transfer HTML for the Web.

IANA (Internet Addressing and Naming Authority)   organization that issues unique names and addresses required for functioning of the Internet Protocol suite.

IAP (Internet Access Provider)   a provider of Internet access.

IEEE (Institute of Electrical and Electronics Engineers)   international technical/professional society; produces a series of technical standards which include specifications for local area networks.

IETF (Internet Engineering Task Force)   organization that provides technical standards and implementation guidance for the Internet Protocol suite.

insertion order   the document that contains online or off-line media-buying agreements.

integrity   property of a system or data unit indicating it is intact or whole, in other words, not compromised from a security standpoint.

Internet   the global set of interconnected networks that uses the Internet Protocol suite.

intranet   a corporate internet which may or may not be connected with the Internet.

inverse DNS   function of the Domain Name System that returns a DNS name, given an IP address.

IP (Internet Protocol)   primary network layer protocol of the Internet Protocol suite; defines format and procedures for transmission of packets between Internet hosts and routers; the Internet currently uses IPv4.

IP address   network address used by the Internet Protocol; for IPv4, it is 32 bits, for IPv6, 128 bits.

IPv4 (Internet Protocol version 4)   current version of the Internet Protocol.

IPv6 (Internet Protocol version 6)   proposed new version of the Internet Protocol; currently in trials.

IRC (Internet Relay Chat)   a protocol and a communications method similar to live chat.

ISDN (Integrated Services Digital Network)   a communications standard for transferring voice, video, and data over telephone lines; supports transfer rates of 64 Kbps.

ISOC (Internet Society)   an international nonprofit society of users and professionals dedicated to the promotion, development, and growth of the Internet.

ISP (Internet Service Provider) organization that operates a network providing access to the Internet.

ITU-T (International Telecommunication Union—Telecommunication Standardization Sector) standards body responsible for the OSI network standards.

Java a programming language used to create programs that run on Web client computers and interact with the users of Web browsers.

JPEG (Joint Photographic Experts Group) standard for compression of still images.

Kbps (kilobits per second) U.S. standard for bandwidth speed measurement.

LAN (local area network) data communication system that interconnects multiple stations in a geographically small area.

leased links data communication links leased from a carrier; also called leased lines and leased circuits.

LEC (Local Exchange Carrier) any local telephone company or telephony entity that provides telecommunications facilities within a local area.

list etiquette acceptable standards of behavior and conduct by list members on an e-mail list.

list member anyone who subscribes to an e-mail list; can also be called a list subscriber or just plain subscriber.

list server an e-mail server that distributes and manages e-mail lists; typically used for e-mail newsletters or e-mail discussion lists.

log off to leave the network you were just logged on to.

log on used over networks and usually requires you to enter a username and password to get access to a set of resources.

MAE (metropolitan area internet) a network access point where ISPs connect with each other.

mail alias list of e-mail addresses intended to be substituted by an e-mail server for some incoming message and transmitted; provides a simple form of list server.

Mbps (megabits per second) a measure of data-transfer speed.

message the information passed between sender and receiver via a communication system.

modem (modulator-demodulator) device or program that allows computer data transfer over telephone lines. A modem converts digital computer data to analog and from analog back to digital, which is then transmitted as data over phone lines.

moderated list list server operation where a human reviews e-mail messages and decides which ones are to be forwarded to the list.

MPEG (Motion Picture Experts Group)   family of standards for compressing of moving images.

MSIE (Microsoft Internet Explorer)   a browser designed by Microsoft.

MTU (maximum transfer unit)   the largest data unit allowed by a particular network or protocol.

multimedia   communication involving more that one medium.

NACK (negative acknowledgment)   aspect of a message that confirms nonreceipt of some other message.

NANOG (North American Network Operators Group)   a group of Internet operators who participate in an e-mail discussion list and meet regularly in North America.

NAP (network access point)   ISPs connect through NAPs in peering arrangements that dissipate or create congestion for their users.

netiquette   unwritten and written rules for acceptable behavior when interacting with others on the Internet in many different forms, such as e-mail, Web, or chat.

Netscape   a browser designed by Netscape Corporation, which was acquired by AOL.com.

network   collection of processing elements (nodes) that have the ability to communicate with each other through links.

NNRP (Network News Relay Protocol)   protocol used to relay network news from an NNTP provider.

NNTP (Network News Transfer Protocol)   protocol used to transfer network news.

NOC (network operations center)   the core or room of a network.

node   network element interconnected by links; processing takes place here.

non-facilities-based ISP   an ISP that does not own its own dial-up access switches or services, but rather outsources this function to wholesale dial-up access providers.

NSF (National Science Foundation)   a U.S. government organization that funded the operation of the NSFnet network from 1986 through 1995.

NSP (Network Service Provider)   entity that provides Internet access to ISPs.

online service   a business that provides subscribers with many functions of the Internet; usually connected via dial-up accounts. America Online, CompuServe, and MSN are all examples of online services.

password   a secret series of characters that, if necessary, allows a user to access files, open programs, log on to networks, and so forth.

ping   Internet program that lets you verify a particular Internet address exists and can accept requests; often used in troubleshooting network problems.

pixel   abbreviation for *picture element;* an individual gray scale or colored dot in an image.

PPP (Point-to-Point Protocol)   a means of establishing dial-up links that can work with Internet routers.

PRI (primary rate interface)   contains twenty-three 64-Kbps B-channels and one 64-Kbps D-channel. Transmitted through a T-1 line in the United States and E-1 lines in Europe.

Profit pillar   any profit center that supports your ISP.

protocol   a set of rules for transfer of information under a specified set of conditions.

PSTN (Public Switched Telephone Network)   term for the architecture of the public telephone network based on copper wires that carry analog voice data.

QoS (quality of service)   specification for network performance providing acceptable levels of different network standards.

RADIUS (Remote Authentication Dial-In User Service)   authentication and accounting service used to determine the authentication of a username and password when a user dials in to an ISP.

RBOC (Regional Bell Operating System)   Interchangeable with the term LEC.

receiver   the destination in a communication process.

redundant   duplicative; in data communication systems.

RFC (Request for Comments)   Internet standards documents.

router   computer that performs packet switching, that is, forwarding arriving packets toward their destination.

routing   process of selecting paths to relay data traffic; in a packet network it results in creating or updating a routing table.

server   software (and/or the associated computer) that provides application services over the network to software at other stations (the clients).

SMTP (Simple Mail Transfer Protocol)   Internet standard for e-mail.

SNMP (Simple Network Management Protocol)   Internet standard for network management.

SOHO (Small Office Home Office)   a small business run out of the home.

SONET (synchronous optical network)   standard term for connections of high-speed fiber-optic transmission systems.

spam   unwanted Internet e-mail; otherwise referred to as UCE (unsolicited commercial e-mail)

subscriber (1) a customer of an ISP; (2) a list member of an e-mail list.

switch network element that determines which of two or more possible paths will be used to send data.

T-1 a WAN phone connection or transmission circuit supporting data rates of 1.544 Mbps. Transfers DS1-formatted data; generally used to connect ISPs to other Internet providers.

T-3 a WAN phone connection or transmission circuit supporting data rates of about 43 Mbps.

tariffs fees that telecommunications companies are allowed to charge their customers by law.

TCP (Transmission Control Protocol) primary transport protocol of the Internet Protocol suite which provides for reliable transport using a stream model of data and multiplexing of streams using ports.

telecommunication passing information from a sender to a distant receiver by electronic means.

teleconferencing meeting conducted by people at different locations using telecommunication.

telnet application protocol for remote terminal emulation via the Internet.

thin client a client-server approach where programmed functionality in the client is designed to be small, placing a correspondingly larger burden on the server.

top gun a salesperson who outsells everyone else and is the best sales rep for a company.

TOS (type of service) similar to an AUP (Acceptable Use Policy) as to the level of service a business offers.

traceroute application that allows a user to observe the sequence of routers that will be used by the Internet to reach a given IP address.

upstream provider vendor who provides you with Internet access. Every ISP has an upstream provider unless it is a tier-one backbone.

URL (Uniform Resource Locator) a domain name or IP address that can be commonly accessed via a browser.

USENET collective name for hosts supporting network news distribution.

username a set of characters, usually used in conjunction with a password, used to log on and access a network.

USP (Unique Selling Proposition or Proposal) one sentence that defines the unique value a company delivers its customers.

venture capital money that is available from a venture capital fund which has an expectation of a high return along with many restrictions on the use of the investment.

VPN (virtual private network)   a network that uses public wires to connect nodes but encrypts the network so only authorized users who log on will have access.

WAN (wide area network)   a network that spans a sizable geographic area; its links normally are leased from carriers.

Web   *see* **WWW (World Wide Web)**

Wholesale Dialup Access Provider   a company that resells its dial-up access ports.

WWW (World Wide Web)   virtual network of sites that use the Internet to exchange multimedia files in HTML using HTTP.

Yahoo! (Yet Another Highly Organized Oracle)   one of the best Internet search engine/directories.

Bibliography

Abraham, Jay, *Mr. X—Money-Making Secrets of Marketing Genius Jay Abraham and Other Marketing Wizards*, Newsletter Systems.

Blanchard, Kenneth, and Spencer Johnson. *The One Minute Manager*, Berkley Books, ISBN 0-425-09847-8.

Brown, Paul. B., and Carl Sewell. *Customers for Life*, Pocket Books, ISBN 0-671-74795-9.

Burke, Charles H. *How to Build an Internet Service Company From A to Z*. Social Systems Press, ISBN 0-935563-03-2.

Caples, John. *Tested Advertising Methods*, Prentice-Hall, ISBN 0-16-906891-0.

Chase, Larry. *Essential Business Practices for the Net*, Wiley Computer Publishing, ISBN 0-471-25722-2.

Covey, Stephen R. *Principle-Centered Leadership*. Simon & Schuster, ISBN 0-671-79280-6.

Debelak, Don. *Marketing Magic*. Bob Adams, Inc., ISBN 1-55850-351-X.

Gerber, Michael E. *The E-Myth*. HarperBusiness, ISBN 0-88730-472-9.

Hopkins, Claude C. *My Life in Advertising & Scientific Advertising*. NTC Business Books, ISBN 0-8442-3101-0.

Hopkins, Claude C. *Scientific Advertising*. ISBN 0877541485.

Hopkins, Tom. *How to Master the Art of Selling.* Tom Hopkins International, ISBN 0-938636-03-0.

Hopkins, Tom. *The Official Guide to Business.* Warner Books, ISBN 0-446-39112-3.

Huston, Geoff. *ISP Survival Guide.* Wiley Computer Publishing, ISBN 0-471-31499-4.

Lasker, Albert Davis. *The Lasker Story: As He Told It.* NTC Business Books, ISBN 0844230995.

Levinson, Jay Conrad. *Guerrilla Advertising.* Houghton Mifflin Co., ISBN 0-395-68718-7. Levinson, Jay Conrad. *Guerrilla Marketing.* Houghton Mifflin Co., ISBN 0-395-64496-8.

Levinson, Jay Conrad. *Guerrilla Marketing Attack.* Houghton Mifflin Co., ISBN 0-395-50220-9.

Levinson, Jay Conrad. *Guerilla Marketing Weapons.* Plume, ISBN 0-452-26519-3.

Moore, Geoffrey A. *Crossing the Chasm.* HarperBusiness, ISBN 0-88730-717-5.

Nelson, Bob. *1001 Ways to Reward Employees.* Workman Publishing, ISBN 1-56305-339-X.

Reeves, Rosser. *Reality in Advertising.* ISBN 0394442288.

Rice, Craig S. *Marketing without a Marketing Budget.* Bob Adams, Inc., ISBN 1-55850-986-0.

Ries, Al, and Jack Trout. *The 22 Immutable Laws of Marketing.* HarperBusiness, ISBN 0-88730-592-X.

Williams, Art. *Pushing Up People.* Parklake Publishers, ISBN 9996455416.

Index